Human Resource Management: People and Organisations

2nd edition

Edited by Stephen Taylor and Carol Woodhams

The Chartered Institute of Personnel and Development is the leading publisher of books and reports for personnel and training professionals, students, and all those concerned with the effective management and development of people at work. For details of all our titles, please contact the publishing department:
tel: 020 8612 6204
email: publishing@cipd.co.uk
The catalogue of all CIPD titles can be viewed on the CIPD website:
www.cipd.co.uk/bookstore
An e-book version is also available for purchase from:
www.ebooks.cipd.co.uk

Human Resource Management: People and Organisations

2nd edition

Edited by Stephen Taylor and Carol Woodhams

Chartered Institute of Personnel and Development

Published by the Chartered Institute of Personnel and Development
151 The Broadway, London SW19 1JQ

This edition first published 2016

© Chartered Institute of Personnel and Development, 2016

Designed and typeset by Exeter Premedia Services, India
Printed in Great Britain by Ashford Colour Press Ltd.

British Library Cataloguing in Publication Data
A catalogue of this publication is available from the British Library

ISBN 9781843984160
eBook ISBN 9781843984412

The views expressed in this publication are the authors' own and may not necessarily reflect those of the CIPD.

The CIPD has made every effort to trace and acknowledge copyright holders. If any source has been overlooked, CIPD Enterprises would be pleased to redress this in future editions.

Chartered Institute of Personnel and Development

151 The Broadway, London SW19 1JQ
Tel: 020 8612 6200
Email: cipd@cipd.co.uk
Website: www.cipd.co.uk
Incorporated by Royal Charter.
Registered Charity No. 1079797

Shelfie

A **bundled** eBook edition is available with the purchase of this print book.

CLEARLY PRINT YOUR NAME ABOVE IN UPPER CASE

Instructions to claim your eBook edition:
1. Download the Shelfie app for Android or iOS
2. Write your name in **UPPER CASE** above
3. Use the Shelfie app to submit a photo
4. Download your eBook to any device

Contents

List of figures and tables

CHAPTER 8

Contributor biographies

Stephen Taylor is a Senior Lecturer in Human Resource Management at the University of Exeter Business School and also a Chief Examiner for the Chartered Institute of Personnel and Development (CIPD). He previously taught at Manchester Business School, at Manchester Metropolitan University Business School and worked in a variety of HR management roles in the hotel industry and in the NHS. He teaches HRM and general management subjects as well as employment law at postgraduate and undergraduate level. He has authored and co-authored several books on HRM and employment law.

Professor Carol Woodhams is an Associate Professor of Human Resource Management at the University of Exeter Business School. She has held a number of positions within CIPD including National Examiner for Designing and Delivering Training, External Moderator for the Advanced Qualification and Editor of the flexible learning materials at Intermediate and Advanced levels. She previously taught at Plymouth University and Manchester Metropolitan University. Her specialist teaching subjects are employee resourcing and equality and diversity. Her research topics include studies of gender and disability discrimination in the UK and China. Prior to her academic career she held posts in management in the hospitality sector.

The late **Dr Ted Johns** served as a Chief Examiner at the Chartered Institute of Personnel and Development and its predecessor bodies for over thirty years, taking a leading role in a wide range of its educational initiatives and activities. He wrote and co-wrote many books on a range of subjects including customer care, organisational change and ethical leadership. He was a founder director and later Chairman of the Institute of Customer Service, having previously worked in higher education and management consultancy. Ted was also a noted conference and seminar speaker.

Dr Graham Perkins is a Lecturer in Human Resource Management at the University of Exeter Business School. Alongside interests in the areas of learning and development, knowledge management and reward management, Graham conducts research into how small-medium enterprises encourage creativity. Graham is also involved with the marking of CIPD examinations, and has several years' of operational HR experience with a variety of organisations.

Dr. Krystal Wilkinson is a recent PhD graduate, with a specific focus on work-life balance and qualitative research methodologies. She is a Senior Lecturer in HRM at Manchester Metropolitan University and has been a National examination marker for the CIPD for several years. Prior to commencing her doctoral studies, she worked in operational HR in a range of sectors including construction, retail & hospitality.

Gail Swift is an Organisational Development and Learning Specialist with extensive experience in the public sector. She currently works independently combining this with working part–time as an Experience Assessment Assessor for the CIPD and Associate Lecturer in HRM at Manchester Metropolitan University. A former Deputy Director of OD in the NHS she has held senior organisational responsibility for strategic learning policy and HR and educational governance, together with leadership and management development and talent management. She has also previously held a variety of HR and management roles in the NHS and the retail sector. She regularly provides executive coaching support for senior leaders and is an Associate Examiner for the CIPD.

Cecilia Ellis is Principal Lecturer in Human Resource Management at the Manchester Metropolitan University Business School. She teaches postgraduate and undergraduate students and is course leader for the MSc HRM and IHRM full time programme. Cecilia holds Fellow membership of the Chartered Institute of Personnel and Development (FCIPD) and previously worked as a HR Business Partner for a multinational company.

Claire Roberts is a practitioner in HR, L&D and OD, and has worked in multinational organisations in the UK and Spain, at a national and global level. She is a CIPD Associate Examiner and a visiting lecturer in HRM and HRD at various universities teaching at postgraduate and undergraduate level.

Walkthrough of textbook features and online resources

KEY LEARNING OUTCOMES

By the end of this chapter, you should be able to:

- understand the reasons why organisations change the structure and location of HR service provision by analysing the changing context of human resource service delivery
- critically evaluate different models of HR service delivery available to contemporary organisations
- critically discuss the reason for measuring the impact of service delivery and the measurement indicators used
- understand recent thinking on HR service delivery.

KEY LEARNING OUTCOMES

At the beginning of each chapter a bulleted set of key learning outcomes summarises what you expect to learn from the chapter, helping you to track your progress.

CASE STUDY 1.3

CAPITA WINS BBC'S HR OUTSOURCING CONTRACT

Capita has won a ten-year contract to manage the BBC's HR services. Under the contract, Capita will deal with BBC staff recruitment, pay (excluding pensions), occupational health and other services including some training and development. The work will be handled by Capita's Belfast office and will create 100 new jobs in the city.

programmes and services for our audiences.'

The BBC claims it will save more than £50 million over the ten-year contract period. The decision on whether or not to outsource HR services is debatable and contentious in literature and practice.

CASE STUDIES

A range of case studies from different countries illustrate how key ideas and theories are operating in practice around the globe, with accompanying questions or activities.

? REFLECTIVE ACTIVITY 1.2

Reflect on your organisation or one you know well. Which people-related issue is the most common source of tension between line managers and the HR function? Why do you think this is the case?

REFLECTIVE ACTIVITY

In each chapter, a number of questions and activities will get you to reflect on what you have just read and encourage you to explore important concepts and issues in greater depth.

FURTHER READING

CIPD (2005) *HR outsourcing: the key decisions.* London: Chartered Institute of Personnel and Development (Scott-Jackson, W., Newham, T. and Gurney, M.).

CIPD (2006) *The changing HR function: the key questions.* London: Chartered Institute of Personnel and Development (Tamkin, P., Reilly, P. and Strebler, A.).

CIPD (2007) *The changing HR function: transforming HR.* London: Chartered Institute of Personnel and Development (Reilly, P., Tamkin, P. and Broughton, A.).

CIPD (2011) *Next generation HR: insight-driven.* London: Chartered Institute of Personnel and Development.

CIPD (2015) *Changing HR operating models.* London: Chartered Institute of Personnel and Development.

REILLY, P. (2000) *HR shared services and the realignment of HR.* Brighton: University of Sussex, Institute of Employment Studies.

ULRICH, D. (1997) *Human resource champions: the next agenda for adding value and delivering results.* Boston, MA: Harvard Business Review Press.

FURTHER READING

Further reading boxes contain suggestions for further reading and useful websites, encouraging you to delve further into areas of particular interest.

ONLINE RESOURCES FOR TUTORS

- PowerPoint slides – design your programme around these ready-made lectures.
- Lecturer's guide – including guidance on the activities and questions in the text.
- Additional case studies – these can be used as a classroom activity, for personal reflection and individual learning, or as the basis for assignments.
- Multiple choice questions – a series of questions for each chapter to test your understanding of the text.

ONLINE RESOURCES FOR STUDENTS

Please visit our new student website: http://books-taylorwoodhams.cipd.co.uk

- Videos – access a range of videos including:
  - Ulrich's model
  - Reflections on performance appraisal systems
  - What kind of rewards have motivated you?
- Podcasts – access a range of our podcasts including:
  - Induction
  - Total reward
  - Employer branding
- Annotated web-links – access a wealth of useful information sources in order to develop your understanding of employment law issues.
- Multiple choice questions – a series of questions for each chapter to test your understanding of the text.
- Glossary of key terms.

EBOOK BUNDLING

CIPD have partnered with BitLit to offer print and eBook bundling. BitLit has built a free eBook bundling app called Shelfie for iOS and Android that allows you to get a highly discounted eBook if you own a print edition of one of our titles.

Visit **www.bitlit.com/how-it-works/**

CHAPTER 1

Human Resource Service Delivery

GAIL SWIFT

CHAPTER CONTENTS

- Introduction
- The changing context of HR service delivery
- Models of HR service delivery
- Challenges to the Ulrich model
- Outsourcing HR services
- The delivery of HRM by line managers
- Measuring the impact of HR services
- Future developments in HRM service delivery
- Conclusion

KEY LEARNING OUTCOMES

By the end of this chapter, you should be able to:

- understand the reasons why organisations change the structure and location of HR service provision by analysing the changing context of human resource service delivery
- critically evaluate different models of HR service delivery available to contemporary organisations
- critically discuss the reason for measuring the impact of service delivery and the measurement indicators used
- understand recent thinking on HR service delivery.

1.1 INTRODUCTION

One of the key variables in achieving the aims of HRM is the way the service is delivered. We know from studies of contingency variables in organisations and management that no two organisations utilise the same functional structure and involve the same levels and roles of staff in delivering HRM. Each HRM department is subject to different forces, producing a unique approach to HR service delivery. Our purpose in this chapter is to introduce the reader to the models of HR service delivery that are available to contemporary organisations, together with the reason why organisations have changed the structure and location of HR service provision.

Over the past two decades the role and structure of the HR function in organisations has been debated, with some research studies claiming that 95% of organisations have undergone some form of HR transformation in the past 10 years (Boroughs 2015). Dave

Ulrich's ground-breaking model of human resources services delivery in his book *Human Resource Champions: the next agenda for adding value and delivering results* (1997), spurred many senior HR leaders to restructure the delivery of their services to meet the challenges of changing national and international business conditions. It is now 19 years since Ulrich offered a powerful re-interpretation of the personnel function, which outlined the significance of HR as a change agent in championing competitiveness in US firms (Caldwell 2001). Debate has continued into the success or otherwise of this model and the question 'What comes after Ulrich?' has failed to deliver few coherent propositions of alternative operating models for HR (Fry and Fishman 2015). External challenges to the role and purpose of the HR function continue, ranging from the recent debate generated by Ram Charan's proposal that HR be 'split' (Charan 2014) to David Ulrich's recent comments on the need for HR to be structured in a way that reflects the business and delivers outcomes that focus on the capabilities that organisations require to win in the marketplace (Ulrich 2015). However, the need for HR to continue to exert strategic boardroom influence and work with their organisations to drive change and engagement remain the principal drivers for HR structural change.

1.2 THE CHANGING CONTEXT OF HR SERVICE DELIVERY

No two HR departments are configured in the same way to deliver their service, even though they share the same predominant aim. A recent CIPD report (CIPD 2006) concluded that the primary driver for the **structural transformation** of HR was the desire for the function to be a more strategic contributor and to maximise HR's contribution to business performance. This trend appears to have continued over recent years with the CIPD's 2014/5 Winter Outlook citing 'becoming a more strategic contributor' as the main reason for changes to HR structures (CIPD 2015f).

Business leaders have also come to perceive the link between talent management and business success and to recognise HR's potential role in unlocking the **discretionary effort** of employees as a source of competitive advantage. The link between HR and customer service has strengthened over recent years, with those in the vanguard of change moving to increase the value HR offers to its business customers (CIPD 2006). HR has been charged with developing and organising 'human capital', and the ways in which employees are recruited, developed and managed are seen as key to this. Talent has also become the number one issue for CEOs, with the HR function being asked to lead the transformation of most companies towards a more engaging, high performing, well aligned and highly capable organisation (Bersin 2015). Employee engagement continues to be the top current priority for HR functions (CIPD 2015a), reflecting a recognition of the importance of employee satisfaction in delivering effective services. The link between well-organised and well-managed teams and business success appears to be well recognised in many organisations. However, there continues to be debate as to HR's success in delivering value to the organisation and whether there is definitive evidence of the impact of HR structures and staffing on organisational performance (CIPD 2006). More recently some HR commentators optimistically see the profession sitting 'at the centre of some of the most important decisions in any business' with the function 'rapidly expanding its influence' in the workplace (Brown 2015). Their view is that 'organisations across the globe recognise HR as a way to elevate acceptable business practices up to exceptional business performance' (Brown 2015). What is clear is that current business conditions demand a greater delivery of competitive advantage via HR agendas and require HR to have true strategic influence that is internally coherent with the values of the business and aligned to its goals and objectives (Becker and Huselid 1999). With the world of work growing ever more complex, diverse and ambiguous together with the continuing change in the norms of managing the employment relationship, the way the HR function operates must continue to evolve (CIPD 2015g). It may be concluded therefore that the way in which HR is structured to deliver its services is a key factor in determining its operational success.

? REFLECTIVE ACTIVITY 1.1

Consider your organisation or one that you are familiar with. How is HR delivered? Is it delivered in partnership with other organisations or are certain activities totally outsourced to expert organisations such as consultants? In particular, how involved are line managers in the delivery of HR services?

This question pivots firstly on the extent to which the organisation you are considering retains in-house HR expertise, and secondly on the nature of the relationship between the HR function and the organisation's line managers.

Each organisation is different and the models of delivery are affected by variables such as:

Organisation-level factors

- Organisation size: larger organisations are likely to utilise more innovative features of delivering HRM – for example, more partnerships, shared arrangements and outsourcing.
- Sector: private sector organisations are also more likely to consider arrangements such as those listed above.
- History, traditions and structure: bureaucratic, layered, staid and static organisations, which may also have a longer history and maturity to them, are more likely to have a traditional line-manager-associated delivery model.
- Culture of the organisation – such as the difference between organisations that encourage decision-making at a low structural level and those that are paternalistic and more supportive.

HR-level factors

- Level of organisational representation and responsibility for input into strategy – it is suggested that outsourced transactions, for example, can give the HR manager more time for strategic input
- Size of department
- The history and traditions of HR operations

Personal factors

- The power, influence and perspective of the HR manager/director
- Their experience and background
- The CEO's previous experience of HR

1.3 MODELS OF HR SERVICE DELIVERY

How HR is structured to deliver its services has been the subject of considerable debate and discussion over recent years. A variety of ways in which HR functions have been organised have been examined and whether services should be organised on a best-practice or a best-fit basis is at the centre of much of the debate. Research carried out by the CIPD highlighted the views of practitioners that HR should be structured to reflect the business and what its business customers want (CIPD 2006). What emerges from the literature are two approaches to HR structures that continue to dominate the way in which services are currently organised, which are discussed in further detail in this section of the chapter:

- traditional approaches of a single team of generalists, specialists and administration, or a corporate strategy team aligned by business units or locations
- the 'three-legged stool' model of business partners, shared services and centres of expertise.

1.3.1 TRADITIONAL HR STRUCTURES

A traditional structure of HR services, consisting of a single team with generalists, specialists and administration, is still common in many organisations. In this type of structure, an integrated HR team generally looks after line managers and employees at specific locations or within specific units of the business. Within these teams, depending on their size, there may also be specialisation by work area or by employee grade or group (CIPD 2006). HR staff in these structures may look after administrative and clerical staff as opposed to managerial grades, or look after technical specialities – for example, medical staff in the NHS.

Evidence from the CIPD research suggests that this is still the most common structure for HR functions, with 43% of respondents reporting that their HR departments are structured like this. This model of HR delivery appears to be particularly prevalent among small and medium-sized organisations (SMEs), with 55% of respondents in the report stating this to be the case. The private sector also appears to favour the single HR team structure (CIPD 2015f). Additional research into SMEs found that HR teams in SMEs have to be versatile and deal with both the strategic and the operational work, deploying a combination of generalist and specialist knowledge with wide-reaching demands on their knowledge and agility (Miller 2015). Smaller and less complex organisations in particular continue to have generalist HR staff covering a range of tasks (CIPD 2006).

A similar study from Crail (2006) of the HR function in 179 UK organisations concluded that a 'standard' HR department might typically have the following characteristics:

- It would have a team of 12 people serving a workforce of around 1,200.
- This team would consist of an HR director, three HR managers, one HR supervisor, three HR officers and four HR assistants.
- The department would spend a lot of its time on HR administration, despite some activity as a 'business partner' and strategic contributor.
- Attempts would have been made to shift some HR responsibilities to line managers, not always successfully.
- The department would enjoy some influence over the way the organisation was run and HR's standing in the organisation would be generally high, partly because the external contexts have changed and HR is seen as the source of knowledge and expertise on legal and regulatory requirements.

As this piece implies, the connection between the HR function and operational managers can be fraught. The HR department might attempt to shift HR responsibilities because doing so is in line with a model of ownership and buy-in from managers to the goals of HRM. However, managers are often reluctant to embrace these responsibilities. We investigate this issue later in the chapter.

1.3.2 ULRICH'S 'THREE-LEGGED STOOL' BEST PRACTICE MODEL

The concept of HR Business partnering, or strategic partnering, emerged in the late 1990s when the US business academic Dave Ulrich set out his model of human resource services delivery. This has proved to be hugely influential, particularly its core idea that the HRM function in larger organisations is most effective when it is 'divided up' into distinct areas of activity. In its original incarnation, published in 1997, Ulrich suggested that there are four major roles played by HR managers in organisations:

- strategic partners
- change agents
- administrative experts
- employee champions.

In recent years Ulrich's model has become regarded as best practice, although there is ongoing debate about how his theories should be interpreted and put into practice and Ulrich himself has reviewed and developed his original theories in subsequent work (CIPD 2015a).

The most common interpretation of the model is based on three means or mechanisms of service delivery: HR business partners, HR centres of expertise and shared HR services, commonly referred to as the 'three-legged stool' model or the 'three box' model.

These are discussed in turn in more detail in the following sections.

HR business partnering or strategic partners

The CIPD states that HR business partnering is the process in which HR professionals work closely with business leaders and/or line managers to achieve shared organisational objectives, in particular designing and implementing HR systems and processes that support strategic business aims. Business partners are senior or key HR professionals. They are usually embedded in the business unit where they work in partnership with operational managers within that business unit to influence and steer strategy and strategy implementation. Research has found that in practice the activities that HR business partners are likely to be involved in can vary enormously depending on factors such as 'organisational size, company culture and business priorities' (CIPD 2015a). According to a recent CIPD survey, over a quarter of organisations surveyed use the Ulrich model, with this being more prominent in large organisations, particularly those in the public sector who seem more likely to adopt this model. However, varying definitions and interpretations of the model have made it hard to empirically demonstrate the extent to which it has been adopted in practice (CIPD 2015a).

The benefits of the business partner role appear to be that it allows the HR practitioner to become a more strategic contributor, with increased business focus, greater engagement with line managers and the ability to move people management issues higher up the business agenda (Reilly et al 2007). When HR professionals are embedded in business units, research appears to suggest that they are more easily able to select and implement HR practices that are most appropriate to developing the business strategy for that unit. This structure allows HR partners to utilise their 'unique' knowledge and skills to support and drive change in people management practices. They can also be well placed to support local managers in considering the people consequences of changes to strategy or policies (CIPD 2015a; Ulrich et al 2008). HR business partners can also work with line managers on longer-term people resourcing and talent management planning issues. Their role in intelligence-gathering and understanding of good people management practices, internally and externally, enables business partners to raise issues which managers may be unaware of (CIPD 2015a).

Although many professionals have welcomed the move to a more strategic role, there have also been challenges to this approach. Pritchard (2010, p183) suggests that the transition from generalist to business partner has often not been easy for HR professionals, who can find it 'difficult to step away from day to day activities, in which they had been involved for many years'. Whereas the business partner role has 'given freedom from previous generalist work and enabled a more strategic focus', Pritchard (2010, p181) has observed that in some cases business partners continued to remain involved in generalist work. Some practitioners, however, feel that this is an 'essential stepping stone' to a more strategic role (Pritchard 2010, p184). Being able to understand how the **transactional** side of the agenda works and having the ability to continue to resolve HR issues was regarded as essential to building trust with line managers. This was seen by some practitioners involved in the study as a prerequisite to successful partnerships (Pritchard 2010). More recent research has found that the failure to understand the business partner role and match it to existing HR capability had been a key issue in introducing business partnering to organisations. The single fact being that the demands of the role have 'risen faster than the capacity of many in HR to deliver it' (Holley 2015). If business partners are not seen to be delivering success in their first few months then they can revert to being perceived a 'simply helpful generalist' (CIPD 2015a).

Ulrich et al (2008) suggested that a new competence of 'strategic architect' is required for the role, which in essence means 'embedded HR professionals being able to diagnose what needs to be done; broker resources to get things done; and monitor progress to ensure things are accomplished' (Ulrich et al 2008, p842). This new skill set, together with a perceived natural reluctance to give up an area of work that had previously been seen as adding value (Pritchard 2010), suggests that the introduction of business partnering has not been without its difficulties. Despite this, business partnering remains a popular and widespread approach to organising the HR function (CIPD 2015a).

Centres of expertise

Centres of expertise in Ulrich's model usually comprise 'a team of HR experts with specialist knowledge of leading edge HR solutions' (CIPD 2015a). The role of centres of expertise is to 'deliver competitive business advantage through HR innovations in areas such as reward, learning, engagement and talent management' (CIPD 2015a). Evidence of implementation of centres of expertise suggests that they are accessed on a corporate, regional or national basis. In the 'three-legged stool' model they offer their services either to HR business partners or in some circumstances directly to line managers (CIPD 2007). They often act like businesses in themselves and can have a number of business units using their services. In some organisations some method of internal recharging for these expert services and products is used.

Ulrich et al (2008) suggest that the role of the HR professional in centres of expertise covers a number of important areas, notably in creating **menus of intervention** aligned with the capabilities required to drive the strategy for the business forward. These include:

- diagnosing needs and recommending the most appropriate solution
- working collaboratively with HR business partners to select and implement the right services
- researching and creating new offerings
- acting as guardian of the learning community within an organisation.

There are also some risks inherent with operating centres of expertise that must be guarded against. They include:

- relying on programmes that the centres are familiar with but that are not tailored to the needs of individual business units
- isolation from day-to-day business, so that solutions can appear to be out of touch with the reality of the business
- a tendency to 'craft single solutions' (Ulrich et al 2008, p844), which are then applied to numerous business units

- excessive demands placed on the centre by working for numerous business units, each business unit believing that its own demands are the most important and the most deserving of an immediate response
- an assumption that in creating a centre of expertise business units will be happy to use them. In some organisations line managers and business partners are required to access the central expertise before seeking outside help, but in others managers may pick and choose between the central service and external consultants, especially if there is a high degree of devolved budgets for learning and support activities.

Recent research into experiences of implementing the Ulrich model has found that surprising shortcomings in the area of HR support for talent management, in the areas of recruitment, performance, learning, succession and reward. Many of these functions sit within the centres of expertise part of the model in many organisations. The results of this study reported satisfaction ratings that were less than half of those for HR operations, leading to the view that this was an area of 'major missed commercial opportunity' for organisations (Boroughs 2015, p9).

Shared services

Shared services emerged in the late 1990s as HR leaders realised that many administrative tasks could be performed in a centralised, standard way (Reilly 2000). Its introduction has frequently been one element of a wider restructure of HR services, often associated with the introduction of the three-legged stool service model.

The CIPD's definition of shared services is based on a single, often relatively large, unit that handles all the routine 'transactional' services across the business. An HR shared service would typically provide the routine administration of HR processes such as recruitment administration, changes to contracts, administration of leavers and absence monitoring. Some organisations may also advise on HR policy and practice and simpler employee relations issues. The remit of shared services is to provide low-cost, effective administration (CIPD 2015b).

Reilly (2000) found that there were three principal reasons for the introduction of shared services – cost, quality and **organisational change** – development in technology being the facilitator of the movement to shared services rather than the driver for it. A 2007 CIPD survey also found that just over a quarter of organisations had introduced a centralised provision of shared administrative services. Typically, these services are located in-house although they can be outsourced to specialist third-party providers (see the section on outsourcing later in the chapter). Often the use of shared services centres is also associated with the move to devolve people management activities from the HR department to individual managers or employees by the use of **self-service technologies**. Typically HR shared services are organised around a number of tiers (Figure 1.1):

As can be seen from Figure 1.1 **employee self-service** systems often underpin this tiered approach to shared services (Tier 0). These are secure web-based computer systems that allow employees access, via the company's intranet or the Internet, to manage their own personal records and payroll details. Typically employees are able to update their own personal details when their circumstances change, usually through a portal or intranet, and without any need for external intervention from a line or HR manager. Some organisations also have separate systems for managers which allow them to view records for their staff, such as absence records. Some systems, such as 'Snowflake' also allow employees to schedule and request their own holiday leave.

Although these systems allow HR to harness technology to support the shift to a more strategic role, significant pressure can be placed on line managers, who may be unsure or unwilling to take on more responsibility for day-to-day people management. Experience at companies such as Marks and Spencer and British Nuclear Fuels when they implemented employee self-service systems also highlighted a number of issues, including the impact on staff who lacked computer skills and those who have limited access to office facilities. They also suggested that the savings that could be made within HR also needed to include the (hidden) costs of the impact on line managers' workloads (*People Management* 2000). However, benefits to both employees and HR have also been observed. For example, Aviva Insurance Services reported savings in its HR staff costs and an improvement in its HR operations. Marks and Spencer also installed computer booths in staff areas and introduced more training in IT skills for staff to support the implementation of their e-HR system, with notable improvements to process such as scheduling leave over the Christmas period which was 'no longer the mountain-of-paper nightmare of the past' (Churchard 2009).

Figure 1.1 Tiered structure of HR services

Tier 3	• Some organisations also have 'process owners' who has overall responsibility for a particular process area and can be the final point of escalation
Tier 2	• Teams aligned to specialisms, such as recruitment, performance management, payroll and benefits, etc
Tier 1	• A contact centre where employees and managers can access the services provided by emails or telephone
Tier 0	• An HR portal/intranet providing 'self-serve' options to employees and managers

Source: CIPD (2015b)

At Tier 1, organisations also utilise HR contact centres (or **call centres**) to support line managers and employees with a range of employee relations issues. These are dedicated centres which use voice-to-voice contact, usually supported by computer-based systems. They can be located in-house as part of an organisation's existing HR or corporate service delivery, outsourced or off-shored. The following case study, taken from *People Management* (1998), describes Lloyds TSB's HR Call Centre model:

CASE STUDY 1.1

LLOYD'S TSB'S HR CALL CENTRE MODEL

Lloyds TSB set up a centralised call centre to deal with all personnel enquires from line managers aimed at relieving pressure on managers and ensuring consistency of response to enquiries. The centre sets strict standards, including answering 80% of calls in 10 seconds, and can handle up to 1,000 calls a day in busy periods. Employees are also told that they should not contact the centres directly as HR recognises the importance of the relationship between the employee and their line manager and encourages line managers to try and resolve issues with their staff directly in the first instance. Importantly, the call centre only discusses what options for action are available to the line manager, leaving the line manager to make the final decision. The calls taken by the centre have also identified gaps in existing bank policies, leading to the review of policies such as parental leave, career breaks and the employee share options scheme. The service estimated to have saved Lloyds TSB more than £100,000 a year and internal surveys suggest that 94% of callers are satisfied or very satisfied with the service.

The benefits of shared services reflect many of the reasons why organisations looked to implement them in the first place (Reilly 2000):

- lower costs
- more efficient resourcing
- an improved quality of service
- increased customer satisfaction
- a single point of contact
- an integrated 'total solution' approach
- greater transparency of costs
- more consistent management information
- economies of scale for investment in technical and communications infrastructure
- the release of time to spend on strategic issues.

CIPD (2007) research has identified that shared services, as would be expected, are mainly found in large rather than small organisations. Two thirds of organisations employing over 5,000 employees cite that they have some

degree of shared services, as opposed to 17% of organisations that employed 250–1,000 staff. The research cites several high-profile private sector companies that have recently entered into shared service arrangements and an increased interest in take-up in the public sector.

To demonstrate this idea in practice, an interesting illustration is provided in the following case study of how a joint venture between Liverpool City Council and BT delivered HR services in a new way. Evidence in the case suggests that through a radical overhaul in providing services and the appointment of a new HR leader, the joint venture has been useful in providing HR services that:

- are more cost-effective
- are united behind a single product
- provide HR jobs that are varied and skilled
- free up in-house provision to focus on strategic matters
- build joint commitment to solutions
- construct green shoots of a commercial model that can offer services to other organisations.

 HR SERVICES AND THE JOINT VENTURE: LIVERPOOL CITY COUNCIL AND BT

CASE STUDY 1.2

When David Henshaw took over as chief executive of Liverpool City Council in October 1999, he had his work cut out. The Council was third from bottom in the local authority performance league table, with only the London boroughs of Hackney and Lambeth deemed to provide poorer services for their residents. Not only that, Liverpool also had the most expensive Council Tax in the country.

His brief was to cut costs and bureaucracy, stabilise the Council Tax and improve services and information for the local community and the Council's staff. Henshaw set in motion a modernisation process that saw the

authority's eight directorates condensed down to five portfolios, a new executive team and 2,700 jobs shed – 10 per cent of its workforce.

He also focused his attention on what he saw as one of the major obstacles to delivering better services and value for money – the Council's inefficient business processes. The state of the HR function at the time provides a good example. It was split into eight units, each providing day-to-day operational support for a directorate, plus one central corporate unit. The eight units were basically doing the same job, but all had a different way of doing things and had their own interpretation of corporate policies.

'There were 200 people in HR, but it wasn't a good service,' Henshaw says. 'Personnel officers in different units were spending their time arguing with each other about different versions of the truth.'

Henshaw's aim was to get down to one version, not only for HR but for the whole Council, and to ensure that everyone had access to it. To do this, the Council's information and communication technology (ICT) needed considerable improvement. ICT had been underfunded for years. But the Council's previous outsourcing experience had not been encouraging.

'Outsourcing can and does go wrong,' says Henshaw. 'You can outsource a problem and end up with an outsourced problem, rather than a solution.' Instead, he took a different approach and started looking for a private-sector partner to form a joint venture with.

In May 2000 BT was chosen as preferred bidder to help run the business support services, and Liverpool Direct Limited (LDL) was born.

BT would invest £60 million in the company over a 10-year period, and provide the much-needed computer systems and software. The Council would pay the company £330 million to run all its business support (including ICT, HR and payroll) and its front-line customer services, such as benefits and advice services. All these services would be restructured to benefit from the technology. This would allow mundane processes to be automated and information to be shared, saving time and money.

The HR department was to play a major part in the change to the new model. First, it would be involved in the overall restructuring, handling the redundancies, overseeing the selection of executive directors and recruiting the second tier of assistant executive directors. Second, it would go through a fundamental transformation, taking on a new structure and ways of working as it became part of LDL.

A new HR management team of seven was set up, and the old system in which each HR team supported a single directorate [akin to a department] was scrapped. In its place four new teams based on expertise (employment relations, resourcing, learning and development, and payroll and pensions) were formed.

The redundancy programme was judged a success: the target of losing 10 per cent of the workforce through voluntary redundancy was achieved. HR is now part of LDL, and the latest stage of its transformation has been the launch of the intranet, allowing all staff and line managers to access HR policies and other information online, and the opening of the HR service centre, which went live in January 2001.

Although 81 per cent of LDL is owned by BT and 19 per cent by Liverpool City Council, Henshaw stresses that the Council is in the driving seat in terms of the direction and management of the company. In fact, beyond providing the hardware, BT's involvement seems to be limited to advice on setting up and running business service administration systems. The staff who are actually providing the services have all come from the Council and were already working in similar areas. They have been seconded to the company but, crucially, are still employed by Liverpool City Council.

For Henshaw the joint venture is a positive way of accessing private money and know-how without the disadvantages of outsourcing. 'Our sector has to think differently about what it does, and move away from stale outsourcing deals,' he says. 'When outsourcing goes wrong, people reach for the lawyers rather than working to solve the problems. In our contract with BT we have very clear targets for service improvements and cost reductions, and we have to work together to achieve those.'

He adds that LDL has plans to provide services for other authorities. The extra business would bring in revenue for the Council, as well as BT, and create more jobs. They are currently in discussion with two authorities.

'There are few private companies that have managed to make this work on their own,' he says. 'The public sector has a huge amount to contribute. If we can harness that with the private sector, that's good for everybody.'

Liverpool Direct Limited's HR service centre handles telephone enquiries and, where necessary, refers callers on to someone with greater expertise in the back office. The intranet and service centre have removed the burden of process-related tasks from the 70 back office staff.

Front-line call centre staff were previously HR administrators and say the change in

role has been a positive one. Customer services adviser Peter Lynskey says that the job is more varied and has given him new computer skills.

The new structure has also freed up the HR management team. HR project manager Mike Evans, who was responsible for setting up the intranet, was previously manager of one of the HR units – a job that had little impact on the Council at large or the community. Now the projects he runs are all about improving the way the Council works and the services it delivers.

'LDL has opened up opportunities for people throughout the organisation to do things with real scope,' he says.

Adapted from Hammond (2002)

1.4 CHALLENGES TO THE ULRICH MODEL

A great deal of the debate, since Ulrich first introduced the concept of business partnering, has centred on the perceived success of the model within business and the extent to which it has enabled HR practitioners to adopt a more strategic approach. Holley (2015) puts forward the view that the three box model is fundamentally sound and has taken HR forward, but his research at Henley Business School found a big gap between intention and reality, especially in the role of HR business partner. Pitcher (2008) argues that the business partner model has not resulted in strategic thinking, and is little more than superficial 'spin'. He cites the example of Elizabeth Arden, in which the HR director, Gabriele Arend, disagreed with any model that splits HR professionals into recruiting, training and employee relations experts. Her company is moving towards a traditional structure, where HR employees are trained to develop generalist operational knowledge. The CIPD (2015a) recommends exercising caution when adopting the business partner model and suggests that partnering should mean a paradigm shift for most HR functions, resulting in changes to HR's values, operation and skills, and not simply a repackaging of good HR practice. Perhaps the key question comes down to HR's credibility and contribution, summed up succinctly in a Deloitte Report (2009, p8):

> The business partners' greatest failing has been their inability to convince senior managers that they have the necessary business acumen to contribute to the strategic debate.

This view is supported by research from KPMG which show that a fifth of business leaders fail to see any tangible outcomes between the HR function and business outcomes (Bolton and Payne 2013).

Research conducted by the Roffey Park Institute into the use of business partners revealed that 55% of HR professionals thought that it had been a success but 32% remained unsure, with a further 10% claiming that it had not been successful at all in their organisations (Hennessey 2009). Reilly et al's work for the CIPD (2007) found a wide variety of ways in which organisations have implemented this model, and which differed greatly from Ulrich's original model.

Figure 1.2 Variants in implementation of the three-legged stool model

A large number of business partners and a shared service centre but no centres of expertise because business partners are expected to be conversant with most HR issues	A small number of HR teams, led by a business partner, a support unit/shared service centre and a policy strategy unit	A corporate HR function, an insourced shared services operation and a well-staffed business unit
Business partners for each of the main departments, and centres of expertise – including an employment support line – which pick up the administrative work; a shared payroll operation but no shared service as such	A small number of business partners – one for each department – a policy unit, a separate learning unit and a development design unit, a call centre, a 'duty desk', case work section and a project team; administration is carried out by a shared service centre located outside HR	Business partners, together with learning and development advisers embedded in business units, with a corporate 'service delivery' unit and a strategy consultancy group
Shared services (where appropriate globally), business partners (aligned to global business units, regions or individual locations) and centres of expertise	Business partners, an advisory call centre, a global shared service centre and different levels of centres of expertise at global (principles and strategy), regional (guidance on implementation) and local level (actual delivery)	Business partners, regional administrative service centres, together with call centres but with payroll executed locally, no centres of expertise but with core HR strategy units and delivery teams

Source: Reilly et al ([CIPD] 2007, pp13–14)

Despite the undoubted popularity of Ulrich's model, many commentators remain sceptical as to its true success and unconvinced of it as 'the right way forward for people management'. Some critics have maintained that it has all too often only involved a 'change of title only' for HR managers (Hennessey 2009, p26) and has not resulted in any improvement in strategic thinking on HR issues within business (Pitcher 2008). Ulrich claimed, however, that poor implementation and a lack of understanding had let the model down (Peacock 2008). Real concerns were expressed that many practitioners have rushed into implementing the Ulrich model without properly considering whether it met the needs of the business first. Where the Ulrich model has been introduced, it is the business partner leg of the stool that has proved the most popular, whereas centres of expertise and shared services are less frequently found (CIPD 2007). Most commentators agree that 'the Ulrich model can be a useful starting point'; however, the segmentation of the HR function into distinct streams may work for some organisations but create silos in others – 'no one size fits all' (CIPD 2015g, p4).

The CIPD advocate that 'no matter what model the business chooses it is important for HR to remain united as a function, sharing knowledge and insights from different parts of the organisation and remaining focused on the business needs, regardless of the roles that HR practitioners hold' (CIPD 2015b).

1.5 OUTSOURCING HR SERVICES

According to the CIPD Executive Briefing (2005), this is the practice of transferring some, or all, of the HR service provision from an in-house team to one or more external providers. It is also utilised by a number of small organisations that, unable to carry their own internal resource, form an agreement to finance a common service to which they all have an equal, or agreed, access. HR services may be transferred on an anticipated long-term basis, or may be outsourced for the completion of a specific piece of work or project (CIPD 2005).

There has been significant growth in this type of external provider, firms such as Capita, Accenture, Hewitt and Exult taking large chunks of HR business. To illustrate, the following case study, taken from *People Management* (2006), announces a BBC deal with Capita.

CASE STUDY 1.3

CAPITA WINS BBC'S HR OUTSOURCING CONTRACT

Capita has won a ten-year contract to manage the BBC's HR services. Under the contract, Capita will deal with BBC staff recruitment, pay (excluding pensions), occupational health and other services including some training and development. The work will be handled by Capita's Belfast office and will create 100 new jobs in the city.

'This deal marries both our expertise in HR with the resource and expertise of a leading player in business process outsourcing,' said Stephen Dando, director of BBC People. 'The value created from this deal is a significant step for us in ensuring that the BBC continues to invest in creating innovative

programmes and services for our audiences.'

The BBC claims it will save more than £50 million over the ten-year contract period. The decision on whether or not to outsource HR services is debatable and contentious in literature and practice. A typical outsourcing arrangement allows HR services for an organisation to be transferred out of ownership of the organisation to a third-party supplier to be re-provided back into the organisation. Alternatively HR services are purchased outright from a specialist firm, such as Capita in the UK, who offer such services. Typically, these are the transactional elements of services.

1.5.1 REASONS FOR OUTSOURCING DECISIONS

Organisations usually decide on an outsourcing option for one or more of the following reasons:

- It can enable access to specialist skills and knowledge not possessed by the in-house team and which the outsourcing organisation is unable or unwilling to develop for it.
- It can be seen as a means of achieving levels of service quality and efficiency, which, for one reason or another, are not considered to be achievable within the outsourcing organisation itself.
- There may be an anticipation of significant savings on an ongoing basis, which is attractive to any organisation seeking to reduce its overall costs.

According to a CIPD survey on outsourcing activity (CIPD 2009) the incidence of outsourcing extended to around 29% of the survey respondents and was said to be increasing, especially over the five years prior to the study. Outsourcing appeared to be most prevalent in the private sector, around 69% of the survey respondents engaging in the practice. It was apparently less common among public service organisations, where it extended to only 25% of the respondents.

The survey also demonstrated a clear link between organisational size and outsourcing activity. Large organisations, with more than 10,000 staff, outsourced up to 71% of at least some of their HR activity, retaining 29% in-house. Smaller organisations, employing fewer than 250 staff, retained only 11% for provision on an internal basis.

HR outsourcing is most commonly used in the transactional and specialist functions. Typically, these are recruitment, training, pensions, payroll, legal services, information systems and compensation and benefits. All of this, taken together with the findings in the preceding paragraph, fits neatly with the reasons why organisations opt to engage in outsourcing, outlined in the bullet points above.

1.5.2 SKILLS REQUIRED BY HR PRACTITIONERS IN OUTSOURCING DECISIONS

HR outsourcing is perceived to require a particular set of skills and knowledge on the part of those involved in the process. These include the ability to properly plan, specify and cost the services that are to be provided externally. Thereafter, the process requires that contracts have to be made, tendered, awarded and then monitored carefully on an ongoing basis if the expected benefits are to be achieved and maintained. According to the 2009 CIPD survey, HR professionals involved in outsourcing considered themselves as having the necessary level of competence in those areas deemed to be important. However, vendor management – which involves partnership working, together with an understanding of the way in which commercial organisations operate on a day-to-day basis – was not regarded as crucial to a successful outcome. The survey in fact indicated that HR professionals only ranked this fifth in terms of importance.

Further, 13% of HR outsourcers lacked vendor management skills and 6% lacked any financial skills.

The stated results of HR outsourcing seem to be quite mixed. If the intended objective was to outsource the transactional elements of HR activity to allow an in-house concentration on strategic work, the findings show that this appears not to have been the result. CIPD's recent Winter Outlook found that nearly four in ten professionals in the UK reported that their HR function does not outsource any work, which was a fall from almost half reported in a similar survey in 2012. Over half reported that the incidences of outsourcing work had remained the same and interestingly incidences of outsourcing were also consistent across organisational size. Payroll remains the main area of outsourcing activity, with 57% of respondents reporting this, followed by external support for complex advice (including case management) which was outsourced by 26% of respondents. The survey also found that SMEs are significantly more likely to outsource complex case management and advice together with other areas of specialist advice such as reward. Other common areas that are outsourced include recruitment and legal advice (CIPD 2015e).

The general conclusion is that HR outsourcing is one potential means of HR functions achieving the aim of improving the efficiency of administration services as part of a shift to undertaking more strategic and influential activities which can be perceived to add more value to the organisation. However, to ensure that it is successful it must be carefully planned and targeted. It must be aimed at those areas where it can make a viable contribution, and it must be well monitored once it is in operation. HR outsourcers must have developed the necessary skill sets required for successful engagement, and outsourcing must be regarded positively as an integral and strategic aspect of HR activity generally.

1.5.3 OFF-SHORING

Aligned to outsourcing is the practice of **off-shoring** services, although that the two terms can sometimes be used, incorrectly, interchangeably. This involves the moving of HR services or activities to an overseas third party, or to another country as a direct or indirect employer (CIPD 2015e). The term 'nearshoring' is sometimes also used in respect of services moved to another country close to or bordering the country of operations. The main reasons given for these decisions are usually cost considerations, such as lower labour costs or more favourable economic considerations in the other country. One of the first examples of this was IBM's move of its HR Services Centre in Portsmouth to Budapest. The centre covered HR services for IBM's operations in Europe, Middle East and Africa (EMEA) and the reason given for the move was that Budapest offered an ideal location on the grounds of cost, language and political stability. The migration started with the transfer of HR administrative services but proved so successful that the company accelerated the transfer of tier two HR jobs. Overall this resulted in a loss of 100 HR jobs (Pickard 2004).

1.6 THE DELIVERY OF HRM BY LINE MANAGERS

Line managers have taken increasing responsibility for the delivery of HR practices over the last few decades and now play a critical role in people management in most organisations. Significantly, the way line managers implement these practices can influence employee attitudes and behaviour. Line managers are therefore the important link between employee experiences of HRM and the formation of their attitudes towards their job and the organisation. This relationship has been subject to a number of changes and tensions in recent years with many core activities that were previous viewed as the province of HR shifting to the line. In addition, 'the trend to towards the individualisation of the employment relationship has placed new burdens and opportunities in the hands of line managers' (CIPD 2015d).

Line managers have appropriately been called 'HR agents' of the organisation because they mediate between individuals and HR practices (Truss 2001). Research from Crail (2004) makes it clear that first-line managers are increasingly expected to have the solution to everything, from absence management to productivity. The research listed 23 areas of responsibility and asked respondents whether these were the responsibility of first-line managers alone, a shared responsibility, or not their responsibility at all. Only a handful of the 62 employers contacted said that the following had nothing to do with line managers:

- absence management
- appraisals
- grievance
- health and safety
- planning/allocating work
- recruitment
- staff deployment
- team briefing
- team development
- ongoing training
- welfare.

This is similar, at headline level, to a survey issued in 2000, although there has been a substantial increase in the number of organisations identifying each of these areas – and a still greater increase in those saying that these areas are now the sole responsibility of line managers. The importance of line managers in the delivery of HRM, however, is far greater than a quantitative survey can reveal. The work of Appelbaum et al (2000) and Purcell et al (2003) emphasises that the likelihood of employees' engaging in discretionary effort is influenced by the role of line managers. For example (Appelbaum et al 2000, p235), plant managers who invest in the skills of front-line managers and include these workers in decision-making activities elicit discretionary effort by employees. This effort increases operational efficiency and competitive advantage.

This is an important conclusion. It suggests that there is a direct link between line management training and the willingness to work beyond contract and 'go the extra mile' on the part of employees.

The increased focus on employee engagement also means that the line management role is now particularly influential. The CIPD 'Shaping the Future' project which looked at sustainable organisational performance, highlighted the crucial impact that line managers have on engagement as their roles are the interface between the organisation and its workforce. The more positive the employee relationship with the line manager, the more likely employees are to demonstrate higher levels of job satisfaction, commitment and loyalty. Given that this in turn leads to higher levels of performance and engagement, organisations need to 'pay close attention to the way they select, develop and manage the performance of line managers' (CIPD 2015d), not just in terms of skills and knowledge or people processes and management, but also paying particular attention to their people management behaviours and organisational values. A great deal is now expected of line managers who are already busy dealing with operational responsibilities. HR's role is to ensure that line managers have sufficient training and coaching to enable them to confidently fulfil their people management responsibilities, together with ensuring that there is an organisational environment that clearly supports line managers' roles in this respect (CIPD 2015d).

> ### ? REFLECTIVE ACTIVITY 1.2
>
> Reflect on your organisation or one you know well. Which people-related issue is the most common source of tension between line managers and the HR function? Why do you think this is the case?

1.7 MEASURING THE IMPACT OF HR SERVICES

Why measure HR performance? It could be said that on one level the effectiveness of – or the necessity for – HR activity speaks for itself. Clearly, if an organisation cannot recruit, retain, develop and deploy its staff efficiently, it will not survive. But this, in itself, is not enough of a contribution. The HR function has to show that it is part of the general movement towards greater efficiency and cost reduction. This in turn demands the development of viable measurement processes and techniques with which it can demonstrate its effectiveness.

This is particularly important given the pressures under which modern organisations now operate, with an increasing emphasis on good business practices, the development of new technology and the extensive use of management information systems. Customer and stakeholder requirements have become sharper and much more closely defined, which gives providing organisations increasingly less room for manoeuvre. Inefficient practices cannot be concealed or buried and so must be identified and addressed.

The HR function must therefore, in so far as it is possible, seek and apply ways of indicating efficiency, if it is to achieve and maintain any degree of credibility in the organisation in which it operates.

1.7.1 MEASUREMENT INDICATORS

The measurement of human resource efficiency may be somewhat difficult, and indeed thought by some not to be possible at all (Brewster and Tyson, cited in CIPD 2005). 63% of HR professionals in response to a CIPD survey (2015) said that they felt that their HR data did inform business decisions and stimulate change and improvement in the organisation (CIPD 2015f). A recent report by KPMG recognised that most HR teams understand the value of using HR measures to support their HR decisions, but was of the view that this was often at the level of generic and basic operational and transactional measurement, rather than developing metrics that provided 'predictive data and insights that could have a positive impact on the success of the organisation' (Bolton and Payne 2013, p2). This view is supported by the CIPD 2015 survey which concluded that there was less agreement from respondents about whether HR effectively communicates and interprets its people measures to relevant stakeholders.

Many commentators have highlighted the key role HR analytics has to play in the future of work. Speaking at an HR Directors summit in February 2015, Charlotte Harding, Human Capital Project Manager at Mercer and the World Economic Forum emphasised its importance, saying that 'workforce analytics could help build the links between HR programmes and business strategy to ensure that initiatives are having the desired impact' (Harding 2015). There are a number of measures that can move towards a greater understanding of the contribution of HR to overall organisational effectiveness. These range from the general to the more specific and quantitative.

Overall, general tests of HR effectiveness rely firmly on the extent to which HR objectives are directly linked to the aims of the organisation as outlined in its strategy and its associated operational plans. If this is well done – that is to say, if the workforce plan is developed along with the organisational strategy and seen as integral to it and not as a post-planning 'add-on' – then it may be said to be effective if the organisation as a whole is seen to be succeeding. This of course is a somewhat indirect measurement of HR effectiveness, but is nonetheless considered to be viable.

If, for example, the organisational strategy demands a workforce of a particular character and shape, possessing a defined skill mix, and the HR function is able to provide this through effective recruitment, retention, training, development and employee relations policies, then it must be seen to be making a valuable contribution. This descends from the introduction and maintenance of sound HR policy and procedure at the senior level to a committed application on the ground with a rigorous attention to detail, fairness and consistency. A good example of HR outcomes in practice is found in research reports from Michael West et al (2006) who strongly suggest that good HR practices can be seen to affect the performance of hospitals, as evidenced through a reduction in the mortality rate.

In a study of 61 hospitals in England, West et al (from the Institute of Work Psychology at Sheffield University) found strong associations between HR practices and business performance measured through patient mortality. The Chief Executive and HR directors completed a questionnaire asking them about their hospital characteristics, HRM strategy, employee involvement strategy and practices, and other HR policies and practices covering the main occupational groups, such as doctors, nurses and midwives, professions allied to medicine, hotel services, professional and technical staff, administrative and clerical, and managers. Data was also collected on the number of deaths following emergency and non-emergency surgery, admissions for hip fractures, admissions for heart attacks, and re-admission rates. Care was taken not to bias the data and account was taken of the size and wealth of each hospital and of the local health needs. In particular, the researchers found that:

- appraisal has the strongest relationship with patient mortality
- the extent of teamworking in hospitals is also strongly related to patient mortality
- the sophistication of training policies is linked to lower patient mortality.

Specific and quantitative indicators include the use of **staff turnover** and **stability figures**, sickness absence rates, the incidence of discipline and grievance cases and personal performance and appraisal outcomes. These provide strong clues to the overall health of an organisation from which the motivation and commitment of the workforce directly stems.

Making comparisons through **benchmarking** these and other indicators between organisations can indicate relative efficiency or otherwise. Care must be taken, however, to ensure that correct and valid comparisons are being made and that there is due regard to any operational, structural or cultural differences that may affect the outcomes.

Other measures may include the study of response rates in the recruitment and grievance-handling process, customer and stakeholder feedback, both formal and more casual, **employee engagement** and output, and the detailed costing of HR activity with which to make informed decisions on the way in which HR services should be provided. That is on an in-house or external basis.

It may be difficult to determine the right balance between specific and more general HR performance measures, or indeed choosing the right ones to use in the circumstances – not made any easier by the existence of over 1,000 human capital indices (Hartley and Robey, cited in CIPD 2005). However, according to KPMG's report now is the perfect time for HR to 'up its analytics game'. They believe that three are three trends creating the current momentum in this are:

- HR systems are increasingly integrated and allow easier access to both input measures, for instances people's characteristics and output measures, such as sales data.
- The general buzz around big data and data analytics across the business world.
- The availability of social data.

(Bolton and Payne 2013)

HR analytics is an increasingly important process for HR functions to develop and is a growing discipline amongst HR teams. Organisations who are investing in developing these skills have 'seen dramatic changes in the way HR systems and policies are implemented and have in some cases shown demonstrable impact on HR activity' (CIPD 2015c). Once established and used, HR performance indicators should be kept under continuous review in order to ensure their ongoing value and effectiveness. Used positively and confidently, good HR indicators may be a powerful determinant in the direction taken by the organisation as a whole and in the credibility of the HR function in particular.

> ## **?   REFLECTIVE ACTIVITY 1.3**
>
> Carefully read the following quotation from CIPD's conversation with Roger Bolton, partner and leader of global HR transformation at the centre for excellence for KPMG, taken from the CIPD podcast on how HR can influence strategy through data (3 April 2013).
>
> Roger is a firm believer that HR should be doing more with analytics to enable HR to develop strategically differentiated functions that can prove the value that they bring to the business. So

why does he think that the value HR can add is still often underestimated by senior management:

'I can best convey the issue from quoting Terry Leahy when he was chief executive of Tesco who said that when the marketing manager comes to me he brings insightful and predictive information about our customers. We know what our customers are thinking and feeling, what they're going to do, how they see Tesco in relation to their needs and wants. It's hugely insightful and we make decisions on it. When the HR Manager comes to our meetings, it's not predictive, it's not insightful, it's rear view mirror and we can't make decisions on it.'

Sir Terry Leahy gave that quote to KPMG about five years ago but Roger thinks that the challenges he laid down still exist in many organisations up and down the country. He concludes that HR needs to start to take the information that it has and to really drive insight, explore it, work with it, and integrate it with other sources of information and 'it's only then it will start to tell a story'.

Now see if you can answer the questions that appear below. Log on to the CIPD website to hear the discussion on the podcast in more detail if you have the opportunity.

1   Why might organisations have struggled to make use of measurement data in the past?

2   What measure of HR services is used in your organisation (or an organisation that you are familiar with)?

3   If you were to design a 'dashboard' of metrics for your organisation (or an organisation that you are familiar with) to show how HR measures are linked to business outcomes, what would your dashboard look like? What are the reasons behind your choice of performance metrics?

Source: Adapted from Analytics – How HR can influence strategy through data (2013). CIPD Podcast available at: www.cipd.co.uk/hr-resources/podcasts/77-analytics.aspx

1.8 FUTURE DEVELOPMENTS IN HRM SERVICE DELIVERY

This chapter has discussed the models of HRM service delivery that are currently found in operational practice, and has concentrated on discussion of the results of research and academic thinking that demonstrate their relative effectiveness.

The popularity of Ulrich's model stemmed in part from the desire of HR professionals to become more closely aligned with the business and promote efficiency and effectiveness. Models of shared services, centres of expertise and outsourcing have allowed HR practitioners to concentrate their efforts at a more strategic level. Ulrich's model had dominated the debate about HR structures for the past few decades but the CIPD report *Changing HR Operating Models* (2015g) acknowledges that it is time for the profession to move on and focus more on effectiveness. The report suggests that this will require us to challenge our current HR operating model to 'ensure that they align with the business and the business needs and that we have the right capabilities in the right places'. The report invites a number of leading thinkers (academics, practitioners and consultants) to share their views on the future of the HR function to stimulate this debate, with a number of key themes emerging. The link between strategy, **organisation structure** and HR structure is increasingly evident (Sparrow 2015), as is the need for HR to focus on 'High Impact', bringing specialist skills to the business where they can drive most value (Bersin 2015). The need for HR to be more realistic about what it can deliver based upon the capability of the function and its business partners is also explored (Holley 2015), together with the need for centres of excellence to be significantly developed to meet business needs to develop and retain organisational capability and talent (Boroughs 2015). The report concludes that the strong message coming from all contributors is that 'although the Ulrich model is a good starting point, there is not one model that fits all'.

The debate on the future of the HR function has also been joined by a number of other prominent commentators. Peter Capelli, in his article 'Why we love to hate HR' (2015, pp55–61), highlighted HR's perceived bureaucracy and operational focus and commented on the lingering effects of the 2008 recession. He suggests that this has effected executives' views on HR's contribution resulting in them not seeing an urgent need for new HR initiatives. A great deal of debate has also recently been generated by Charan's (2014, p34) proposal that HR corporate functions should be split. He proposed one function to support the administration that manages compensation and benefits reporting to the Chief Finance Officer together with one focused on leadership and organisational development. He applauded the value of HR and saw his proposed split as facilitating a 'new all-powerful triumvirate' at the top of the organisation. This would include the CEO, CFO and Chief HR officer with the aim of 'putting people before strategy'.

The CIPD's *Next Generation Research* (2011) also challenged us to think about where the HR profession is headed and suggests that 'a comparable deeper shift in mind set and focus' is now required (CIPD 2011, p5). It observes that a good deal of current HR practice is still strongly concerned with service and process delivery. 'Getting things done' with 'intervention-led delivery and high-volume activity' is still seen as the measure of success for many HR and business leaders (CIPD 2011, p5). It proposes that HR practitioners will need to become 'business savvy; context savyy and organisation savvy to develop a deeper understanding of the businesses within which they operate'.

How this research and comment will impact on the future structure of HR services remains to be seen and has the potential to be the source of as much debate as that raised by Ulrich's model 19 years ago.

1.9 CONCLUSION

This chapter has highlighted key elements of the way an organisation structures its HR service delivery. At the start of the chapter the context in which HR services are delivered was explored. A range of variables that impact on the delivery of HR services was considered. Following on from this, the current models of HRM service delivery were explored, with a particular focus on a discussion of the introduction of Ulrich's three-legged stool model as opposed to the continued use of more traditional HR structures, together with a consideration of its success or otherwise. This section concluded that no one-size-fits-all model appears to be evident from the research, even though the Ulrich model has recently been considered to constitute best practice. The introduction of HR business partners appears to remain a popular method of HR service delivery. This has allowed the HR function to become more closely aligned with business practice. The chapter went on to look at HR outsourcing and its place in the provision of HR services. In particular, it focused on its role in supporting HR to realign its services as an aid to cost reduction and to concentrate resources on strategic issues within the organisation. Towards the end of the chapter we reviewed the connection between line managers and HR services. We also analysed the measurement of HR services, including their accompanying methods, and concluded that, used well, good HR indicators may be a powerful determinant in establishing the credibility of the HR function. The chapter ended with a look at the potential challenges to the way HRM services may be delivered in the future, including an exploration of the CIPD's report *Changing HR Operating Models*, together with a glimpse of the CIPD's Next Generation research into **insight-driven** HR.

FURTHER READING

CIPD (2005) *HR outsourcing: the key decisions*. London: Chartered Institute of Personnel and Development (Scott-Jackson, W., Newham, T. and Gurney, M.).

CIPD (2006) *The changing HR function: the key questions*. London: Chartered Institute of Personnel and Development (Tamkin, P., Reilly, P. and Strebler, A.).

CIPD (2007) *The changing HR function: transforming HR*. London: Chartered Institute of Personnel and Development (Reilly, P., Tamkin, P. and Broughton, A.).

CIPD (2011) *Next generation HR: insight-driven*. London: Chartered Institute of Personnel and Development.

CIPD (2015) *Changing HR operating models*. London: Chartered Institute of Personnel and Development.

REILLY, P. (2000) *HR shared services and the realignment of HR*. Brighton: University of Sussex, Institute of Employment Studies.

ULRICH, D. (1997) *Human resource champions: the next agenda for adding value and delivering results*. Boston, MA: Harvard Business Review Press.

REFERENCES

APPELBAUM, E., BAILEY, T., BERG, P. and KALLEBERG, A. (2000) *Manufacturing advantage: Why high performance systems pay off*. Ithaca, NY: ILR Press.

BECKER, B. and HUSELID, M. (1999) Overview: strategic human resource management in five leading firms. *Human Resource Management*. Vol 38. pp287–301.

BERSIN, J. (2015) A modern HR operating model: the world has changed. In: CIPD (ed.). *Changing HR operating models*. London: Chartered Institute of Personnel and Development.

BOLTON, R. and PAYNE, T. (2013) People are the real numbers. HR analytics has come of age. KPMG International [online]. Available at: https://www.kpmg.com/NL/nl/IssuesAndInsights/ArticlesPublications/Documents/PDF/Management-Consulting/People-are-the-real-numbers.pdf [Accessed 2015].

BOROUGHS, A. (2015) The future is centres of expertise: What impact has 18 years of the Ulrich model had on the HR operating model and what does it tell us about the future? In: CIPD (ed.). *Changing HR operating models*. London: Chartered Institute of Personnel and Development.

BROWN, D. (2015) What does the Future hold for HR? *Personnel Management*, August 2015 [online]. Available at: www.cipd.co.uk/pm/peoplemanagement/b/weblog/archive/2015/08/25/opinion-what-does-the-future-hold-for-hr.aspx [Accessed 2015].

CALDWELL, R. (2001) Champions, adapters, consultants and synergists: the new change agents in HRM. *Human Resource Management Journal*. Vol 11, No 3. pp39–52.

CAPPELLI, P. (2015) Why we love to hate HR and what HR can do about it. *Harvard Business Review*. Vol 93, No 7/8, July/August. pp55–61.

CHARAN, R. (2014) It's time to split HR. *Harvard Business Review.* Vol 92, No 7/8, July/ August. p34.

CHURCHARD, C. (2009) Aviva cuts costs with self-service HR system. *People Management.* December.

CIPD (2005) *HR outsourcing: the key decisions.* London: Chartered Institute of Personnel and Development (Scott-Jackson, W., Newham, T. and Gurney, M.).

CIPD (2006) *The changing HR function: the key questions.* London: Chartered Institute of Personnel and Development (Tamkin, P., Reilly, P. and Strebler, A.).

CIPD (2007) *The changing HR function: transforming HR.* London: Chartered Institute of Personnel and Development (Reilly, P., Tamkin, P. and Broughton, A.).

CIPD (2009a) *HR outsourcing and the HR function: threat or opportunity.* London: Chartered Institute of Personnel and Development.

CIPD (2011) *Next generation HR: insight-driven.* London: Chartered Institute of Personnel and Development.

CIPD (2015a) *HR business partnering.* Factsheet. London: Chartered Institute of Personnel and Development.

CIPD (2015b) *HR shared services centres.* Factsheet. London: Chartered Institute of Personnel and Development.

CIPD (2015c) *HR analytics.* Factsheet. London: Chartered Institute of Personnel and Development.

CIPD (2015d) *The role of line managers in HR.* Factsheet. London: Chartered Institute of Personnel and Development.

CIPD (2015e) *HR outsourcing.* Factsheet. London: Chartered Institute of Personnel and Development.

CIPD (2015f) *HR outlook winter 2014–5.* London: Chartered Institute of Personnel and Development.

CIPD (2015g) *Changing HR operating models.* London: Chartered Institute of Personnel and Development.

CRAIL, M. (2004) Welcome the multi-tasking all-purpose management expert. *IRS Employment Trends.* No. 793, February.

CRAIL, M. (2006) HR roles and responsibilities 2006: benchmarking the HR function. *IRS Employment Review.* No. 839, January. pp9–15.

DELOITTE (2009) *Shaping up: evolving the HR function for the 21st century.* New York/ London: Deloitte MCS.

FRY, B. and FISHMAN, A. (2015) Owning our HR operating model: an enterprise centre's organisation design methodology for HR. In: CIPD (ed.). *Changing HR operating models.* London: Chartered Institute of Personnel and Development.

HAMMOND, H. (2002) A dynamic duo. *People Management.* 21 March.

HARDING, C. (2015) The future of HR and the role of analytics. Report from the 14th HR Directors Business Summit.

HENNESSEY, J. (2009) Take your partners and advance. *People Management.* 29 January. pp24–7.

HOLLEY, N. (2015) You can't put in what God left out: not everyone can be a strategic HR Business Partner. In: CIPD (ed.). *Changing HR operating models.* London: Chartered Institute of Personnel and Development.

MILLER, J. (2015) What does the future of HR look like in an SME? In: CIPD (ed.). *Changing HR operating models.* London: Chartered Institute of Personnel and Development.

PEACOCK, L. (2008) Dave Ulrich's model defence. *Personnel Today.* 15 April.

PEOPLE MANAGEMENT (1998) Centre stage. 12 November.

PEOPLE MANAGEMENT (2000) Self service is hard work. 23 November.

PEOPLE MANAGEMENT (2006) Capita wins BBC's HR outsourcing contract. 17 February.

PICKARD, J. (2004) Unchartered shores. *People Management.* December 2004.

PITCHER, G. (2008) Backlash against HR business partner model. *Personnel Today.* 29 January.

PRITCHARD, K. (2010) Becoming an HR strategic partner: tales of transition. *Human Resource Management Journal.* Vol 20, No 2. pp175–88.

PURCELL, J., KINNIE, N., HUTCHINSON, S., RAYTON, B. and SWART, J. (2003) *Understanding the people and performance link: unlocking the black box.* London: Chartered Institute of Personnel and Development.

REILLY, P. (2000) *HR shared services and the realignment of HR.* Brighton: University of Sussex, Institute of Employment Studies.

REILLY, P., TAMKIN, P. and BROUGHTON, A. (2007) *The changing HR function: transforming HR.* Research into Practice. See CIPD (2007).

SPARROW, P. (2015) Living in a collaborative world: implications for HR operating models. In: CIPD (ed.). *Changing HR operating models.* London: Chartered Institute of Personnel and Development.

TRUSS, K. (2001) Complexities and controversies in linking HRM with organizational outcomes. *Journal of Management Studies.* Vol 38, No 8. pp1121–49.

ULRICH, D. (1997) *Human resource champions: the next agenda for adding value and delivering results.* Boston, MA: Harvard Business Review Press.

ULRICH, D. (2015) Reflecting on the past and looking to the future: the importance of business structure. In: CIPD (ed.). *Changing HR operating models.* London: Chartered Institute of Personnel and Development.

ULRICH, D., YOUNGER, J. and BROCKBANK, W. (2008) The twenty-first century organization. *Human Resource Management.* Vol 47, No 4, Winter. pp829–50.

WEST, M. A., GUTHRIE, J. P., DAWSON, J. F., BORRILL, C. S. and CARTER, M. R. (2006) Reducing patient mortality in hospitals: the role of human resource management. *Journal of Organizational Behavior.* Vol 27. pp983–1002.

CHAPTER 2

Employment Law

STEPHEN TAYLOR AND KRYSTAL WILKINSON

CHAPTER CONTENTS

- Introducing UK employment law
- Recruiting and promoting people
- Change management
- Pay and working time
- Managing discipline and poor performance
- Other major employment rights

KEY LEARNING OUTCOMES

By the end of this chapter, you should be able to:

- understand the purpose of employment regulation and the way it is enforced in practice
- manage recruitment and selection activities lawfully
- manage change and reorganisation lawfully
- manage issues related to pay and working time lawfully
- ensure that staff are treated lawfully when they are at work
- manage performance and disciplinary matters lawfully.

2.1 INTRODUCING UK EMPLOYMENT LAW

In recent years it has become essential for HR managers to gain and then to maintain a good working knowledge of employment law. This is because the amount of employment law has increased greatly, creating many more situations in which management decisions or a lack of management oversight can lead employees, ex-employees and failed job applicants to challenge an employing organisation in a court or **employment tribunal**. While the introduction of claim fees in 2013 served to reduce the number of cases very considerably, it remains the case that a failure to act lawfully when handling the employment relationship is risky. When cases come to court considerable organisational costs are almost always incurred, as well as reputational damage arising from media coverage.

There are now over 80 distinct types of claim that can be brought to an employment tribunal, in addition to many more that are employment-related but that are heard in the County Courts (Shackleton 2005). Many of the most important of these have either been introduced or expanded in the past ten years (for example, discrimination on the grounds of age, religion or belief and sexual orientation, paternity leave, rights for agency workers, etc), giving people more potential grounds for launching legal claims. Employers have also contributed by sacking more people. It is estimated, for example, that 2.7 million people were made redundant during the economic downturn between 2008 and 2012, receiving severance payments of £28.6 billion (CIPD 2012).

Employment law can affect and influence a huge range of HR decisions, policies and practices. It requires us to think carefully before going ahead with plans that make complete operational sense but that carry a legal risk. It restricts what we are able to do in practice and accounts for a great deal of our time – 20% on average, according to a CIPD survey (2002).

Employment law is also the subject of a great deal of debate and fierce political controversy. This is because people disagree hugely about its economic benefits and about how far it is in practice desirable to protect employment rights through state regulation.

In this chapter we begin by introducing some core debates about employment law in general terms. We go on to focus in particular on the ways in which law affects practice in the fields of recruitment and promotion, the management of change, pay and working time issues, managing discipline and poor performance, health and safety and relationships with trade unions.

2.1.1 DEBATES ABOUT EMPLOYMENT LAW

The arguments in favour of extensive employment law are rooted in the desire to enhance social justice. While we tend to presume that employers and employees are equal parties, free to negotiate contractual terms as they see fit, this is a long way from being the reality of the position for most. In truth, employers are many times more powerful than their employees and in a position, should they wish to, to exploit them unreasonably. Were it not for employment law, many employers would be tempted to compromise on health and safety, to pay unfairly low wages, to work their staff far too hard, to sack them for no good reason without compensation and to deny them basic rights such as maternity leave and equal pay for men and women. Minority groups would have fewer opportunities than they do, while all would run the risk of being bullied and harassed by unscrupulous managers. There would also be few guaranteed rights for **trade unions** and their members, and no obligations on employers to consult with their staff about anything at all.

The main arguments against employment regulation are economic. It is argued that although protections of this kind undoubtedly benefit employees, there is a price to pay in higher unemployment and lower economic growth. Employment law places a 'regulatory burden' on employers, often takes the form of unnecessary red tape, and hugely increases the economic risks associated with employing people. It thus serves to act as a major deterrent to smaller employers who might otherwise hire new people and to international companies who choose not to site their operations in the UK because the conditions are more employer-friendly elsewhere. More generally, because employment law adds to UK employers' costs, it makes them less competitive than commercial rivals based in other countries.

Another set of arguments against employment regulation is based on the idea that it actually harms the people it is intended to protect. It is not uncommon, for example, to hear of instances in which prominent business people argue against employing women of child-bearing age because of the many employment rights that they have the potential to claim (Lea 2001; Brewer 2008).

Less commonly expressed, but equally important, are the economic arguments in favour of employment regulation. Some argue, for example, that it is important to make work attractive in order to make sure that employers have access to the skilled staff that they require and who otherwise might choose to take early **retirement** or work in another country. It is also persuasively argued that poor, inequitable employment practices reduce employee commitment and hence productivity. The most productive and efficient economies in the world, it is pointed out, are often the most highly and effectively regulated ones.

?   REFLECTIVE ACTIVITY 2.1

The groups that complain most about the negative impact of employment regulation have always been those who represent the interests of small businesses. They argue that larger organisations can cope much better with it because they have more resources available and because employment law tends to be designed around their needs. This often leads them to argue that there should be major exemptions for small businesses from whole areas of employment law.

1   Why are small businesses less well equipped to deal with increasing amounts of employment regulation than larger ones are?

2   What arguments can be made against the proposition that small businesses should not be required to comply with some employment laws?

2.1.2 THE EMPLOYMENT LAW SYSTEM

Most UK employment law takes the form of **statutes** passed by Parliament. These comprise Acts (such as the Employee Relations Act 1996, the Employment Act 2002, the Equality Act 2010, the Enterprise and Regulatory Reform Act 2013) or Regulations issued under the terms of Acts (such as the Agency Workers' Regulations 2011, the Unfair Dismissal and Statements of Reasons for Dismissal Regulations 2012). In recent years many employment statutes have had a European origin, the UK Parliament giving effect in British law to the contents of Directives agreed by European Union institutions. In some cases the impact has been profound, EU Directives and the subsequent UK regulations that implement them having major implications for HRM practice in many industries. Good examples are the Working Time Directive (implemented in the UK as the Working Time Regulations 1998) and the Acquired Rights Directive which have been implemented in the UK in successive sets of Transfer of Undertakings (Protection of Employment) Regulations.

It is, however, important to grasp that not all of our employment law appears in statutes. Indeed, some of the most significant rights have never been considered by Parliament, let alone made by it. Instead, they come to us via the **common law**, which has been made by judges and which has evolved over many centuries.

This is true of the law of contract, which regulates the fundamental relationship between employers and employees, and of the law of negligence, which provides us with the right to claim compensation when we suffer an injury at work. The common law is made when judges rule on points of principle in cases that are brought before them. These then become precedents, which are followed whenever a similar case is brought in the future.

The UK court system is hierarchical, there being a right to appeal against the outcome of cases to a higher court. Because the rulings of higher courts on points of law are binding on all the lower courts, new law is effectively created whenever a higher court decides that the law is to be interpreted in a particular way. This principle applies when it comes to the interpretation of statutes as well as in common law matters. The practical consequences are highly significant. It means that UK employers have to be familiar not just with what a statute says, but also with what it has been held to mean in practical terms in the case law.

When **claimants** (employees, ex-employees or failed job applicants) wish to pursue claims that concern rights enshrined in an employment statute, they first inform the Advisory, Conciliation and Arbitration Service (ACAS) of their intention. ACAS officials then contact the employer (that is, the respondent in the case) and speak to the claimant or his/her representative with a view to facilitating an out of court settlement. If these attempts fail, the claimant can go ahead and lodge the claim at the local employment tribunal office. A few weeks later, provided the claim is neither withdrawn nor settled, a hearing is convened at which both sides in the dispute present their cases, cross-examine one another's witnesses and ask the presiding Employment Judge to interpret the law in their favour. In some circumstances a panel of three may hear a case, but nowadays it is more common for cases to be heard and decided by judges sitting alone.

For most areas of jurisdiction, **employment tribunals** are only able to accept a case and list it for a hearing if the claim form arrives at the tribunal office within three months of the incident about which the claimant is complaining, less the time that ACAS officials have spent seeking a settlement. In the case of contested dismissals the cut-off date is three months from the date at which the dismissal took effect (the effective date of termination). In the case of ongoing disputes the rule is that a case must be brought within three months of a date at which it is alleged a detriment was suffered by the claimant. So, for example, an employee who believes that he or she has not been paid at the level of the National Minimum Wage has up to three months from their leaving date to pursue a claim.

Appeals from the employment tribunal can only be made on points of law. You cannot appeal simply because the judge found your witnesses to be less credible than those of your opponents or because of the way particular facts were interpreted. However, if you believe that the judge has misapplied or misinterpreted the law – case law as well as statutes – an appeal can be made to the next court in the hierarchy. This is the **Employment Appeals Tribunal** (the EAT), which has responsibility for deciding how new employment statutes will be interpreted, and thus makes highly significant rulings that affect all employers in the country.

Disputes that relate to the common law do not generally go before an employment tribunal. Instead, they are heard by judges of the County Courts or, when high levels of compensation are being sought, by the High Court. Here no three-month rule applies, most claimants having up to six years to bring a claim before they are timed out.

Appeals from the EAT, County Court and High Court are heard by the Court of Appeal in England or the Court of Session in Scotland. It is rare for cases to go further, but when major issues of public interest are at stake, cases can be appealed to the **Supreme Court** (formally known as the House of Lords). This happens in an employment matter perhaps three or four times a year. The Supreme Court is the final court of appeal as far as UK law is concerned. However, when a case concerns a principle of European law there is the possibility of a further appeal to the **European Court of Justice** in Luxemburg.

This is where disputes about the implementation and interpretation of EU Directives are settled.

2.2 RECRUITING AND PROMOTING PEOPLE

HR managers are obliged to take account of the possible legal consequences of their actions across all areas of their activities. The law permits people who have a range of 'protected characteristics' to claim compensation when they suffer from unfair discrimination. So when recruiting, selecting and promoting staff, managers need to ensure not only that they treat everyone who applies for a job equitably and fairly, but also that they are seen to do so.

Another area of employment law that has to be taken account of when recruiting new staff is the law of contract. When a new employee is hired, a **contract of employment** is established, which is legally binding on both parties and enforceable in the courts. Importantly, this means that employers are not lawfully able to reduce someone's pay or employment conditions unilaterally without first securing their agreement. So it is essential that great care is taken to offer terms that will subsequently be honoured.

2.2.1 DIRECT AND INDIRECT DISCRIMINATION

The Equality Act 2010 provides protection from unfair discrimination for people with the following protected characteristics:

- age
- disability
- gender reassignment
- marriage and civil partnership
- pregnancy and maternity
- race, ethnicity and national origin
- religion or belief
- sex
- sexual orientation.

In addition, further EU law provides some protection for the following groups:

- part-time workers
- fixed-term workers.

Further UK law also extends some protection on the following grounds:

- being ex-offenders
- union membership or non-membership.

In the case of the protected characteristics covered by the Equality Act, a clear and important distinction is made between direct and indirect discrimination.

Direct discrimination occurs at the recruitment stage when an employer fails to shortlist or to appoint a well-qualified person purely on grounds of a protected characteristic. Appointing a woman because she is a woman, or a white person because of his or her ethnicity would be examples of direct discrimination. In the case of most protected characteristics, actions such as these, if they are proven on the balance of probabilities to have occurred, are unlawful. In other words, the case goes against the employer and compensation must be paid to the claimant.

Importantly, no defence can be heard. However reasonable or justified an employer considers its actions to have been, rejecting a candidate on one of these grounds is simply not lawful.

There are nonetheless some exceptions to this general rule. Firstly, it is lawful for employers to reserve some jobs for particular groups. These are jobs that have what are known as 'occupational requirements' (formerly 'genuine occupational qualifications'), which mean that they have to be done by people of a particular gender, race or age. Acting and modelling jobs are common examples, as is work in ethnically themed restaurants and where, for reasons of decency, a job can only practically be carried out either by a man or a woman. Secondly, in the case of discrimination on grounds of disability and age (and not the other protected characteristics), employers are entitled in law to deploy a general justification when they directly discriminate. In other words, an employer can argue that a disabled person was turned down for a job on grounds of disability or that a 65-year-old was turned down on grounds of age, but that there is a good, genuine business reason that justifies the decision. In the case of disability discrimination the tribunal must be satisfied that there are no 'reasonable adjustments' to working practices or to the working environment that the employer could make in order to accommodate the needs of a disabled candidate. In the case of age discrimination the following question is asked:

> Did the decision not to appoint/shortlist/promote the claimant amount to a proportionate means of achieving a legitimate aim?

This same legal test is used to determine cases of indirect discrimination, although here the defence can be deployed in the case of all the protected characteristics. An act of indirect discrimination occurs when an employer has in place 'a rule, criterion or practice' that has an adverse effect on a substantially greater number of people with a protected characteristic than it does on others.

A simple example is a height requirement. Were an employer to state that applicants for a particular role had to be over six feet tall, it would be applying a rule that many more men are able to comply with than women. That is indirect discrimination. The same of course would be true in reverse were an employer to stipulate that only people under six feet could apply for a role. Indirect race discrimination in recruitment occurs when an employer stipulates that it will only consider applications from people who hold a specific UK qualification, while indirect religious discrimination occurs when an employer requires staff who are prepared to work on religious holiday days. Indirect age discrimination is most common of all, happening whenever a person specification requires a set number of years' experience before a job application will be considered. This is because fewer younger people are able to comply with the condition than older people. In all of these cases the employer is acting unlawfully unless it can satisfy the tribunal that its rule, criterion or practice represents 'a proportionate means of achieving a legitimate aim', namely that there is a good, genuine business justification for it.

The Equality Act also permits employers to discriminate positively in favour of 'under-represented groups' when they are recruiting, but only in circumstances in which they have interviewed candidates who are equally appointable. So an organisation with no women on its board of directors could, if it wished to, select a female candidate over a male rival provided the two were of equal merit. The reason given could, quite lawfully, be that she was chosen because she is a she.

? REFLECTIVE ACTIVITY 2.2

Which of the following recruitment decisions, in your view, would be lawful, which unlawful, and why?

- Only shortlisting people of Chinese ethnicity to work as waiting staff in a Chinese restaurant
- Stipulating that cabin crew employed to work on an aeroplane must be under six and a half feet tall
- Refusing to interview a man aged 55 who has applied to join a company's graduate training scheme
- Turning down an application from a disabled woman who, while well qualified, could only perform the job in question if she is assisted by other employees in doing so
- Insisting that all applicants for a teaching job in a Roman Catholic school are baptised Roman Catholics
- Selecting a well-qualified male candidate for employment as a primary school teacher because all the existing staff are women and a more balanced team is sought

- Only recruiting people to a driving job who can demonstrate that they possess 'a full, clean UK driving licence'.

2.2.2 FORMING A CONTRACT OF EMPLOYMENT

Discrimination law of the kind described above generally applies to all workers, whatever their contractual status. However, this is not true of all employment law, some of which applies only to people who are employed to work under 'contracts of service', commonly known as 'contracts of employment'. This includes the right not to be unfairly dismissed as well as a host of other important protections that employees enjoy thanks to the law of contract, such as the right to a relationship of mutual trust and confidence. Moreover, of course, once a contract of employment is established, it cannot generally be altered without both sides agreeing to an amendment.

For these reasons managers must take great care when recruiting staff to ensure that both sides are fully aware of the type of relationship they are entering into and the legal rights and obligations that it entails.

Establishing a contract of employment is remarkably easy. There is no need for any written documentation or even a handshake. A contract can be formed during a telephone conversation or via an exchange of emails. Obviously, it is preferable for the main terms and conditions to be spelled out unambiguously on paper so that everyone knows where they stand, but this is not a prerequisite in UK law for the establishment of a legally binding contract. In fact there are only five major conditions that must be in place in order for a contract of employment to exist:

- an unconditional offer
- an unconditional acceptance of the offer
- an intention to form a legal relationship (that is, not an informal agreement between friends and family members)
- consideration (payment or payment in kind)
- certainty (that is, clarity about the main terms and conditions).

One or two further regulatory restrictions ensure that minors are not bound to contracts that operate against their interests, that the contract is not 'tainted by illegality' and that both parties are 'of sound mind' when the contract is formed. It is also important to note that 'consideration' is not always a requirement under Scottish law. Otherwise, provided all five conditions are satisfied, a contract of employment exists with all the legal rights and obligations that follow.

Some types of contractual arrangement between workers and their employers are defined in law as amounting to 'contracts for services' rather than 'contracts of service'. These are not full contracts of employment and mean, as we explained above, that the job-holder does not enjoy the full protection of all employment law.

The distinction between 'a contract of service' and 'a contract for services' is not always clear. Self-employed people can fall into the second category, but do not always do so, giving rise to further complications about who exactly has what legal rights and about when and where they can be enforced.

We do not have the space in this chapter to discuss these complex legal issues at any length. You will find a proper, full explanation of the situation in Taylor and Emir (2015, Chapter 3). But it is important that you appreciate one key point.

When deciding who falls into which category, the courts look at the reality of the relationship that has been established between the worker and the employer. It is not possible to deny people their full employment rights simply by labelling the relationship 'self-employment', 'an agency contract' or 'casual employment' and providing documentation to that effect. Employers are often tempted into this in order to avoid paying employers' National Insurance contributions (a payroll tax on employees paid by employers), but they are often acting unlawfully in doing so. As far as the law is concerned, what matters is what happens in practice. If a worker works under the control of an employer and uses its tools for the job, cannot substitute someone else when he or she cannot work and cannot turn work down if it is offered without risking losing the job, there is in all likelihood a contract of employment in place with all that this entails legally for both parties.

2.3 CHANGE MANAGEMENT

Here too great care must be taken in order to avoid breaching employment law and running the risk that staff (or former staff) will seek damages for compensation in court. Managers need to take particular care to avoid pushing through changes in terms and conditions unlawfully, but it is also necessary in many cases of reorganisation to take account of redundancy law and the Transfer of Undertakings (Protection of Employment) Regulations.

2.3.1 CHANGING CONTRACTS LAWFULLY

As we explained in the previous section, a core principle of the law of contract in the UK is that once formed, a contract of employment is legally binding on both parties. An employer cannot lawfully make detrimental changes without first securing the agreement of the employee any more than the employee can announce a unilateral change. However, the law recognises that from time to time employers have to make changes for good, strong business reasons. We do not have the space here to discuss all these situations in depth, but the following are the most important and the most common:

- Including a flexibility clause in the contract that gives the employer the right to make reasonable changes to terms and conditions from time to time in accordance with business needs. Mobility clauses are a common form of flexibility clause, which allow employers lawfully to relocate their staff provided reasonable notice is given.
- Writing to the employee setting out contractual changes, while anticipating that there will be no negative response. This is an uncertain approach but can work if the employee's response is to continue to come to work without objecting to the change. There is no specific time stipulation, but after two months or so an employer is entitled in law to assume that the employee has signalled 'acceptance through practice'.
- Negotiating changes with a trade union when there is a collective agreement in place that has been incorporated into all individual contracts of employment.
- Dismissing staff before rehiring them instantly on new terms and conditions of employment. This is a risky option because it raises the possibility that employees will bring unfair dismissal cases and, if successful, require reinstatement of their original contracts. Sometimes, however, there is no choice if contractual change is to be forced through against the wishes of affected employees. The key is to remember that in doing this the employer must act 'reasonably' if it is to defend itself successfully in court. Usually this means only moving to 'dismissal and rehire' as a last resort.

Employers are entitled in law to make technical changes to working arrangements that fall short of contractual amendments. This includes the introduction of new machinery or of new working practices provided they do not impact on core contractual terms such as hours of work or pay rates. It is also important to remember that a breach of contract claim will only succeed if a claimant can satisfy the court that a genuine detriment has been suffered. Causing staff relatively minor inconvenience is therefore unlikely to lead to a court case – as, of course, are changes that on balance work in the employee's favour, such as pay rises.

A final point to make in this section concerns the law of **constructive dismissal**. This can only be claimed by employees with over two years' service behind them, but they can win substantial compensation if successful. A constructive dismissal occurs when the following conditions (set in the case of *Western Excavating (ECC) Ltd v Sharp*, 1978) are all satisfied:

● The employer must, through its action, be in actual or anticipatory breach of the contract of employment.
● The employer must be guilty of 'a significant breach going to the root of the contract' or show through its action that it no longer intends to be bound by an essential term of the contract.
● The employee must decide to resign shortly after the breach.
● The employee must resign in response to the breach.

This means that an employee who chooses to resign rather than to accept an employer's breach of contract is able to pursue their claim for compensation at the employment tribunal and is not required to go to the County Court at considerable expense. Employers can defend themselves in cases of constructive dismissal by demonstrating that a reorganisation was necessary for a good business reason and otherwise carried out reasonably, but there are considerable, potential financial risks associated with failing to satisfy the tribunal that this is the case.

These days many constructive dismissal claims relate to breaches of implied terms on the part of employers, and in particular the very broad 'duty to retain a relationship of trust and confidence' which we will be revisting again later in the chapter. The evolution of this implied term means that employees are able to resign in protest following all kinds of situations in which they feel that their employer has treated them dishonestly or in some other unpleasant manner and have their case treated as if it were a dismissal. While the employers' actions can not be trivial in any way in order that such a case can be sustained, there is often no way of predicting what a particular Employment Judge will see as constituting a fundamental breach of trust and confidence.

2.3.2 REDUNDANCY

A well-established employment right that applies to all employees who have completed two years' service is the right to receive a severance payment when they are made redundant. There are also a range of procedural requirements that employers must follow when making redundancies in order to avoid claims of unfair dismissal.

A **redundancy** occurs when an employer is reducing its headcount for economic reasons. People are dismissed, albeit with compensation, because the employer can no longer afford to continue their employment. While individual conduct and performance may well determine who is selected for redundancy and who continues to work, these are not the reason that the dismissals are occurring.

Redundancies are part and parcel of many change management episodes. It is not difficult to carry them out lawfully when you know what you are doing, but this does not prevent many thousands of cases going to the employment tribunal each year. The key requirements are:

● The employer must identify a pool of 'at risk' employees from whom it will select those who are going to be made redundant. The decision about who should and should not be in the pool is for the employer to determine, but it must be reasonable.
● The employer must consult with those who are at risk about the proposed selection method and about ways of minimising the number of redundancies. Individual consultation is always required. Collective consultation with a recognised trade union or other elected representatives is required when more than 20 redundancies are proposed.

- Redundancy selection must be objective and reasonable. In practice this means either selecting those who have the shortest service ('last in, first out'), scoring everyone according to performance measures or requiring 'at risk' staff to apply competitively for jobs in a new structure.

Minimum levels of redundancy compensation are set out in the employment statutes. These increase somewhat each year, but are based on the employee's age, length of service and current salary. At the time of writing (2015) the maximum payment that employees can claim under the statutory scheme is £14,250. In practice many employers pay considerably higher sums, particularly when they are contractually obliged to do so.

2.3.3 TUPE

The Transfer of Undertakings (Protection of Employment) Regulations derive from two European 'acquired rights' Directives dating from 1977 and 2001. In the UK the law in this area has long been referred to as 'TUPE' (pronounced 'tupey').

It is complex and unsatisfactory in many ways, although matters were clarified to an extent with a new set of Regulations that came into effect in April 2006. The aim of the law is to help ensure that in most respects employees do not lose out when the identity of their employer changes, and to protect them from dismissal or redundancy when a business transfer takes place. TUPE now applies in two distinct types of situation:

- where a business, part of a business or part of another type of employing organisation is merged with or taken over by another employer
- where the contract to provide a service is either lost by one provider and won by another, or otherwise outsourced/insourced by an organisation.

The TUPE Regulations thus have to be taken account of in many cases of structural change, in any situation in which the identity of someone's employer changes, or when a contract that a group of staff work on most of the time transfers from one provider to another.

The key employment rights/legal duties that apply in TUPE situations are:

- Employees affected by a transfer have the right to be consulted formally before, during and after the transfer by both the transferor and transferee organisations.
- Employees have the right to have their continuity of service recognised by their new employer.
- The contents of contracts of employment transfer with the employees to whom they apply. It is usually unlawful to force changes to contracts as a result of a TUPE transfer.
- Employment-related liabilities and benefits as well as collective agreements transfer along with employees in TUPE situations.
- It is usually unfair in law to dismiss an employee for a reason related to a TUPE transfer.
- There are obligations placed on transferors to give specific information to transferees about the employees who are transferring.

The TUPE Regulations are usually seen as providing important legal rights protecting the interests of employees. It is important to remember, however, that in one very major respect they favour the employer's interest. This is because they deny employees the right to object to being transferred across to another employment except where the regulations are not fully complied with. If an employee does object and resigns at the point of transfer, however many years' service he/she has, there can be no case for unfair dismissal or constructive dismissal unless there is a reduction in the level of terms and conditions (ie TUPE is not followed) after the transfer.

The TUPE regulations sometimes create situations which employers find difficult to accept. The most common example occurs when one company merges or takes over another and seeks to gain efficiency savings as a result. In such situations two groups of employees who are often used to working in very different cultural settings and also have different terms and conditions of employment are brought together and asked to form a single, cohesive team. Building a single, harmonised culture is hard enough in such situations, particularly when one group feel dominated by another and are obliged to make more compromises. But tensions are often heightened by the fact that post-merger, the two groups must continue to be employed on their original terms and conditions. This typically means that rates of pay are different, and the same may well be true of things like holiday entitlement, redundancy terms and sick pay arrangements. The former employees of Company A might be paid a great deal more, be paid well when off sick and enjoy longer holiday entitlements than their new colleagues who used to be employees of Company B. However, the management of the newly merged Company A&B are restricted by the TUPE regulations from harmonising terms and conditions in the most efficient manner. Unless everyone is given the most generous package, they run the risk of legal action if any changes are made.

2.4 PAY AND WORKING TIME

How much we are paid and the amount of work we do are for most people the most significant elements of their contract of employment. They are also fundamental factors in determining our productivity and hence our value to our employers. They are therefore key sources of potential conflict between staff and their organisations and are, unsurprisingly, regulated quite heavily in important respects.

2.4.1 THE NATIONAL MINIMUM WAGE (NMW)

Since 1999, each year, a body called the Low Pay Commission has advised ministers on an appropriate level for the NMW. It is required to recommend a wage that will maximise living standards for the lowest-paid workers but which is not so high as to have a serious adverse impact on levels of employment.

In fact the government sets four separate minimum hourly rates for different groups of workers. In most years these rise on 1 October. At the time of writing (late 2015) the rates are:

Main adult rate: £6.70

Lower rate for those aged 18–22 or 22+ who are in training in a new job: £5.30

Youth rate for 16–17-year-olds: £3.87

Apprentice rate: £3.30

From April 2016 a new National Living Wage (NLW) is being introduced for people who are over 25 years old. It is initially being set at £7.20 an hour, the plan being that it should rise to £9 an hour by 2020.

2.4.2 EQUAL PAY LAW

One of the longest-established employment regulations stipulates that men and women should be paid the same for doing 'like work, work which is rated as equivalent and work of equal value', provided they work for the same employer, the same group of companies or are covered by the same industry-level collective agreement. This right is enshrined in the major European treaties and is generally considered to constitute a fundamental human right. The law in the UK has a number of complexities that can be confusing, but the fundamental rights are easily stated and readily explained.

The term 'like work' means any work that is either the same or broadly similar. So two people, one male and one female, should be paid the same amount for doing the same job. 'Work of equal value' refers to a situation in which a man and a woman are employed in the same organisation but do different jobs. The law states that if the work they do is nonetheless broadly equal in terms of the level of skill, experience and effort required, as well as the level of responsibility the jobs carry, then their pay should also be the same. Where this is not the case, a mechanism is provided for a claimant to test his or her case at an employment tribunal. Provided a basic case can be made out, the tribunal is obliged to appoint an 'independent expert' to carry out a job evaluation exercise to determine whether or not the two jobs are of equal value.

The term 'work rated as equivalent' requires more explanation. This plays a part when an employer carries out a job evaluation exercise which results in two different jobs (one held by a man, the other by a woman) being graded at the same level. Sometimes an employer will do this but will then stop short of implementing the new grading system. In such cases a claim can be made to enforce equality. More commonly, work rated as equivalent cases relate to situations in which a new grading system is introduced, resulting in a group of employees being re-graded to a higher level thanks to a job evaluation exercise. If the group is predominantly female, for example, and now finds itself graded at the same level as a group which is predominantly male but which has historically been paid more, then claims for back pay can be made going back for six years.

Employers can defend themselves in equal pay cases by satisfying the tribunal that there is a good, genuine business reason that explains any pay differential between men and women who should, on the face of it, be paid equally under the terms of equal pay law. These are known as 'material factors', the most significant of which are:

- one worker has more/higher qualifications than the other
- one worker is more skilled or has undertaken more training than the other
- one worker is more productive or higher-performing than the other
- one worker has greater seniority/length of service or experience than the other
- regional allowances (such as London weightings) explain the difference in pay
- the shift patterns are different – one worker being prepared to work more unsocial hours, for example
- budgetary constraints at the time of appointment meant that it was not possible to afford to match salaries between the male and the female worker.

2.4.3 DEDUCTIONS FROM WAGES

The right not to have unauthorised deductions made from your pay packet applies to all workers, not just to employees. It is small and simple bit of law but one that accounts for 20% of all employment tribunal cases. Essentially, the law lays out clearly the circumstances in which an employer can make deductions from pay without the consent of the worker. It follows that it is unlawful to make deductions in any other situation. The situations are:

- to recover overpayments of wages
- where a court orders that a deduction is made (for example an attachment order)
- when a worker takes industrial action

- where it is authorised by legislation (for example tax)
- where it is authorised by contract (for example trade union dues).

There are special rules for retailers to deal with cash shortages/stock deficiencies and for the police and army that permit fines to be levied as part of disciplinary procedures. The regulations do not permit fining for disciplinary offences in 99% of organisations. Fines cannot therefore be levied (in cases, for example, of lateness, misconduct, damage to property, etc) unless:

- there is an express term of contract saying it is permitted

  or

- the employee has agreed in writing *in advance* of the incident.

2.4.4 SICK PAY, MATERNITY PAY, ETC

These regulations help ensure that employees who are unable to work for periods due either to sickness, maternity or paternity are nonetheless paid a reasonable daily rate through their employer's payroll for set periods of time. In the case of Statutory Maternity Pay (SMP) and Statutory Paternity Pay (SPP) employers can claim back much of the money from the government through reduced National Insurance contributions. At the time of writing (2015) the rates are:

Statutory Sick Pay (SSP): £88.45 per week

Statutory Maternity Pay (SMP): 90% of salary for the first six weeks of maternity leave, then £139.58 for the remaining weeks.

Statutory Paternity Pay and Statutory Adoption Pay (for parents of newly adopted children) are paid at the same level as SMP.

Some groups do not qualify – mainly people who work part-time and earn too little. They have to claim money from the Benefits Agency instead.

It is important to understand that these are the statutory minimum sums that have to be paid by law. In practice many employers offer much more generous arrangements as part of their benefits packages. Return-to-work bonuses are also relatively common in the UK but are not required by law.

2.4.5 THE WORKING TIME REGULATIONS

These originate in the European Union and are quite complex and lengthy. However, the basic fundamental rights they give are easily summarised:

- a limit of 48 hours' work per week
- four weeks' paid annual leave each year in addition to the eight statutory bank holidays
- 20 minutes' rest in any period of work lasting six hours or more
- 11 hours' rest in any one 24-hour period
- 24 hours' rest in any seven-day period
- night workers are limited to eight hours' work in any one 24-hour period and have the right to free, regular health checks
- special provisions that restrict the working time of young workers (16–18 year-olds).

On the surface this looks clear-cut and straightforward, but this is in fact far from the case. The Regulations are very complex, running to more than 100 pages in length. There are three types of situation in which some or all of the Regulations do not apply. The major sources of complexity are:

- averaging

The regulations allow for considerable flexibility because they allow employers to average time worked over a reference period – in most cases 17 weeks.

- opt-outs

More generally, anyone can if they wish formally 'opt out' of the 48-hour week restriction by signing or writing a written declaration. Employers in the UK are lawfully able to make the signing of such an opt-out a requirement of employment.

Anyone is entitled at any time to opt back in by informing their employer in writing – they have to give three months' notice and cannot be victimised for exercising this right.

- workforce agreements

These allow an employer to seek to vary Working Time Regulations in various ways if it first secures acceptance by its workforce through a workforce agreement. Effectively, this means that whole workplaces can adapt their interpretation of the Working Time Regulations to suit their needs.

2.4.6 MATERNITY LEAVE

The statutory scheme specifies three different types of maternity leave:

- ordinary maternity leave (OML)
- compulsory maternity leave (CML)
- additional maternity leave (AML).

OML applies only to employees, but there is no qualifying period of service. It is now 26 weeks in duration (that is, six months).

OML normally starts on the intended date – that is, on the date the employee informed the employer that it would start. The earliest it can start is the 11th week prior to the Expected Week of Confinement (EWC) – that is, the date on which the baby is expected to be born.

However, it starts automatically at an earlier time in certain situations:

- if the baby arrives early
- if the woman is absent owing to a pregnancy-related illness in the four weeks prior to the EWC.

CML is straightforward: it is simply the two weeks after the birth, during which there is now a compulsory period of maternity leave. The onus is on the employer to make sure that no work is done during this period. Normally, CML and OML overlap – the baby would have to arrive extraordinarily late for this not to be the case – so CML only applies where a woman decides she does not wish to exercise her right to OML. The EU is currently actively considering a proposal to extend CML from two weeks to six weeks. It is too early to say whether or not such a change is likely to happen and, if so, from what date.

There is a general right of return to the same job on the same terms and conditions following CML and OML, all pay rises and other improvements to terms and conditions being honoured. After the return to work, the contractual situation should be as if the maternity leave had not happened. The only exception is where the job becomes redundant during OML, in which case the right is to return to a suitable alternative job with similar terms and conditions.

It is important to remember that the right is to return to the same job and not necessarily to the same work. It may be that changes have been made in the woman's absence that mean the work that she does on her return may be somewhat different. It only becomes a different job if the content is substantially altered. At present there is no general right for a woman to return on a part-time basis or on different working hours unless this is provided for in the contract of employment. But there is just a right to request flexible working, and a requirement that the employer only turns down such requests for defined business reasons set out in the statutes.

AML (additional maternity leave) applies only to employees (that is, women working under a 'contract of service') and it runs for a further 26 weeks following on from the end of OML.

The right to return after AML is to the same job *if reasonably practicable*. Otherwise, it is to a suitable job on no less favourable terms and conditions. During maternity leave the contract of employment continues in all respects except for pay. All benefits continue to accrue (including holidays). Company cars, portable computers and mobile phones are kept, health insurance is retained and all duties owed by employers and employees (mutual trust and confidence, etc) continue.

Since 2007 employers have gained the right to maintain reasonable contact with employees who are on maternity leave. This is to discuss a range of issues – for example their plans for returning to work, or to keep them informed of important developments at the workplace. The employee should also be informed of any relevant promotion opportunities or job vacancies that arise during maternity leave. In addition it is now possible for a woman to return to work on a temporary basis, by mutual agreement, for up to 10 days during her maternity leave in order to 'keep in touch', without this bringing the leave to an end. Pay for these days is something that is left for the individual parties to agree.

2.4.7 PATERNITY AND ADOPTION LEAVE

Fathers of newborn babies have a statutory right to take ordinary paternity leave (OPL) at the time of the birth, the right applying to employees who have been employed for 26 weeks at the start of the 14th week before the EWC and who expect to have responsibility for the child's upbringing. The period is up to two weeks, and it must be taken within 56 days of the birth.

In 2014 a new system was introduced which couples can make use of should they wish to. Under the shared parental leave regulations once a mother has completed her period of CML, she and the father are entitled to divide up the remainder of her paid leave entitlement between them in a flexible way. Importantly this means that both can take leave concurrently for several weeks directly after the baby is born.

The right to return after the leave is the same for mothers and fathers taking SPL as it is for mothers taking AML, as is the right to retain contractual benefits such as cars, laptops and even live-in accommodation.

Parents who adopt children are permitted under the statutory scheme to take leave on the same basis as parents of newly born children. The key date here is that on which the match between parents and child was made. The big difference is that the couple can choose which of them is going to take maternity leave and be paid SMP and which will take the benefits associated with paternity.

2.4.8 FURTHER FAMILY-FRIENDLY EMPLOYMENT RIGHTS

In addition to the rights to take leave that are associated with maternity, paternity and adoption, there are a few other statutory rights that apply in UK workplaces. These are:

- the right to take unpaid time off work to deal with family emergencies
- the right to take four months' unpaid parental leave
- the right to request flexible working.

The latter right permits employees, once a year only, to write to their employer formally asking for a one-off change in terms and conditions, together with an explanation as to how his or her request could be accommodated. Any change made as a result of the request is both contractual and permanent. So, for example, there is no right to request a year's part-time work followed by a return to full-time working.

The employer can turn the request down if it believes there is a good business reason for doing so. There are eight possible reasons given in the statute for legitimately refusing a request:

- the burden of additional costs
- a detrimental effect on the company's ability to meet customer demand
- an inability to reorganise work among existing staff
- an inability to recruit additional staff
- a detrimental impact on quality
- a detrimental impact on performance
- insufficiency of work during the periods the employee proposes to work
- planned structural changes.

?   REFLECTIVE ACTIVITY 2.3

Two brief summaries of cases that relate to family-friendly employment law are set out below. Read the summaries and then answer the questions that follow.

1   Mrs Edgell was employed as a bookkeeper. As part of her job she had the authority to sign cheques up to a specified limit. She also worked without day-to-day supervision, reporting to a senior manager. Following the birth of her child she went on maternity leave.

While she was away Lloyds reorganised their bookkeeping division, bringing in new administrative systems and a new organisational structure. When Mrs Edgell returned to work she was given a bookkeeping role at the same grade as she had been on before her leave, but she was no longer able to sign cheques and now worked under a supervisor. She resigned her post and brought two claims to tribunal:

- constructive dismissal
- infringement of the right to return to the same job following maternity leave.

Do you think Mrs Edgell should have won either or both of these claims?

2   Ms Moore and Ms Botterill both worked as air stewardesses on long-haul flights, both becoming pregnant at around the same time. In accordance with the terms of a collective agreement the two women were transferred to ground-based roles once they reached the 16th week of their pregnancies. The intention of the agreement was to ensure that the company complied with its duty to protect the health and safety of pregnant employees. The ground-based jobs were graded at the same level as the in-flight jobs the women carried out and they were equivalent in terms of skills and status. However, because the women were no longer cabin-crew members, they ceased to receive flying allowances in addition to their basic pay. British Airways argued that these allowances did not constitute pay but were intended to cover out-of-pocket expenses incurred by cabin crew members when staying away from home. The women showed that in practice the allowances were more generous, and that they had long considered them to form part of their regular pay packets.

Were the women entitled to continue receiving their flying allowances during their pregnancies, even when working in ground-based roles?

2.5 MANAGING DISCIPLINE AND POOR PERFORMANCE

A great deal of HR time is taken up with the management of disciplinary matters and of employees who are not performing their jobs to the required standard. We have already discussed some issues in this area, but we now need to focus on it properly. Central here is the law of unfair dismissal. While it is by no means the case that every employee who is guilty of misconduct or poor performance ends up being sacked, managers dealing with such matters always have to have at the back of their minds that the case *might* end up with a dismissal. You therefore always need to handle it from the start in accordance with the expectations of the law. Only then can you be confident that you will be able to defend your actions adequately at an employment tribunal, should that ultimately prove necessary.

Before we look at each main type of situation and at what response the law expects, we must make a few general points about unfair dismissal law.

Firstly, it is important to appreciate that unfair dismissal law only applies to employees. People who work under 'contracts for services' rather than 'contracts of service' cannot bring dismissal claims to an employment tribunal. This includes most casual staff, agency workers and people who are employed on a subcontracted basis. Secondly, for the most part it is only employees who have completed two years' continuous service as employees who can bring claims. There are significant exceptions to this rule deriving from the presence in the statutes of 'automatically unfair reasons for dismissal' such as pregnancy, trade union membership and refusal to work in unsafe conditions. If one of these is the main reason for a dismissal, the right to bring a claim applies from the first day of employment.

It is also always important to remember that some groups of staff are covered by discrimination laws, which protect them from unlawful dismissals even when the law of unfair dismissal does not. Dismissing someone on the grounds of gender, race or sexual orientation, for example, is always unlawful. And, moreover, all workers and not just employees are covered.

Dismissals on the grounds of misconduct and poor performance are very common. In both cases these reasons are classed in law as being 'potentially fair'. This means that an employer has the legal right to dismiss, but must handle the matter in a reasonable fashion. Who wins the case thus hinges on whether or not the employer's actions met the test of reasonableness that has been established in the case law. Above all, this means that the employer must follow the correct procedure. That is why HR managers always 'think legally' from the start when handling these kinds of cases.

2.5.1 ORDINARY MISCONDUCT

Ordinary misconduct is best defined as being a relatively minor breach of an employer's established rules. What exactly comprises a minor breach inevitably varies from workplace to workplace. An airline pilot who had an alcoholic drink prior to flying a plane could not expect his or her employer to treat such a matter as 'ordinary misconduct'. However, if we as university teachers were to have a drink before giving a lecture, it would probably be treated as ordinary misconduct – as long, of course, as we delivered the lecture capably. In most workplaces ordinary misconduct comprises occasional lateness, rudeness to colleagues and minor breaches of health and safety rules.

The response required by the law is:

- conduct a full investigation
- organise a hearing at which the accused employee is able to put his or her case and can be represented by either a work colleague or a trade union representative
- if appropriate, issue a formal warning
- permit an appeal to be made to another/more senior manager.

The key point is that you do not dismiss for a first offence. Instead, a warning is issued, and only if there are subsequent infringements of workplace rules is a lawful dismissal possible.

Some employers have established more complex procedures for dealing with these issues. Sometimes, for example, there is provision for two warnings to be issued before dismissing. Others have policies about the length of time they will hold a warning on file before removing it. None of these is a legal requirement, but as a rule tribunals expect employers to follow their customary procedures and will find a dismissal to have been unfair if they do not.

2.5.2 GROSS MISCONDUCT

Gross misconduct occurs when an employee breaches an employer's rules in a much more serious way, acting intolerably and destroying trust and confidence in the process. In such circumstances, provided procedures are adhered to, an employer has the right in law to 'summarily dismiss without notice'.

Again, what precisely constitutes gross misconduct in any workplace varies, and employers have a good deal of discretion in deciding for themselves what types of misconduct they will treat as 'gross'. It is important, however, that any rules of this type that are not obvious are communicated effectively. This means that employees know at the time that they breach a rule that they may be dismissed as a result – a situation that makes it much easier to show 'reasonableness' if the matter ever comes to court. Gross misconduct in most workplaces includes fighting, drunkenness, use of illegal drugs, fraud and dishonesty of all kinds. Any employee who does one of these things can expect to be disciplined and summarily dismissed, and should know that their employer has every right to do this.

That said, proper procedures must be followed if a gross misconduct dismissal is to be lawful. As with ordinary misconduct, a full investigation must take place, a hearing convened and a right of appeal provided.

2.5.3 POOR PERFORMANCE

Dismissing people on the grounds of their (lack of) capability is something that most managers hate having to do. It is always a difficult process, particularly in cases of ill health, but it is often necessary for the health of the organisation. The legal principles are actually very straightforward. It is putting them into practice that can be challenging.

In procedural terms, cases of poor performance have to be handled in a very similar way to cases of ordinary misconduct. The procedures used are labelled differently, but the principles are the same. That means that a formal hearing has to be set up at which the employee concerned is warned (again formally) about his or her poor performance. A period of time then has to be agreed during which improvements have to be demonstrated. Ideally, specific performance targets must be set and a programme of training or assistance put in place to help the employee meet them. Performance is then reviewed at a later date and a decision taken at a further hearing about whether or not to dismiss, to issue a further warning, or to let the matter drop. Appeals must also be provided for.

Incapability due to ill health or poor attendance has to be handled in the same way when there is no long-term underlying medical condition. You simply organise a hearing and warn the employee that he or she will be dismissed if attendance does not improve. Again it is best to set clear attendance targets and to give an adequate opportunity for an improvement to occur. It is then lawful to dismiss if these targets are not met.

When someone does have a long-term medical condition that is causing substantial absence, you have to tread much more carefully. In such cases the requirement in law to act reasonably means that the long-term medical prognosis must be taken into account. It would, for example, generally be considered unfair in law to dismiss someone who you knew was recovering and would be likely to return to work in a week or two's time. It is also vital in such cases to take account of disability discrimination law. This applies to anyone who has a serious medical condition (physical or mental) that either has lasted, or could reasonably be expected to last, for 12 months or more. In such cases the employer must not dismiss until it has first gone through a process of considering whether or not there are any reasonable adjustments that could be made that would enable the worker to return to work/continue in the job.

2.6 OTHER MAJOR EMPLOYMENT RIGHTS

In the above sections we have summarised and explained many core areas of UK employment regulation. There are, however, several others too. We do not have the space here to go into them in any great detail, so the following paragraphs simply set out the key principles.

2.6.1 HEALTH AND SAFETY LAW

There is a huge body of health and safety law that UK workplaces are obliged to follow, much of it comprising detailed regulations that are of relevance to particular industries. However, there is a single piece of legislation – the Health and Safety at Work Act 1974 – which sets out general principles and places specific obligations on all employers. This Act forms part of the criminal law and is policed by an inspectorate who have considerable powers, including the right to close down an unsafe workplace and to bring criminal prosecutions when serious breaches of the regulations occur. The preamble to the 1974 Act contains the following general statement:

> It shall be the duty of every employer to ensure, as far as is reasonably practicable, the health, safety and welfare at work of all his employees.

The Act then goes on to outline the following duties, all of which apply in all workplaces:

- to maintain plant and equipment and to provide safe systems of working
- to ensure safe arrangements for the handling, use, transport and storage of hazardous equipment and/or substances
- to provide all necessary information, training and supervision in the use of hazardous equipment/substances
- to ensure that entrances and exits to buildings are safe and maintained
- to provide adequate facilities and arrangements to ensure welfare at work.

In addition, the Act requires that all workplaces that employ more than five people have in place a written health and safety policy. Central to health and safety law is the concept of 'risk assessment'. Health and safety inspectors, and indeed the courts, always focus heavily on whether or not these have been carried out. It is far easier for an employer to defend itself if it has done so. Risk assessment simply involves identifying any health and safety hazards and taking appropriate steps to minimise any risks. Such measures must be written down and the steps followed in practice. In recent years the health and safety inspectorate has shown a particular interest in jobs that are unusually stressful and which leave their holders susceptible to mental breakdown. Risk assessments thus now need to include reference to stressors in the workplace.

2.6.2 PERSONAL INJURY LAW

Stress-related breakdowns also play a major potential role in personal injury law, which is concerned with paying compensation to staff who have suffered serious injury at work. Employees looking to sue their employers in such circumstances have a number of potential avenues to choose from, including resigning and bringing a case of constructive dismissal to an employment tribunal. However, most people – particularly if substantial sums by way of damages are being sought – choose to bring a claim of negligence before the County Court or the High Court.

Most employers in the UK are required by law to have employer's liability insurance, so negligence cases are often more effectively fought by insurance companies seeking to limit their exposure. A number of defences are available for employers to deploy. But by far the most significant is summed up in the following sentence:

The injury was not reasonably foreseeable.

As a result, provided full risk assessments have been carried out and implemented, courts are often obliged to find in favour of the employer. Liability for damages only occurs when an employer knew of a risk and took inadequate steps to deal with it.

2.6.3 BULLYING AND HARASSMENT

Two criminal statutes offer some protection for workers who are bullied by co-workers or by managers at work:

- the Criminal Justice and Public Order Act 1994, which makes it an offence, punishable with up to six months' imprisonment, to cause 'intentional harassment, alarm or distress'
- the Protection from Harassment Act 1997, which is mainly about stalking and situations in which someone places another person in fear of violence. This is also punishable with up to six months' imprisonment.

But in truth neither of these statutes is very helpful to someone being bullied at work. The first requires the prosecution to show that the harasser deliberately sought to harass, alarm or distress, which is difficult to prove and easy to defend.

The second requires a genuine fear of physical violence, which is rare in a workplace setting. In extreme cases of bullying these conditions can apply – in which case a report must be made to the police – but most workplace bullying, while distressing, is not in this league.

Much more common are claims made at an employment tribunal accusing a manager or colleague (or more usually a former manager or colleague) of unlawfully harassing. The outcome will be compensation of between £500 and £30,000 if the case is proven, the sum depending on the nature of the harassment suffered and the length of time it was endured.

The problem here, though, is that only a very narrow range of harassment situations qualify and are thus unlawful. The law of harassment forms part of discrimination law, and hence can only cover situations in which detriment is suffered due to one of the protected characteristics listed in the Equality Act 2010 (see above). Nonetheless, this law does offer considerable protection for people who suffer harassment on the grounds, for example, of sex or race.

Generally the primary case is brought against the employer and not the particular harasser, although since 2014 it has been possible simply to make a claim against the individual responsible. When the employer is the respondent it can defend itself by showing that it acted swiftly and appropriately as soon as the complaint was made and that it took all reasonable steps to prevent the harassment from occurring in the first place.

Protection of a more general kind for employees who are bullied at work is provided through the presence in all contracts of employment of a duty on both employers and employees to maintain a relationship of mutual trust and confidence.

Serious bullying is now clearly accepted by the courts, in principle, as constituting a breach on the part of the employer of the duty to maintain a relationship of mutual trust and confidence. And there have been some high-profile cases in this field. The best known is the case of *Horkulak v Cantor Fitzgerald International* (2004), in which a senior manager used threatening and abusive language to a subordinate. Damages were assessed at £900,000 because this was a very highly paid individual.

What does this mean in practice for employers and employees? Firstly, it is possible for an employee or an ex-employee to sue their employer in the County Court or High Court for any financial losses they sustain due to the bullying suffered. There is no need to show that any illness has occurred as a result.

Secondly – and much, much more commonly – it makes it possible for an employee who has suffered from being bullied to resign and take a claim of constructive dismissal to an employment tribunal. This latter course of action is much cheaper and is risk-free from the point of view of the employee.

The key test, of course, is what does and what does not constitute bullying. This is a question of judgement – but it must be quite serious for an employee to win a case. In effect, in order to sustain a case, a claimant has to show that the employer acted intolerably and that this led directly to the resignation.

Damages in constructive dismissal cases are generally quite low, and are limited to compensation for financial loss. But employers do not generally relish defending their actions in court, and so the possibility of constructive dismissal proceedings may act as a deterrent and should help to ensure that others are not bullied in the future.

2.6.4 WHISTLEBLOWING

The Public Interest Disclosure Act 1998 gives a measure of protection to 'whistleblowers' who take action when they become concerned about the activities of their employers. Basically, the Act does no more than give whistleblowers protection from victimisation in certain defined circumstances. It covers all workers except those working in the police and security services. Central to the Act is the notion of a 'qualifying disclosure' – that is, one which gives the discloser legal protection. There are five categories named. The disclosure must concern, or be reasonably believed to concern, one of these:

- a criminal offence
- a failure to comply with legal obligations
- a miscarriage of justice (legally, not colloquially, defined)
- compromised health and safety arrangements
- something to cause environmental damage.

Straightforward incompetence or dishonesty are not included, nor is abuse of power unless one of the above is also involved. Moreover, in order to 'qualify', the disclosure must be made in good faith, and only having first exhausted the possibilities for raising the issue with managers internally. Only at this point should representations be made to the authorities.

The whistle can be blown to any of the following:

- the employer
- a legal adviser
- a Minister of the Crown
- appropriate enforcing authorities
- a media organisation.

However, there are restrictions on media disclosures. The qualifying disclosure must relate to 'an exceptionally serious failure' and, moreover, there must be no personal gain.

2.6.5 COLLECTIVE EMPLOYMENT LAW

In the UK, as in most countries, the law gives particular protection to trade unions. The term 'freedom of association' is used in this context to describe the right to join and form trade unions and to participate freely in their activities without any interference from the employer. Importantly, the right of UK employees not to join trade unions is also protected in law. These protections are achieved in three major ways:

- It is considered automatically unfair (and hence unlawful) to dismiss an employee for being a union member, joining a union, taking part in union activities, not being a member, not joining or not taking part in union activities.
- It is also unlawful to subject an employee to 'action short of dismissal' in the same circumstances.
- It is unlawful to discriminate against trade union members when recruiting new staff, or to maintain industry blacklists of union members.

However, once a union and its members engage in any kind of **industrial action**, including strikes, a different set of employment regulations apply, which are a great deal less union-friendly than those which protect freedom of association. As far as union members are concerned, this means that:

- they can lose pay if they fail to perform their contractual duties due to industrial action
- in the case of unofficial industrial action (that is, wildcat action organised without the knowledge or approval of a union executive committee), employers are free to dismiss at will
- in the case of official action it becomes 'potentially' fair to dismiss after 12 weeks of a dispute.

Union officials who are organising industrial action, as well as unions themselves, are said in law to be 'immune from prosecution in tort' provided they follow set rules about fair balloting, informing the employer about who is going on strike and respecting a seven-day 'cooling-off period' between holding a ballot and the action starting. In practice this means that unions who follow the basic rules on industrial action can never be sued for any damage they may cause to an employer's business by organising it.

Further regulations positively promote union interests. These include measures contained in the Employment Relations Act 1999, which require employers to recognise unions who can demonstrate that they have the support of a good proportion of a workforce, a long-standing right to be consulted on certain types of issue, limitations on how much a union can ever be sued for in court, and the right to represent members in 'serious' disciplinary and grievance proceedings.

 TROUBLE AT THE BIG TOP

CASE STUDY 2.2

All around towns across the country brightly coloured posters proclaim the imminent arrival of Geraldo Pecorino's traditional family travelling circus.

Geraldo's round red face smiles out inviting all to gaze and wonder at Alice and Maximilian's amazing feats on the flying trapeze, to gasp in amazement as Little Fat Stan the human cannonball is propelled at speed across the circus ring, to laugh at the crazy antics of Micky the clown and his chums, and to applaud as Daisy the elephant dances daintily on her hind legs. But in reality, Geraldo is not

smiling at all. He is very worried about the future of his circus. His star performers may help bring in the crowds, but they are also causing him a variety of managerial headaches.

Alice is his longest-serving artiste. For 35 years, partnered by a succession of male trapeze stars, she has nightly swung and somersaulted high in the air above a safety net, before descending to take her bow. Unfortunately, over time, the once lissom Alice has become less agile and has put on a great deal of weight. As a result, when she enters the ring in her leotard and climbs up to her trapeze the audience increasingly see her as a figure of fun. When she carries out her final triple somersault and falls into the safety net, the structure wobbles alarmingly, causing the audience to scream with laughter. The contrast with the much younger and very athletic Maximilian is becoming more and more obvious, and he is not happy. 'Find me a new partner,' he says, 'or I will find a better circus to work for.' But what can Geraldo do?

Alice is well paid and popular among the troupe. For several months he has been able to placate Maximilian by saying that he cannot find a replacement for Alice, but now a perfect new partner for Maximilian has become available. A beautiful 18-year-old trapeze artist called Melanie who has the rare capacity to carry out a Russian style backflip quadruple somersault has left a rival circus and is begging Geraldo for a job. Can he sack Alice? Can he redeploy her? Redeployment would be preferable, but the only suitable job he has for her would involve performing with Micky and his crazy clowns. Alice would get the laughs, but it would much be less well paid work and undignified for a senior artiste with years of loyal service behind her.

Geraldo's second managerial headache concerns another long-serving employee. Jethro has for many years acted as keeper and trainer of Daisy the elephant. They are devoted to one another. Every day Jethro feeds her, cleans her wagon, takes her for walks, washes her and then, in the evening, the two of them perform together to the delight of the audience. For many this act is the highlight of the circus. But six months ago an unfortunate accident occurred. In the middle of their act a large light bulb exploded above the circus ring, which gave Daisy a terrible fright. She panicked and instead of continuing to dance, she charged at Jethro and tossed him into the air. He sustained serious back and neck injuries in this accident and has been in and out of hospital ever since. Geraldo now realises that Jethro will not be able to

return to work again for many more months. Daisy is back to her old self and has apparently bonded well with her new keeper, Geraldo's daughter Romola. Jethro visits her when he can, but he comes with his carer and is unable to get up out of his wheelchair.

What should Geraldo do? He is still paying Jethro but cannot afford to continue doing so for ever. Can he dismiss him? Should he try to reach a financial settlement, and if so, would his insurance company reimburse him?

And finally, what is Geraldo to do about Little Fat Stan, his much-loved but increasingly awkward human cannonball? Stan has worked in the circus for years, delighting generations of audiences with his acts. He started out as a tumbler. Then as he got older he turned to fire-eating and knife swallowing, before winding up being fired nightly from a cannon across the ring through several paper hoops and landing spectacularly in a meticulously placed bouncy castle. Stan is not happy. He feels his life is unfulfilled and he wants to change direction. Stan has dealt with his depression in the past by drinking heavily, but has now managed to stop. Instead, he has found great solace by becoming an active Christian. He attends churches in each town that the circus visits and continually regales the other performers with stories about how his faith has changed his life. But this has caused difficulties for Geraldo because Stan has said that he will not in future be available to perform on Sundays or at any time over the Christmas and Easter periods. He has asked Geraldo if he could give up performing and assist him in a management role, taking responsibility for publicising the circus. Failing that he would like to run the box office. But these jobs are already taken and are not, in truth, suitable for Stan. Geraldo insists that he can only employ him as a specialist performer.

What should Geraldo do? Mondays and Tuesdays are the days the circus does not put on a performance and on which everyone takes time off. Two performances are mounted every Sunday, and Easter and Christmas are periods when audiences increase substantially. Should he threaten to sack Little Fat Stan? Could he employ someone else to be a human cannonball on Sundays, and reduce Stan's wages to compensate?

The worry of what to do about Stan, Jethro, Maximilian and Alice causes Geraldo to suffer many sleepless nights.

Questions

Geraldo decides that he has no choice but to employ Melanie as a replacement for Alice. He tells Alice that from next week onwards she will have to perform alongside Micky and his clowns. Her role will be to act as his foil and a victim of his many practical jokes. For the next six months she will be paid the same salary that she currently earns. After this date it will be reviewed.

1   Assuming that she is unhappy with Geraldo's decision, what possible legal claims might Alice be able to

bring? What defences might Geraldo be able to deploy were Alice to take her case to an employment tribunal?

Geraldo decides to dismiss Jethro, offering him a one-off payment of £25,000 by way of a full and final settlement.

2   What possible legal claims could Jethro bring were he to reject Geraldo's offer? What action could Geraldo take to minimise his chances of losing these cases in court?

Geraldo decides to allow Little Fat Stan to take Sundays off and to take his annual leave over the Christmas and Easter periods. Another performer will be trained up to take his place at these times. In return Geraldo will reduce Stan's pay by 20%.

3   What possible legal claims might Stan be able to bring? How might Geraldo be able to defend himself were the dispute to reach a tribunal hearing?

FURTHER READING

Two books that provide excellent introductions to the key debates about employment law are *Perspectives on labour law* by Anne Davies (2009; Cambridge University Press) and *Great debates in employment law* by Simon Honeyball (2011; Palgrave Macmillan).

More general introductions to employment law that have primarily been for people who are not studying law include *Employment law: an introduction* by Stephen Taylor and Astra Emir (2015; Oxford University Press), and *Essentials of employment law* by David Lewis and Malcolm Sargeant (2015; Chartered Institute of Personnel and Development).

REFERENCES

BREWER, N. (2008) Speech at the launch of the 'Working Better' consultation, 14 July. Equal Opportunities Commission.

CIPD (2002) *Employment Law*. Survey report. London: Chartered Institute of Personnel and Development.

CIPD (2012) Work audit research. Cited in *People Management*, April. p13.

DAVIES, A. (2009) *Perspectives on labour law*. 2nd ed. Cambridge: Cambridge University Press.

EMPLOYMENT TRIBUNAL SERVICE (2011) *Annual report and accounts*. London: ETS.

HONEYBALL, S. (2011) *Great debates in employment law*. Basingstoke: Palgrave Macmillan.

LEA, R. (2001) *Work–life balance and all that: the re-regulation of the labour market*. London: Institute of Directors.

LEWIS, D. and SARGEANT, M. (2015) *Essentials of employment law*. 13th ed. London: Chartered Institute of Personnel and Development.

SHACKLETON, J. R. (2005) Regulating the labour market. In: BOOTH, P. (ed.). *Towards a liberal utopia?* London: Institute of Economic Affairs.

TAYLOR, S. and EMIR, A. (2015) *Employment law: an introduction*. 4th ed. Oxford: Oxford University Press.

CHAPTER 3

Resourcing and Talent Planning

KRYSTAL WILKINSON AND STEPHEN TAYLOR

CHAPTER CONTENTS

- Introduction
- Labour market trends
- Core talent planning
- Developing resourcing strategies
- Managing recruitment and selection
- Maximising employee retention
- Managing retirement, dismissal and redundancy

KEY LEARNING OUTCOMES

By the end of this chapter, you should be able to:

- understand key contemporary labour market trends and their significance for different kinds of organisation and in different contexts
- undertake the various different activities involved in core talent planning
- contribute to the development of organisational resourcing strategies
- design and deliver recruitment and selection activities that are appropriate for the organisation and meet the expectations of the law and good practice
- understand how to maximise employee retention
- appreciate how to manage dismissals, redundancy and retirement effectively and lawfully.

3.1 INTRODUCTION

A fundamental part of the human resource (HR) management role is concerned with the mobilisation of a workforce. This means taking responsibility for ensuring that the organisation has the right number of people, with the right skills, at the right time, working in the right places to drive sustained organisation performance. It involves a number of activities including workforce planning, attracting potential employees, selecting the best individuals, retaining employees, succession planning, and managing the departure of staff from the organisation for a number of reasons including retirement, redundancy and dismissal. Achieving this requires well-considered strategic and operational activity.

Organisations are obliged to compete with each other to secure the services of a workforce in labour markets that are continually evolving. One of the major aims of this chapter is thus to introduce you to the strategic approaches that organisations take to position themselves as employers in the labour market and plan effectively so that they are able to meet their current and anticipated organisational skills needs. Another is to introduce the operational tools, techniques and practices that organisations need to use to resource their organisations.

3.2 LABOUR MARKET TRENDS

The term '**labour market**' is a key concept in employee resourcing. The traditional definition of a market is 'an actual or nominal place where forces of demand and supply operate, and where buyers and sellers interact (directly or through intermediaries) to trade' (www.businessdictionary.com). Thus in marketing, organisations are concerned with the market(s) for their products or services – identifying which people or companies might be willing and able to purchase, and determining what these groups are looking for. A labour market concerns the market for potential employees – which people may be willing and able to work for the company, and what they are looking for in terms of employment.

3.2.1 SOURCES OF LABOUR

There are a number of different sources of potential employees in the overall labour market. Sources of labour include:

● job-seekers in the local market

These are people who are actively looking for employment and to live in the local area. They are especially useful where companies are looking to fill low skill roles.

● job-seekers in the national market

These are people who are actively looking for employment anywhere in the country. They tend to be more suited to companies that are looking to fill skilled/specialist roles – where salaries are likely to be higher, and individuals are willing to relocate for the right job.

● job-seekers in the international market

These are people who are actively looking for employment anywhere in the world. These tend to be more appropriate again for higher-skilled specialist or shortage roles, especially following the changes in immigration laws that have made it harder for job-seekers to enter the UK.

● individuals working in other companies

These are people who are not actively looking for employment but who may well have the skills and experience that another company wants. They may be interested in changing employer if the right package is offered.

● graduates

These are people who are highly educated, who are actively looking for employment, and who often want some form of structured development plan.

● school- or college-leavers

These are people who are new to the world of work. They are actively looking for employment but might require more investment from an organisation in terms of training and development.

- the economically inactive

These are people who are not currently either in employment or looking for employment, but who could enter the workforce if the appropriate incentives or provisions were made available. The group includes people who have retired, people with long-term health problems, and those with childcare or eldercare commitments. More attention has been paid to this group, and how they can be brought into the workforce, over the last decade or so – as competition for workers has increased.

It is important to be aware that different companies therefore focus on different labour markets when coming up with their recruitment strategies – something we discuss further later on.

3.2.2 TIGHT AND LOOSE MARKETS

When considering a labour market, one of the main things to understand is that the ease with which organisations can recruit employees depends on the nature of the market they are targeting at that specific point in time – whether it is 'tight' or 'loose'.

A **tight labour market** refers to a situation in which there are more job opportunities available than there are active job-seekers, meaning that companies find it more difficult to fill their vacancies because job-seekers have a considerable degree of choice. A **loose labour market** therefore refers to the opposite situation – in which there are many job-seekers competing for a smaller number of opportunities.

When markets are tight, employers are required to be more creative with their people management recruitment strategies, often focusing on the following:

- employer branding

We cover this in more detail later, but the term basically refers to activities designed to formulate a specific (and attractive) personality for the company, and to promote it to potential employees.

- recruitment initiatives

Investing money in innovative recruitment techniques, targeting a broader pool of potential applicants.

- retention strategies

Investigating the reasons for departures from the company, and finding ways to tackle those that suggest or constitute a problem.

- reorganisations

Changing the way that job tasks are allocated in order to minimise the need for hard-to-recruit staff. A 'skill-mix review' can be carried out to ensure that the people who are the hardest to recruit (usually with specific skills) can spend all of their time on the tasks that only they can complete, and that other things are delegated to others.

- development initiatives

Enhancing the skills of the current workforce, and bringing in people who do not have the required skills yet but who are interested in developing them.

- long-term resource planning

The company could collaborate with local universities or training providers to increase the number of people with the relevant skills in the future.

3.2.3 TRENDS IN THE DEMAND AND SUPPLY OF SKILLS

Over time, the national labour market and specific parts of it (different regions and industries) can be seen to expand (loosen) and contract (tighten) owing to a range of factors. These include:

- the economic context

An economic downturn usually has a significant effect on the labour market, because many companies will be forced to close or to downsize, resulting in either case in staff redundancies.

- demographic changes

The number of births and deaths, inward and outward migration from the country, population ageing, etc.

- political changes

Things like immigration policies and investment in national skills development have an effect on the number of people in the labour market and their usefulness to employing organisations.

- legislative changes

Employment laws limiting working hours can increase the demand for numbers of employees, and legislation concerning non-discrimination can open up the labour market to groups traditionally excluded (such as those who are disabled or past retirement age).

- technological developments

Advancements in automation can make a lot of workers superfluous in certain industries while at the same time increasing the demand for those with technical expertise.

- natural disasters, epidemics or international events (such as war)

These can wipe out or divert a considerable proportion of the labour force. At a local level, the introduction or removal of competitors can have an impact.

In recent years, largely as a result of the sharp economic downturn that hit most countries in 2008 and the subsequent need for governments to cut spending so as to reduce levels of public borrowing, labour markets in countries such as the UK tended to be relatively loose. For several years unemployment remained high and wage levels stagnant, meaning that it was not difficult for most employers to hire people with the skills and experience that they required. In addition to recessionary conditions, other factors such as the fairly open immigration policies that prevailed, increased international competition, jobs being exported to cheaper countries, and the development of labour-saving technologies also contributed to a loosening of labour markets. In such conditions organisations often pay little attention to employee recruitment and retention, simply because employees are unlikely to voluntarily leave a job, and when they do the chances that a replacement will be hired quickly are much less.

This situation contrasted significantly with the tight labour market conditions which prevailed in the fifteen years or so prior to 2008 when the economy grew steadily and it became very difficult to recruit and retain people. Staff turnover levels were high and wages grew in response. At the time of writing (2015) employment levels are rising quite rapidly in the UK, along with average wages, as the economy is going through a period of recovery and growth. The result is a re-tightening of labour markets as skills shortages once again resume. Indeed, the long-term trend has been for increasing levels of employment. When data on the number of jobs in the UK was first recorded in 1960, the figure stood at 26.1 million. In the 50 years that followed, this figure grew to 31.4 million and now stands at 33.5 million. Relatively tight labour market conditions thus look likely to be with us for the foreseeable future.

So will this be a problem? During the past 50 years, the ongoing increase in the number of jobs available has not been problematic because the number of people seeking employment has also been rising – a result of three social and demographic trends:

- a steady increase in the number of women entering the workforce
- the 'baby-boom' generation (which refers to the large cohort of individuals born in the years following the end of the Second World War) being of working age
- increasing numbers of immigrants entering the UK for work.

Assuming that the economy continues to grow steadily, and the long-term trend for increasing jobs resumes, where does this leave us in terms of the ability of supply to meet demand? All three of the trends cited above are unlikely to continue – meaning that labour markets are likely further to tighten considerably – and organisations and their HR teams will need to respond.

3.2.4 SOCIAL AND DEMOGRAPHIC TRENDS

The two main demographic factors that affect the labour market are the age profile of the population, and trends surrounding migration. It is widely known that the UK, alongside most countries in Europe, has an ageing population. In the decades since the 'baby boom' of the 1960s there has been an ongoing reduction in the number of children being born each year. When combined with the trend for young people to stay in full-time education for longer than they used to, it means that considerably fewer young people are entering the labour market each year than they did in the past.

This becomes a significant problem when we combine it with the fact that many of the 'baby-boom' generation are approaching retirement age – which means a considerable loss of skilled workers from the labour market at the other end of the cycle. The government has introduced a range of provisions to encourage older workers to remain in employment for longer, such as the removal of the default retirement age and the introduction of employment protection from discrimination on the grounds of age, but this is unlikely to be enough to stop the volume of the working-age population reducing year on year.

In terms of immigration levels, the trend for the last 50 years has been a steady increase in the percentage of the UK population that was born overseas – from around 4% in 1951 to over 8% in 2001 and around 15% today. This trend may slow somewhat in the future because the UK population as a whole has been growing at a rate that is not economically sustainable (in terms of housing, transport and public service provision). One way that the government has responded is to tighten immigration policies for people from outside the European Union – so that only migrants who have specific skills (that are in short supply in the home market) are permitted to enter the country and live here.

3.2.5 GOVERNMENT AND STATE SKILLS STRATEGIES

Given the concerns about a discrepancy between the nature of the skills needed by UK employers and the level of skills available in the working-age population, and the failure of the UK to compete on a global scale owing to skills levels, the former government put in place a wide-ranging and formal skills review in 2004.

Led by the Chairman of the National Employment Panel, Sandy Leitch, the final report was published in 2006, detailing two key areas for action: improving levels of basic skills, and improving levels of higher-level specialist, professional and technical skills.

'Basic skills' refers to basic literacy and numeracy. In response to this part of the Leitch Report, the government published the *World-Class Skills* White Paper, which set some ambitious targets for skills levels to be reached by 2020. Targets included having 95% of adults functionally literate and numerate (currently 85% and 79% respectively); over 90% of adults having gained a Level-2 qualification – GCSE or equivalent (currently 69%); and having 500,000 people on apprenticeship schemes. In support of such targets, the government set in motion an increase in the education-leaving age (this will be 18 years from 2015), and has focused on collaboration with educational providers and employers.

In terms of improving higher-level specialist, professional and technical skills, the focus of the government has been on 'turning the old system on its head', so that training and development provision are demand-led (determined by the needs of business) rather than via bureaucratic central planning and regulatory control.

3.2.6 LABOUR MARKET FLEXIBILITY AND THE IMPORTANCE OF FLEXIBLE WORKING

In addition to improving overall skills levels in the UK, another way to maximise the potential of the labour market is to ensure that organisations are as flexible as possible. Flexibility is actually one of the key emerging issues for organisations of the twenty-first century, closely associated with the rate of change in the wider environment and the requirement for organisations to be able to adapt to such changes quickly. The terms 'labour market flexibility' and 'flexible working' are associated with a considerable number of strategies that companies can use to get maximum value out of the individuals working for them.

One of the leading authors in the field is John Atkinson (1984a), who noted four types of flexibility strategy used by modern companies:

- external numerical flexibility

This involves the company having the ability to increase or decrease the total headcount of the organisation based on peaks and troughs in demand. It is usually achieved by supplementing a minimal permanent workforce with a periphery group of workers on various forms of 'atypical' contract (including temporary contracts, fixed-term contracts, seasonal contracts and 'zero-hour'/casual contracts).

- internal numerical flexibility

Sometimes referred to as 'temporal flexibility' or 'working time flexibility', this involves the company adjusting the working hours or schedules of the people already employed in the firm. It therefore includes part-time, flexitime, flexible working hours/shifts (including nights, weekend shifts, split shifts) and overtime. One of the main benefits to the business is the ability to cater for the 24/7 nature of much modern business without needing to employ more people.

A number of people on different, relatively short shifts can often provide more effective cover than a smaller group of full-time staff, but the wage cost is the same.

- functional flexibility

This involves the company increasing the extent to which employees can be transferred to different activities and tasks within the firm. It has to do with the organisation of operations (job rotation) and the training of workers (multi-skilling), and enables the company to allocate staff to where they are most needed on a day-to-day basis.

● financial or wage flexibility

This refers to a system in which pay levels are not decided collectively, so that employment costs can reflect the supply and demand of labour. It can be achieved by rate-for-the-job systems or an assessment-based pay system, or individual performance wages.

Although the primary aim of flexibility strategies is to make the organisation more responsive and they are therefore said to be 'employer-friendly', it should be noted that some of the strategies are also said to be 'employee-friendly'.

?   REFLECTIVE ACTIVITY 3.2

Think about your own organisation, or one that you are familiar with, and consider the following questions:

1   Which of these overall flexibility strategies are in operation at the moment?

2   What are the specific provisions in operation?

3   How do you think the different provisions are perceived by those within the company? Are they seen to be 'employee friendly' or only beneficial to the company?

In a different publication, Atkinson (1984b) described the ultimate 'flexible firm', which combines different types of flexibility in a core/periphery model:

The organisation employs a relatively small 'core' workforce, which consists of permanent full-time employees, who are trained to be functionally flexible and are responsible for carrying out the company's key firm-specific competencies. Because the organisation wants to develop long-term relationships with these individuals, they are offered considerable reward and employment security.

In order to protect the employment of this core workforce, the company then makes use of a 'periphery' workforce that acts as a buffer to the core group – in that they can be easily up- or down-sized as required. Rather than functional flexibility, the key strategies employed for this group are internal and external numerical flexibility.

3.3 CORE TALENT PLANNING

Now that we have examined the idea of labour markets and different sources of potential employees, we can move on to the issue of talent planning. Sometimes described as 'workforce planning' or 'human resource planning' (HRP), this refers to the activities carried out by a company to consider the specific employees and skills that it will need in the future, and to put in place strategies to ensure that it can meet these requirements – which may well involve turning to the labour market for more people. It involves ensuring that the company will have 'the right people, with the right skills, in the right places at the right time' to fulfil the company's strategic objectives.

Talent planning can vary in terms of both scope (one department, one site, national or international) and timescale (are we thinking next year or ten years' time?). There are, however, four stages that should be followed:

- forecasting the organisation's future demand for skills
- forecasting what skills the organisation will have in the future
- identifying any gap between the future demand and supply of skills
- making plans to fill any gap.

3.3.1 FORECASTING DEMAND

Forecasting the demands that the organisation will have for skills in the future is the first stage of the talent planning process. It involves asking the following questions:

- What tasks will need doing?
- How can these best be divided into individual job roles? We need to consider the type of role (part-time, full-time, contract) as well as numbers.
- What skills are needed for each role?

So how do we get started in answering these questions? How can we know what our requirement will be in the future? There are a number of approaches that can be taken:

- *systematic techniques*, which can include things like (a) looking at past trends to predict future needs; and (b) working back from the outputs desired
- *managerial judgement*, which is based on the knowledge and experience of senior staff of the specific company, the industry and the external environment
- *working back from costs*, which begins with the future budget and then determines how many staff can be afforded.

From such activities we should be able to identify roughly what job roles are needed, how many people are needed in each and what skills are needed. From this we can draw up specific job descriptions and person specifications (covered below).

3.3.2 FORECASTING SUPPLY

When we know how many people we need, and with what skills, the next thing we must do is look at the current resources of the organisation. We must consider the composition of the current workforce, the skills of this workforce and the proportion of this workforce that is likely to remain at the time that we are forecasting for.

In terms of understanding the current workforce, we need to identify the total number of people employed, the total wage cost, the workforce composition (percentages employed in each department, at each grade, in different age groups and with different lengths of service) and the levels of sickness absence (and the impact this has on the ability to deliver services).

After looking at the people that we currently have, we must assess the skills they have, which can be done by consulting person specifications for current job roles (more on this later), appraisal information and internal training records.

Finally, we must estimate the number of these employees that are likely to still be employed in the future. The most important thing to think about here is general trends in employee turnover – how many people tend to resign each year, how many people are approaching retirement age? More sophisticated analyses will also consider the roles that people will be working in, considering the number of lateral moves and promotions that are likely as well.

3.3.3 IDENTIFYING GAPS BETWEEN DEMAND AND SUPPLY

Once we have information on the job roles and skills that we will need in the future, and on the job roles and skills we have in the present, we can conduct a skills audit for the majority of the common roles in order to determine the extent of the mismatch between the two. Put simply, there are three steps to this activity:

1   Create a competency framework for each of the common roles. This would be a list of all of the competencies (desirable human characteristics) that are required for the role, and an indication of the level of skill required. An example for a call centre operative might be:

2   Assess each current employee using an audit form. Each individual's line manager is best placed to complete the audit, and should base assessments on personal judgement, observation and discussion with the individual (including scenario-based questions on how they would handle a situation).

3   Summarise the results for the whole workforce to identify the total skills currently available, and the extent to which this matches the skills base needed for the future.

3.3.4 ADDRESSING THE GAPS

There are two main areas that must be considered next. The first is to determine how the organisation can best use its existing resources. This might involve moving people, training people (in the current or in a different area), encouraging knowledge-sharing (coaching and mentoring), ensuring the retention of valued people (discussed below), and removing some individuals if their skills and aspirations unfortunately do not match future needs (discussed below).

The second is to identify what external sources of skills can be utilised. This involves assessing the nature of the local labour market, contemplating recruitment from further afield, and considering the usefulness of bringing people in on a contract basis or collaborating with other organisations (charities/universities, etc) in relation to work experience programmes. Another angle is to consider the value of outsourcing or off-shoring certain activities. The former refers to securing an external provider for an activity rather than doing it in-house, and the latter to securing a foreign provider.

3.3.5 SUCCESSION PLANNING

One activity that is often cited interchangeably with talent planning – but which actually refers to a distinct activity – is succession planning. Whereas talent planning refers to overall staffing considerations, succession planning refers to a group of activities that aim to ensure that at any time an organisation has sufficient numbers of people with the ability, knowledge, personal attributes and experience necessary to step into roles at the next level when they become vacant.

The original focus of succession planning was at the very highest levels of an organisation – to ensure a smooth transition when a director or a very senior manager departs, and to avoid having to react quickly and ask someone to 'act up' for a temporary period, to promote someone who is not prepared or to recruit someone from outside the organisation who doesn't know the organisation and the way things are done. The process therefore concerned the selection and grooming of a chosen few. It has since been extended to cover the whole workforce, however. Rather than targeting specific individuals for specific roles, the aim is to develop 'pools of talent' from which a replacement can be selected as and when a vacancy becomes available.

Appraisal meetings are central to the process – identifying the aspirations of employees, assessing current skills levels and agreeing development plans moving forward. A range of development activities can be utilised to help furnish individuals with the skills they will need at the next level, including formal training programmes, on-the-job training and coaching, work shadowing, mentoring schemes, experience in different departments, supervised 'acting up', and things like attendance at committees and ownership of special projects.

One long-standing debate in the field of HR planning is how to balance succession planning with a desire for 'new blood' – bringing in people from outside the business who may have fresh ideas and perspectives. The CIPD factsheet (CIPD 2012a) suggests that companies should aim for a ratio of around 80:20 between insiders and outsiders, and should avoid appointing outsiders at board level, where an awareness of corporate culture is key.

3.3.6 FAIR ACCESS TO OPPORTUNITY

When considering activities in the field of talent planning (deployment, development and career management), it is essential that organisations give all employees fair access to the opportunities available. There are several ways to help ensure this:

- extensive communication of opportunities to all
- mechanisms whereby anyone can express an interest in opportunities
- fairness in selection – open competition for opportunities and formal selection criteria (as opposed to management discretion)
- regular appraisals for all employees – with development goals to help them move towards longer-term aspirations
- positive action initiatives: forms of assistance for those who may be disadvantaged in some respect. For example, if women are under-represented at management level in a company, a management skills course targeted at female staff might be developed
- auditing of training records and/or the inclusion of training and development questions in any employee satisfaction surveys
- making a variety of development provisions available so that all employees are catered for – including those with different learning styles, those with atypical working patterns and those at different stages of their careers
- in the case of redeployment, making certain that all individuals involved are fully consulted
- working with all management staff on the importance of equality of opportunity and on career management in general. It is important that managers are not, for example, blocking the development of a promising subordinate for fear that the individual might move to another department or even take over their own job.

3.4 DEVELOPING RESOURCING STRATEGIES

When an organisation is faced with the task of developing a targeted resourcing strategy, it must be aware that it is not operating in isolation. To be successful, the resourcing strategy of an organisation should be based on attracting the right people, and differentiating the company from the competition. In this brief section of the chapter three key activities are examined: competitor analysis, organisation positioning in relation to the labour market, and **employer branding**.

3.4.1 COMPETITOR ANALYSIS

Before any decisions are taken in relation to the optimum resourcing strategy for the organisation, it is important to be aware of what competitors are doing.

'Competitors' here refers to labour market competitors, which are not necessarily the same as product market competitors. If, for example, your organisation is a food-processing factory and you need to recruit a number of low-skill local workers, the companies that you should consider are not necessarily the dominant food-processing companies in the UK but rather the other companies in the local area that employ low-skill workers (shops, restaurants, other factories, etc).

When conducting an analysis, you need to think of both the strengths and the weaknesses of the employment deal offered by each competitor – which includes things like the salary offered, other benefits, employment security, job role, working environment, and opportunities for training and development.

Once you are aware of what the competition is offering, you are in a better place to consider what you can offer to potential employees that may make your company stand out from the crowd.

3.4.2 ORGANISATION POSITIONING

Although it is up to the individual organisation to decide how it would like to present itself to the labour market, it has been noted that there are some common overall approaches. Taylor (2011) cites the following useful typology offered by Higgs (2004).

The approaches are differentiated based on two factors: *reward* (the amount of money the employer is willing or able to pay its employees) and *culture* (the extent to which employees are respected and treated ethically).

An 'employer of cash' tends to treat employees quite harshly, perhaps autocratically or expecting them to work excessive hours, but compensates them by paying them well.

An 'employer of values' is the polar opposite – it often cannot afford to pay people the going market rate but is committed to treating employees very well (offering fair treatment, rewarding work, job security). The approach tends to be associated with the public and voluntary sectors.

An 'employer of churn' tends to both pay poorly and treat employees harshly. The result is often high staff turnover levels, which means that such an approach is only a viable possibility in loose labour market conditions – when staff can be easily replaced. Target groups are often those with low skill levels (and with little choice of alternative employment), workers recruited from overseas and students looking for temporary work.

To be an 'employer of choice' is perceived to be the optimal strategic aim, especially where labour markets are tight, and involves both paying well and treating people positively. Companies with this approach tend to make it on to the annual *Sunday Times* list of the '100 best companies to work for'.

3.4.3 EMPLOYER BRANDING

Employer branding is about presenting your organisation to the labour market in the best possible light so that potential employees would like to work for you more than your competitors. The CIPD's definition of an employer brand is:

> a set of attributes and qualities, often intangible, that makes an organisation distinctive, promises a particular kind of employment experience, and appeals to those people who will thrive and perform best in its culture. It is based on the principles of product branding and advertising developed in marketing.

(Walker 2007)

There has been a lot of interest in employer branding in recent years, and a degree of consensus has emerged on how organisations should go about it. The most important thing appears to be that the brand message that is developed *must* reflect the reality of working for the organisation. If the employer markets itself by making false claims, all that will follow is that any new recruits will be disappointed, current employees will be confused and cynical, and gradually the reputation of the organisation will suffer. To ensure that the brand reflects the reality, the starting point of any activity in this area should be research into the perceptions of existing members of staff. The key things to discover are what aspects of the employment experience are perceived to be both positive and unique (different from that of other employers).

There are some useful frameworks available for managers to consult when deciding how best to present themselves to potential employees. The idea is that there are different 'personalities' that organisations can align themselves with.

Lievens et al (2007), for example, offer the following five options:

- sincerity – branding based on being honest and friendly
- excitement – branding based on being trendy, spirited and innovative. An example is Google, who state the following on their website:

> In every Google office, you will find challenging projects and smart people with potential to change the world. Googlers relish the freedom to create the next generation of web technologies in an environment designed to foster collaboration, creativity, health, and happiness.

- competence – branding based on being reliable and successful
- sophistication – branding based on being prestigious
- ruggedness – branding based on being masculine and tough.

Once the analysis is complete and the key factors that differentiate the employment experience have been clearly established, the next step is to develop slogans and statements that can be used to communicate the key messages to existing and to would-be staff. A feature of employer branding is the need to repeat the core message again and again and again over a prolonged period using every available opportunity.

Organisations that are able to sustain a really positive position in their labour markets over a long period of time can reasonably claim to have achieved the status of 'employers of choice'. Such organisations are well-respected as employers and tend to attract a large number of outstanding applications whenever they advertise vacancies. University students compete strenuously for places on their graduate training programmes and they tend to have low staff turnover rates. Such a status is hard won, but hugely valuable from a talent management perspective. Provided employee selection processes work effectively and an intelligent, employee-focused style of management is preserved, being an employer of choice all but guarantees the presence of a highly talented and well-motivated workforce who are likely to help it perform very well.

Some now argue that in the tightest labour markets where 'talent wars' exist between employers looking to recruit outstanding people, it is not enough for organisations to settle for 'employer of choice' status. This is because all the leading organisations offer similar deals and will always match the employee value propositions (EVPs) that their rivals make available to recruits. What is needed is something more special still so that would-be recruits do not just find the prospect of working for the organisation desirable, but truly irresistible (Ladjemi 2014). Achieving this is very challenging, requiring organisations to invest heavily in highly sophisticated employer branding activities and to segment the labour market in the same way that marketing professionals segment target markets for products and services. Recruitment messages then have to be crafted carefully so as to appeal to the right people at the right time.

TRANSFORMING AN EMPLOYER BRAND

CASE STUDY 3.1

McDonald's is truly a global brand – being one of the largest and most successful food chains in the world, operating over 31,000 outlets spread across 119 countries. It would be almost impossible to dispute the success of the McDonald's corporate brand – but what about the employer brand?

Traditionally, McDonald's has had a poor reputation as an employer. This derives from the cost leadership strategy employed, most jobs being of the entry-level, low-skill, low-autonomy variety, and relatively poorly paid.

Although McDonald's has by no means been alone in offering this type of employment, its sheer prevalence made it a commonly cited example – leading to the unfortunate term 'McJob' appearing at the end of the 1990s, being used in

connection with any low-prestige, low-benefit, no-future type of employment, usually in the service sector.

Aware of the damage such a reputation would do – to both the morale of the existing workforce and efforts to attract new employees – McDonald's has been working hard to systematically redefine the 'McJob' term and improve its employer brand image since. It has done this by continually working on the benefits it offers to employees, and ensuring that these are well promoted.

The current employee benefit portfolio includes a range of work–life balance provisions, a range of recognition programmes, and impressive training and development provision, including its own corporate 'Hamburger University'.

? REFLECTIVE ACTIVITY 3.3

What would you say was the employer brand of your own organisation (or an organisation that you are familiar with)?

3.5 MANAGING RECRUITMENT AND SELECTION

Recruitment and **selection** tend to be lumped together as contributory parts of a process of bringing new employees into a company. It is important to be aware, however, that the terms refer to two different sets of activities. 'Recruitment' refers to advertising the company and the vacancy to potential employees, and trying to encourage suitable individuals to apply, whereas 'selection' refers to choosing the most suitable candidate from those who have applied.

3.5.1 MANAGING THE RECRUITMENT PROCESS

Recruitment is a required activity in two different circumstances: when a new job role is created within a business, and when an existing employee leaves the business. Before any recruitment activities commence, however, it is important that thorough consideration is given first to determining that a vacancy has definitely arisen (and that the job tasks cannot be distributed among existing employees), and second, if a vacancy has arisen, to knowing exactly what skills and experience are needed to fill it.

In order to determine the skills and experiences needed for a role, some form of job analysis is generally undertaken, which collects information from a range of sources on job duties, job responsibilities, the equipment, tools and materials used, controls over work, interactions with others, performance expectations, the working environment, and any prerequisites in terms of education/experience.

The range of sources from which such information can come is wide. If the role is not a new one, information on it can come from current role-holders (via observation of them at work, via interviews or via the completion of work diaries). Information can also be collected from the line manager for the role, from other organisation stakeholders who would have contact with the individual, from documentary evidence such as appraisal results and training manuals, and from external experts in the specific field.

After the job analysis, the steps described below are commonly followed.

Developing a job description

The job description is one of the key documents in recruitment and selection activities. Based on the job analysis exercise, it summarises the tasks that make up the job, together with statements of reporting lines, areas of responsibility and performance criteria. IRS (2003, p43) found that over 75% of employers include copies of job descriptions in application packs, and that 82% use them when drawing up job advertisements.

Job descriptions tend to follow a standard format from company to company, usually listing the following information:

- job title
- grade/rate of pay
- main location
- supervisor's name/post
- details of any subordinates
- summary of the main purpose of the job
- list of principal job duties together with very brief descriptions
- reference to other documents (such as collective agreements) that may clarify or expand on other items.

Developing a person specification

Whereas the job description focuses on the nature of the role, the accompanying person specification focuses on the human attributes that are considered to be necessary for someone performing the role. IRS (2003) found that 72% of employers make use of person specifications. Person specifications tend to include information under a number of headings, including:

- skills – such as a certain level of IT competence, a foreign language, familiarity with certain tools and techniques
- experience – in a similar job role, company or industry
- qualifications – generally vocational
- education – mostly referring to a specific level (such as GCSEs, A-level or degree)
- personal attributes – such as professionalism, creativity, interpersonal skills.

It is also typical for each specification to be classified as either 'essential' or 'desirable' in the person performing the role.

Identifying useful sources

The most appropriate source for filling a vacancy will depend on the nature of the job. Companies can look to individuals currently working in the company (who may be interested in a promotion or even a sideways move) as well as those in the outside labour market.

Identifying the most appropriate advertising methods

There is a huge range of options available, including:

- internal company methods (staff intranet, noticeboards)
- word of mouth – encouraging current employees to recommend the company to others who may be suitable ('refer-a-friend' schemes)
- a variety of print advertisements (local newspapers, national newspapers, specialist trade magazines)
- online advertisements
- local radio
- job centres
- employment agencies
- educational liaison – careers service, career fairs, college tutors, student societies.

Along with the suitability of different methods for reaching the required labour market, the costs of the different options are likely to be key considerations.

3.5.2 MANAGING THE SELECTION PROCESS

Once the fruits of a successful recruitment campaign have appeared, and a company has a number of eager individuals expressing an interest in the job(s) available, the next task for the company is to identify which individuals are best suited to both the job(s) and the culture of the company.

The first task at this stage is often the development of a **competency framework** to use throughout the selection process (generally produced at the same time as the job description and person specification). This document was mentioned earlier in connection with the skills audit activity in talent planning. Because companies tend to place great emphasis on their 'core values', and want these to permeate throughout the business, many organisations have a fixed list of competencies (linked to the core values) against which all jobs are assessed. It has been noted that the most commonly sought competencies in UK organisations include communication, customer focus, commercial awareness, teamwork, flexibility and problem-solving.

To assess each applicant against the requirements of the competency framework for the role, a number of selection techniques can be used. The major methods are:

Application procedures

Such procedures mostly focus on the instructions given to those interested in the vacancies in terms of registering their interest (usually by submitting a CV or completing the company's standard application form), together with subsequent in-house procedures for sifting through the pile of applications to identify the most promising – a process of shortlisting.

Interviews

A range of options is available:

- telephone interviews

These tend to be common as a first stage in the process, to identify those suitable for a more substantial interview, or where candidates are being recruited from overseas.

- face-to-face, one-to-one interviews

These are usually conducted by a member of the HR department or by the line manager of the vacant role.

- panel interviews

This is where more than one company representative attends the interview.

- group interviews

This approach differs in that it involves a group of applicants being interviewed at the same time by a recruitment team. Sometimes tasks may be set which the interviewers observe, such as one candidate interviewing another.

There is no one set format for any of these types of interview, and the nature can vary considerably from company to company. In the past, interviews tended to be fairly unstructured, different candidates being asked different questions based on the factors cited on their CVs/application forms. Given the concerns about consistency in treatment, however, interviews tend to be more structured these days, the interviewers following a fixed interview schedule but then tailoring the discussion to the specific interviewee when probing and seeking examples.

In line with the popularity of competencies in the workplace cited above, many companies now use competency-based interviewing, where applicants are asked to provide examples of how they have demonstrated a certain competency in the past, or answer a scenario-based question that aims to draw out how they would act in a specific circumstance.

Ability and personality tests

According to the CIPD's 2015 *Resourcing and Talent Management* survey, around half of the UK's larger employers now use some form of ability testing when selecting at least some of their employees. There are different types of tests, including those measuring general ability (such as IQ tests), those measuring literacy and/or numeracy, and those measuring skills in job-specific activities. It is important to be aware that these tests are never used in isolation – their primary purpose is to weed out the poorest performers in shortlisting from huge numbers of applicants (such as in highly competitive graduate recruitment schemes) and to provide supplementary information for consideration alongside the data from other selection techniques.

Along with ability tests, a range of personality tests is also available for use in employee selection (as well as employee development). According to the CIPD's 2015 survey, they are used to some extent by 36% of UK organisations, and are especially common when considering management and trainee management roles – where softer, less tangible skills such as communication, diplomacy and emotional intelligence are often deemed necessary. The tests usually consist of personality questionnaires or inventories that candidates complete either on paper or online. Unlike ability tests, there are no 'correct' answers to questions, but the outcomes are used to determine the extent to which each candidate's natural personality matches the disposition deemed to be most suited to the specific position.

Work samples and assessment centres

Work samples are required when organisations ask candidates to complete some element of the job role as part of the selection procedure to demonstrate their competence.

Assessment centres are perhaps the most sophisticated of all the available selection activities: they are designed to bring together a group of applicants and assess each individual using a range of different selection methods. Assessment centres often include a combination of two or more of the following:

- candidate presentations
- interviews

- individual work samples (such as in-tray exercises)
- ability and/or personality tests
- group activities
- role-playing.

The advantage of the method is that it offers a much more valid measure of each individual's suitability for the role (cross-referencing the results of different information sources). The disadvantages of the method are that it is only viable where there are a reasonably large number of candidates, and that it tends to be very costly.

References

Regardless of the specific selection methods used by a company, once the preferred candidate has been identified, most companies seek to further check the suitability of the candidate by securing references. A reference is a testimonial from someone who knows the candidate well, which comments on the candidate's suitability for employment. It is common practice for a company to request two references prior to making or confirming an offer of employment to a candidate – either both from previous employers (or educational contacts if they are new to the world of work), or one professional and one personal.

In the past, companies would ask for quite a lot of information about candidates when making reference requests. But with fears of backlash from disgruntled ex-employees (including threats of legal action), however, employers have become far more reluctant when it comes to providing information in response to reference requests, especially anything that is subjective (personal opinion on performance/attitude, etc). A common approach these days is therefore to provide simply the job title, dates of employment and overall reason for leaving (whether resignation, retirement, redundancy or dismissal).

3.5.3 KEY LEGAL REQUIREMENTS IN RECRUITMENT AND SELECTION

Under the Equality Act 2010, all employers have a legal responsibility to ensure that no unlawful discrimination occurs in the recruitment and selection process on the grounds of what is known as a 'protected characteristic'. This covers sex, race, nationality, disability, age, marital status, sexual orientation, and religion or belief. Unlawful discrimination can be direct, indirect or even 'positive'. It is also important to be aware that there are additional requirements to consider in relation to applicants with a disability. More details on this subject can be found in Chapter 2, Employment Law.

There are also legal requirements to consider in the induction of new employees once selected, such as checking their eligibility to work in the UK, and ensuring that they are issued with an employment contract (a written statement of the main terms of employment) within two months of starting work.

Diversity and fair access to opportunities

As stated previously, it is a legal requirement that organisations do not make any negative decisions about employment based on a protected characteristic. In order to ensure fair access to opportunity in recruitment and selection, however, organisations should go further than simply ensuring that personal factors do not influence the selection decision. They should also take steps to ensure that all individuals have an equal opportunity to apply. To ensure fair access to opportunity, the following can be considered:

- advertising vacancies via a range of different mechanisms to target a diverse population
- auditing the diversity of the workforce, and making use of positive action campaigns if a certain group is found to be under-represented

- offering alternative options for application – for example, large-print versions of application forms; online and paper submission options – and ensuring that the HR department contact details are clearly displayed for those who would like to discuss their specific circumstances
- offering provisions at the selection stage – for example, allowing candidates to bring a support worker to an interview or to be given more time in tests if they are disabled; people might otherwise be offered a telephone rather than a face-to-face interview if they are based overseas.

3.5.4 THE EVALUATION OF PRACTICES

The final matter to consider before we move on from recruitment and selection is the importance of evaluation. For a start, it is important to ensure that the tools and processes used are proving effective – attracting and identifying the best people for the jobs available. Equally important is to be able to prove that the activities are cost-effective. In the modern business environment, all functions – including human resources – are under increasing pressure to demonstrate to the senior management team how they add value to the business. Employee resourcing can be one of the HR team's most costly activities, and so it is essential that the benefits are seen to outweigh the costs.

So how can we evaluate our recruitment and selection practices?

- By monitoring the statistics – such as the average length of time that vacancies are live, the overall number of applications (are we attracting people?), the percentage of applicants initially shortlisted (are we attracting the right people?), and the percentage of offers accepted.
- By recording the costs of recruitment and selection activities and seeing how they compare to previous years' costs (internal benchmarking) or to the costs of other companies in the industry (external benchmarking).
- By monitoring turnover levels – especially in the first few months of employment.
- By holding focus groups with a group of new starters during the induction process.

3.6 MAXIMISING EMPLOYEE RETENTION

As well as understanding how to bring the right people into the company to fill vacancies, it is essential that the employee resourcing team are competent in maximising employee retention – ensuring that the right people don't leave the company and create more vacancies that need filling.

There are two general approaches that can be taken – usually in tandem – when considering how to maximise employee retention: one looking outside the organisation (considering trends in the labour market and what your competitors are doing) and the other looking inside the organisation (at your current turnover levels and the reasons for voluntary departures).

We focus on the latter here – understanding the current turnover situation in the company. It is important to understand that not all turnover is bad. A certain amount of turnover, sometimes termed 'functional turnover', is desired because it concerns things like the removal of poor performers, savings on wages and facilitating the progression of other employees and the entry of 'new blood' into the organisation.

That said, a lot of employee turnover falls under the heading of 'dysfunctional turnover' – staff departures that have a negative effect on the company, seen in terms of the significant costs involved in replacing employees, the loss of skills and knowledge, etc, and the negative effect on remaining colleagues.

In order to understand the turnover situation, the organisation has to establish the level of turnover, the cost of this turnover and the reasons for it. We explore the different methods available for investigating the reason for turnover in section 3.6.1, but for now let us turn our attention to determining levels and costs. In terms of measuring the level of turnover in a company, a variety of quantitative methods are often used, the most common being the following:

● crude turnover rate calculation – establishing the percentage of the workforce to have left in a year
● stability rate calculation – establishing how long people tend to remain in the organisation. This is important because the action that should be taken if the company tends to lose most people in the first few months of employment is different from the action that should be taken if it is losing people with a considerable length of service
● cohort analysis – establishing the stability rate of one specific group/cohort of employees (such as a specific year's graduate intake) so that the retention of these staff over time can be tracked.

A useful activity to undertake after such calculations is benchmarking – which can be either internal or external. 'Internal benchmarking' refers to the practice of comparing the turnover levels in different areas of the business (to target turnover hotspots), or this year's level with that of previous years (to track trends over time, and monitor the success of retention initiatives). 'External benchmarking' refers to the practice of comparing the turnover level in the company either with national industry averages (via published survey data) or with the levels of turnover in companies in the same area (which can be accessed via forming 'benchmarking clubs' where such metrics are exchanged). Both types of benchmarking can help put turnover information into context. For example, if analysis revealed a turnover level of 10% in your organisation, this might be quite concerning – but it would be considerably less concerning if you knew that the average for your industry was 20%.

3.6.1 THE COSTS OF TURNOVER

Dysfunctional turnover can be extremely expensive for a business, the costs being both direct and indirect. It is important for HR practitioners to try to calculate the costs of dysfunctional turnover – both to understand the extent of the problem and also to gain commitment from senior management in relation to any proposed retention initiatives.

Survey data reveals that few organisations appear to make efforts to calculate what **labour turnover** actually costs them. The CIPD's 2015 *Resourcing and Talent Planning* survey reported that only 15% of the organisations surveyed were currently calculating the cost of labour turnover. One reason for this is the fact that calculating the costs of turnover is a very tricky business. Many of the elements, especially those relating to indirect costs, are not easily quantified; many organisations do not have the records needed; it is sometimes hard to distinguish between functional and dysfunctional turnover; and the activity can take a lot of time.

In many cases, a single instance of dysfunctional turnover may result in a vacancy being created which is filled externally. To arrive at an understanding of the overall cost of this, we must consider a variety of issues, as shown in Table 3.1.

Table 3.1 Direct and indirect costs

Direct costs	Indirect costs
• HR administration time re the leaver • Costs of advertising the vacancy • HR administration time re the recruitment and selection process (sifting CVs, etc) • Selection expenses • Costs of covering the role while it is vacant (paying overtime to other staff or employing a temp) • HR administration time re the new starter • New starter costs • Induction and basic training costs	• Departing employee is less productive in final weeks • New employee is less productive in first few weeks • Loss of morale and productivity in colleagues if sad at departure or annoyed at increased workload • Possible damage to client relationships • Lack of return on investment in relation to any training and development that the departing employee was given • Company information could be used to the advantage of a competitor • Damage to company reputation (if individual leaves on bad terms or turnover level is high)

The simplest way to get an idea of the costs of dysfunctional turnover in general is to estimate the cost of turnover for a 'typical post' in the company, and then multiply this by the number of dysfunctional leavers for the year to reach a final 'dysfunctional turnover cost' for the year. Another approach is to estimate the total cost incurred by all activities related to employee resignation, recruitment, selection and induction over the course of a year – which includes both actual expenses and the cost of HR/management time.

3.6.2 UNDERSTANDING WHY PEOPLE LEAVE

In order to try to reduce levels of dysfunctional turnover, it is necessary to understand the reasons for it. People voluntarily decide to leave organisations for a wide range of reasons, and the first important distinction to be made is between turnover that is unavoidable and that which could have been avoided.

Unavoidable turnover refers to circumstances such as ill health, domestic commitments, moving house or returning to study – where the decision to leave has nothing to do with the company and is therefore out of management's control. Avoidable turnover, however, applies to departures that are caused by some form of dissatisfaction – meaning that it is potentially within management's control. It has been estimated that around 90% of employee departures fall into this category.

If 90% of voluntary resignations could potentially be avoided by the use of appropriate organisational interventions, it is important to do a bit more digging into the factors that are causing these departures, so that the appropriate interventions can be identified. Rather than making assumptions about the causes of turnover (such as assuming that it is all about the rate of pay), a number of qualitative data sources can be used to identify the real reasons. The most common sources of information tend to be exit interviews and general staff satisfaction surveys.

According to a recent CIPD survey, around 90% of organisations make use of some sort of exit interview mechanism – a discussion between the departing employee and a company representative (usually the line manager or a member of the HR team) focused on reasons for leaving, factors that might have encouraged the individual to stay, and improvements that the organisation can make moving forward. Some companies use a questionnaire rather than a face-to-face discussion.

> ### ? REFLECTIVE ACTIVITY 3.4
>
> It is important to be aware that the information collected in an exit interview may not be 100% reliable, especially where the discussion takes place between an employee and their own line manager near to their date of departure.
>
> 1   What issues might influence the likelihood that an employee will be completely honest in their exit interview?

The annual employee attitude or staff satisfaction survey is another useful tool in understanding turnover. This is a mechanism designed for the frequent and systematic gathering of opinions on a broad range of organisation-wide issues from the entire workforce. Such surveys can help an organisation target retention initiatives appropriately because they highlight potential sources of satisfaction and dissatisfaction in all employees, rather than just those who have already decided to leave.

Other methods that can be used include surveys of ex-employees (completed a couple of months after departure), analysis of 'stayers' to see what factors encourage people to remain with the company, and 'last job move' surveys – asking new employees to talk about why they left their last job. Although the latter will not provide information on what your own company is doing right or wrong as an employer, it will provide information on the specific dynamics that operate in key labour markets.

3.6.3 RETENTION STRATEGIES

Once you have ascertained the level of turnover (especially dysfunctional turnover), how much it is costing and the main reasons, you are in a position to start to develop an appropriate retention strategy. There are three key issues here.

The first is securing senior management support for the strategy; the second is identifying the appropriate initiatives; and the third is ensuring alignment. The latter refers to three different forms of alignment – alignment between individual retention initiatives; alignment between the retention strategy and other HR strategies; and alignment with overall organisation strategy.

Because most retention strategies require the investment of considerable financial and human resources – in terms of planning, development, execution and maintenance – it is important that the HR department makes a strong business case outlining the need for action. It is here that the costing calculations will prove most useful – showing exactly how much money employee turnover is costing the company, and how much could be saved were this level to be reduced.

To make sure the issue is given the prominence it deserves, HR departments should aim to include turnover information (along with other key metrics) in monthly HR reports that can be discussed at senior management meetings or be added to the board report.

In terms of the specific initiatives to be included in the strategy, a wide range of things can be considered, the usefulness of each and the most effective combination being dependent entirely on the nature of the turnover issue in the organisation.

A breakdown of common reasons for leaving and their associated retention initiatives is presented in Table 3.2.

In addition to this, because a lot of turnover occurs in the first six months of a new role, it is essential that effective induction and transition mechanisms are in place.

Finally, it is important that the retention strategy is fully communicated to all levels of the management structure – because management has a crucial role in the implementation and consistency of many of the component initiatives. It is also important to communicate any policy changes to all employees – to ensure that they are aware of all of the provisions, and so that they feel their opinions (perhaps as the result of satisfaction surveys) are being listened to and acted on.

3.6.4 THE ROLE OF THE PSYCHOLOGICAL CONTRACT

One concept that is relevant to understanding controllable dysfunctional turnover is the psychological contract. Whereas the employment contract sets out the explicit commitments between an employer and employee (pay for hours worked, etc), the psychological contract refers to the more implicit commitments. The CIPD factsheet on the subject (CIPD 2012b) defines it as 'the perceptions of the two parties, employee and employer, of what their mutual obligations are towards each other'. These obligations are often informal and imprecise, but tend to be seen as 'promises' and 'expectations'.

Table 3.2 Reasons for leaving, with associated retention initiatives

Reason for leaving	Retention initiatives
Lack of development opportunities	Regular employee appraisals Investment in training and development (various forms) Skills development programmes (linked to succession planning) Lateral as well as vertical moves
Bad relationships with supervisors or colleagues	Investment in management training Developing an internal mediation scheme Communication and teambuilding activities Opportunities for internal transfers
Negative opinion of the company in general	Transparency in policies and procedures Communication initiatives Consultation and involvement initiatives A focus on equal opportunities and diversity Investment in ethics and corporate social responsibility (CSR) initiatives
Dissatisfaction with reward	External benchmarking with other companies to ensure that salaries are competitive An internal job evaluation procedure to ensure that reward is equitably distributed A flexible benefits scheme from which each employee can select the package that best suits their needs A focus on intrinsic rewards – job variety, autonomy, etc
Incompatibility of work with other commitments	Flexible working arrangements (hours/location) Assistance for working mothers (investing in a crèche or childcare vouchers, etc) Sabbaticals
Dissatisfaction with the working environment	Investment in maintenance and equipment

The psychological contract is relevant to employee turnover because of the concept of breach. When one party (usually the employer) fails to honour its side of the psychological contract, the other (usually the employee) perceives the contact to have been breached – resulting in feelings of anger, injustice, resentment and distrust.

A range of things can be seen to breach the psychological contract, but one of the main problems is unrealistic expectations – often the result of misleading messages in the recruitment process that cause people to compete for and subsequently accept jobs for which they are in truth unsuited. Ways to avoid unrealistic expectations include:

- ensuring that job descriptions are accurate
- ensuring that during job interviews, both employer and employee expectations are discussed
- offering a realistic job preview (such as an hour shadowing an individual doing the same job role, or a half-day working in the role)
- allowing team member involvement in the recruitment or selection process.

Examples include Northamptonshire Police, who asked current staff to feature in podcasts for the company website, talking about their role and what they enjoyed about working for the organisation; and Prêt A Manger, who include the views of future colleagues in the selection process (after the candidates have all had a job preview with the team)

- considering recruitment from among the company's temps, interns, part-timers and others who are already familiar with the employer
- considering the use of an employee referral scheme. The idea is that the current employee knows both the company and the candidate well, and will know where there is a good fit.

CASE STUDY 3.2

DOES REALITY MATCH THE RHETORIC?

On the topic of employer branding above, we noted the claim made by Google that they offer employees freedom, collaboration and an environment that fosters 'health and happiness'. But is this in fact the reality of working there? The following article extract suggests it might not be – at least, not for all staff.

'In 2008 Google HR set up a private Google Group to ask former employees why they left the company ... The thread shows a brutal honesty about what it's like to work at Google, at least from the point of view of employees who were unhappy enough to resign. [There were a number of complaints ...] but one message stands out in most of the posts – employees thought they were entering the promised land when they joined Google, and most of them were disappointed. Some of them wondered if it meant they were somehow lacking ... "If you can't be happy there, how will you ever be happy? If you can't be productive there, how will you ever be productive?"' (Arrington 2009)

As well as unfulfilled expectations, a range of things can result in a breach of the psychological contract, including a sudden shock or a gradual erosion of the contract as a result of repeated minor violations. In terms of the former, Table 3.3 indicates the sort of shock that might be experienced, and the breach it represents.

3.7 MANAGING RETIREMENT, DISMISSAL AND REDUNDANCY

In section 3.6 we looked at employee turnover – primarily considering the issue of **voluntary turnover**. Before we complete this chapter, it is important for you to be aware of three other types of employee departure: retirement, dismissal and redundancy.

3.7.1 RETIREMENT

'Retirement' traditionally referred to the scheduled departure of an employee from the company because he or she had reached the set age for departure from the overall workforce – which was either 60 (women) or 65 (men) years old. Due to developments in employment law, however, individual employees have a lot more control in the retirement process today. It is no longer lawful for companies to compulsorily retire employees at a certain age unless there is a genuine reason (a justified way of achieving a legitimate business aim), and many individuals choose to take flexible retirement options when the time feels right, rather than leaving the workforce altogether.

Table 3.3 Shocks resulting in perceived breaches of the psychological contract

Sudden shock issue	The breach
Company reorganisation and possible redundancies	Security
Being passed over for promotion	Career enhancement; equity
Abusive treatment by line manager	Trust and respect
Overtime freeze	Remuneration expectations
Relocation	Work–life balance
Changed working hours	Work–life balance
Manager takes credit for your work	Recognition and reward

If an individual becomes unable to meet the needs of the job role through factors related to age, any exit should therefore be managed through the performance and capability procedure.

Good practice in the management of retirement is for there to be ongoing discussions with all employees about their future intentions, and the offer of a range of options when retirement starts to be considered. The range may include the following:

- moving from a full-time to a part-time contract
- stepping down to a role with slightly less responsibility
- winding down – gradually reducing working hours
- atypical contracts, perhaps including an extended period of leave
- retiring from permanent employment but remaining on the company books as a consultant.

Such options have proved very popular. In a survey carried out by the Centre for Research into Older Workers (CROW), it was found that 80% of the respondents (people currently in full-time work) would like to stay in work beyond their expected retirement dates. Only 9% would like to do so on a full-time basis, while most would like to stay on only if they could work part-time, occasionally or on a consultancy basis (CIPD 2011, p12).

3.7.2 DISMISSAL

Along with redundancy (covered below), 'dismissal' refers to **involuntary employee turnover** – where the employment contract is terminated by the employer. Dismissals refer to situations in which employment is terminated because the employee has failed to meet the requirements of the job role. The key issues when managing dismissals are that there is a valid reason for the dismissal, and that a fair and proper procedure is followed.

A valid reason for dismissal tends to fall into one of two categories: conduct or capability. Conduct issues relate to the breaking of company rules in either a minor way (misconduct) or a major way (gross misconduct). Capability issues refer to an inability to do the job – which might be due to either competence or health.

In terms of procedure, the standards expected for dismissals are laid out in the Acas Codes of Practice. More details on this, together with information on the legal claims that can be made by individuals should they feel they have been dismissed unfairly, are set out in Chapter 2, Employment Law.

3.7.3 REDUNDANCY

The second type of involuntary turnover is redundancy. This refers to a dismissal because the job role that the individual performs is no longer viable. The definition of 'redundancy' is set out in Section 139(1) of the Employment Rights Act 1996, but in summary, a redundancy only occurs where there has been, or is going to be, a closure of the business, a closure of the workplace or a diminution in the need for employees doing work of a certain kind.

It is good practice for employees to try to find alternatives to compulsory redundancy. This is obviously preferable for the workforce, but it can also have benefits for the company (in terms of staff morale, reputation and ability to expand in the future). Alternatives to redundancy include the following, some of which may be offered by a company as a matter of course, whereas others may instead be introduced via consultation with the workforce:

- recruitment freeze and redeployment of existing talent (with retraining) where vacancies arise
- overtime freeze
- pay cuts
- reduced days/hours
- sabbaticals
- voluntary redundancy
- voluntary early retirement.

CASE STUDY 3.3

VOLUNTARY OPTIONS AT KPMG

In December 2008, amid concerns over the financial climate and while key competitors were announcing plans to cut hundreds of jobs, Big Four accounting firm KPMG launched an innovative scheme to cut down on wage costs without resorting to redundancy. The firm gave its UK staff the option of applying to work a four day week (with the fifth unpaid) or take a sabbatical of up to 12 weeks (at 30% pay) – something that proved highly popular, with more than 85% of employees signing up for the scheme until the end of 2010.

When such alternatives have been exhausted, and redundancy is the only option, it is important that a company follows the correct procedure for redundancies.

More information is available on the legal requirements of this in the Employment Law chapter (Chapter 2) of this book. It is important for a company to be as communicative and transparent as possible in such circumstances, and to pay attention to those who remain employed (in terms of reassurance and the monitoring of workloads, etc) as well as those who are dismissed.

CASE STUDY 3.4

HAPPY DOG WANTS HAPPY STAFF

Happy Dog is a small chain of hot-dog cafés in Sundale Valley, a rural area that covers three villages and lots of open countryside. The population of Sundale Valley is largely retirees and families (because it has good schools and good transport links with the local city for employment), and is a popular family-day-out destination because of the number of beautiful walking routes in the area.

Happy Dog has enjoyed a steady staff turnover for the three years since it opened, and has successfully operated as an Employer of Churn – being especially popular with the large number of sixth-form students in the area, and university students looking for work during summer holidays (when demand for workers at Happy Dog tends to increase owing to tourism).

A new out-of-town retail and entertainment complex is being built in the area, however, which will include a cinema, a ten-pin bowling alley, a number of fashion stores and two fastfood outlets that are both part of well-established national chains. Mr Terrier, the manager of Happy Dog, is quite concerned because he has seen adverts in the local Job Centre advertising the following roles in these outlets: kitchen assistants, serving staff and cleaning staff. Mr Terrier

is worried because these match the roles in his outlets, the rate of pay is the same, and the benefits will be especially appealing to the local student population: discounts at all entertainment and retail outlets in the complex, and a guaranteed location flexibility policy (so that students can transfer to a different outlet in the chain during university term-time).

Because Happy Dog does not have its own HR function, Mr Terrier has called you up for some advice. He wants to know how he can ensure that his outlets have suitable staff without having to increase pay rates – something he simply cannot afford to do.

Questions

1   In addition to sixth-form students, who else would you advise Mr Terrier to target as potential employees?

2   What provisions could he introduce to make employment at Happy Dog more attractive to both students and other groups, without being too costly?

3   How could he gauge the success of new provisions?

FURTHER READING

CIPD (2012) *Information pages* [Online]. Information pages are available on the website, which provide factsheets, podcasts and survey reports on each of the following topics:

- Labour market: www.cipd.co.uk/hr-topics/labour-market.aspx
- Recruitment: www.cipd.co.uk/hr-topics/recruitment.aspx
- Employer branding: www.cipd.co.uk/hr-topics/employer-branding.aspx
- Selection and assessment: www.cipd.co.uk/hr-topics/selectionassessment.aspx
- Retention and turnover: www.cipd.co.uk/hr-topics/retentionturnover.aspx
- Redundancy: www.cipd.co.uk/hr-topics/redundancy.aspx
- Dismissal: www.cipd.co.uk/hr-topics/dismissal.aspx

Various publications on the topic of the UK labour market are available from the Office for National Statistics: www.statistics.gov.uk/hub/labour-market/index.html

Related to the topic of dismissals, a key resource for HR professionals is the Acas Code of Practice on the recommended procedures for conducting disciplinary and grievance investigations. The relevant document – Code of Practice 1 (April 2009) – can be accessed at: www.acas.org.uk/media/ pdf/h/m/ Acas_Code_of_Practice_1_on_disciplinary_and_grievance_procedures.pdf

The following CIPD textbooks also provide more detail on the subjects covered in this chapter:

TAYLOR, S. (2011) *Resourcing and talent planning*. London: CIPD. Contains detailed chapters on most of the issues covered above.

TAYLOR, S. (2012) *Contemporary issues in HRM*. London: CIPD. Especially useful for information related to the labour market and other pertinent trends in the external environment.

REFERENCES

ARRINGTON, M. (2009) *Why Google employees quit*. Available at: http://techcrunch.com/ 2009/01/18/why-google-employees-quit/ [accessed February 2012].

ATKINSON, J. (1984a) *Flexibility, uncertainty and manpower management*. IMS Report No. 89. Brighton: Institute of Manpower Studies.

ATKINSON, J. (1984b) Manpower strategies for flexible organisations. *Personnel Management*, August. pp28–31.

CIPD (2011) *Managing age*. Guide. London: Chartered Institute of Personnel and Development.

CIPD (2012a) *Succession planning*. Factsheet. London: Chartered Institute of Personnel and Development.

CIPD (2012b) *The psychological contract*. Factsheet. London: Chartered Institute of Personnel and Development.

CIPD (2015) *Resourcing and talent management*. Annual Survey Report. London: Chartered Institute of Personnel and Development.

HIGGS, M. (2004) *Future trends in HRM*. In: REES, D. and MCBAIN, R. (eds). *People management: challenges and opportunities*. Basingstoke: Palgrave Macmillan.

INDUSTRIAL RELATIONS SERVICES (IRS) (2003) Setting the tone: job descriptions and person specifications. *Employment Review*, No. 776. pp42–8.

LADJEMI, K. (2014) 5 irresistible employer brand messages for 2014. *Recruiter*. 28 July.

LEITCH, LORD S. (2006) *Leitch review of skills: final report*. Available at: http://dera.ioe. ac.uk/6322/1/leitch_finalreport051206.pdf [Accessed 21 January 2016].

LIEVENS, F., VAN HOYE, G. and ANSEEL, F. (2007) Organizational identity and employer image: towards a unifying framework. *British Journal of Management*. Vol 18. pp45–59.

TAYLOR, S. (2011) *Contemporary issues in HRM*. London: Chartered Institute of Personnel and Development.

WALKER, P. (2007) *Employer branding: a no-nonsense approach*. London: Chartered Institute of Personnel and Development.

CHAPTER 4

Employee Engagement

TED JOHNS AND CECILIA ELLIS

CHAPTER CONTENTS

This chapter provides the reader with an overview of employee engagement, including:
- Introduction and overview
- What is employee engagement?
- What is distinctive about employee engagement?
- What are the enablers of employee engagement?
- What are the benefits of engagement for organisations, their people and their customers?
- What does the research indicate about employee engagement levels amongst UK employees?
- How can we explain the low levels of employee engagement in the UK?
- How can we devise and implement HRM strategies and practices that will raise levels of employee engagement?
- What about the future for employee engagement?
- Conclusion

KEY LEARNING OUTCOMES

By the end of this chapter, you should be able to:

- understand the concept of employee engagement and its importance as a contributor to positive corporate and performance outcomes
- analyse what is distinctive about employee engagement when contrasted with other related concepts, such as employee involvement
- identify and critically assess the findings of recent studies that purport to demonstrate the incidence of employee engagement in various organisations, industries and sectors, both public and private
- evaluate the processes through which high levels of employee engagement can be secured and sustained within organisations
- implement HR strategies and practices intended to raise levels of employee engagement in a specific organisational context
- explain the principles and applications of high-performance working (HPW) and the role of employee engagement as an element in the realisation of an HPW culture
- outline the future for employee engagement, principally throughout the UK economy but also within the globalised world of work.

4.1 INTRODUCTION AND OVERVIEW

Many years ago the philosopher Sir Isaiah Berlin wrote an essay, 'The hedgehog and the fox', in which he identified two types of thinkers. The fox, cunning and resourceful, knows many things; the hedgehog, diligent and persevering, knows one big thing.

Organisations are the same. They often focus on one big thing – namely, profitability. The public sector is more nebulous because it can't focus on profitability, but it can concentrate on resource efficiencies, service delivery and customer feedback. Organisations begin by claiming to know how to make the company grow, and then work from the top down to get the job done, by building factories, organising offices, creating websites and selling their products.

This can work, provided the vision is brilliant and the execution flawless. But it often falls apart further down the chain of command, especially when front-line managers and customer-facing employees don't share the high-level vision (why should they?) and start picking holes in it, deliberately or otherwise.

The problem is that the hedgehog's insular vision tends to ignore the importance of people as contributors to business success, whereas the fox celebrates them. It's the quality of those millions of one-to-one interactions between manager and employee, and between employee and customer, that typically distinguish the businesses that thrive from those that founder. These are what Jan Carlzon, CEO of SAS, the Scandinavian Airlines System, described as the 'moments of truth' – occurring perhaps 50,000 times a day when staff interact with each other and/or with customers, at events. This is why for employees whose contents cannot be regulated, controlled or micromanaged by their organisations, engagement is important. When employees are engaged their managers can be confident that they will conduct themselves in the interests of the business. There can be no such confidence about the behaviour of employees who are not engaged or who, even worse, are actively disengaged.

Employee engagement is one of those HR topics that could endure to the point where chapters about engagement become a compulsory feature in all respectable HRM textbooks – or it could disappear off the face of the earth in a little while, after all its manifold facets have been exhausted. What you have to do is go through this chapter and determine your answers to these questions:

- Is employee engagement something genuinely new, or is it simply a reworking or a rehash of old ideas dressed up (typically by consultants) to look as if it is something new?
- Is the notion of employee engagement sufficiently different from similar notions such as 'involvement', 'participation' and 'commitment'?
- Is there any worthwhile evidence to show that organisations that consciously strive to produce a workforce that is 'engaged' will then experience superior performance and profitability outcomes – or are the arguments about the supposed benefits of employee engagement simply founded on plausible logic and 'common sense', but nothing more?

We can answer the first of the questions straight away, because it is now widely accepted by both practitioners and academics that employee engagement is not merely a fad (Schaufeli and Bakker 2010). As Purcell (2010, p1) observes, 'it would be a waste of time to launch a national awareness campaign and commit government funded organisations to action if employee engagement was just another "flash in the pan"'. Therefore, employee engagement merits further consideration.

4.2 WHAT IS EMPLOYEE ENGAGEMENT?

The first thing we must do is define what we're talking and writing about. And that's where our problems begin, because there are several definitions we could use, and none of them is absolutely definitive.

Kahn (1990) is associated with the start of the academic interest in the engagement concept. Kahn (1990, p694) commented that 'in engagement, people employ and express themselves physically, cognitively and emotionally'. This depicts engagement as a three-dimensional concept. **Physical engagement** could be expressed through high levels of energy and mental resilience while working and the willingness to invest effort in one's work. Cognitive engagement could be being fully concentrated and happily engrossed in one's work, whereby time passes quickly and one has difficulty detaching oneself from work. Emotional engagement could entail strong involvement in one's work, and experiencing a sense of significance, enthusiasm, inspiration, pride and challenge. This three-dimensional nature of engagement suggests that it is a complex concept.

In its Factsheet on *Employee Engagement*, the CIPD (2014) describes employee engagement as 'a combination of commitment to the organisation and its values plus a willingness to help out colleagues (organisational citizenship)'. So far, so good – and the CIPD definition continues:

> It goes beyond job satisfaction and is not simply motivation. Engagement is something the employee has to offer: it cannot be 'required' as part of the employment contract.

This definition highlights the discretionary nature of engagement which means that engagement cannot be assumed; employees will not automatically be engaged.

In 2008, employee engagement became an area of interest for the UK government when they initiated a review of employee engagement which culminated in the publication of the MacLeod Report (2009). MacLeod and Clarke (2009) build on the ideas of David Guest in constructing their own model of employee engagement as a workplace approach designed to ensure that employees are committed to their organisation's goals and values, motivated to contribute to organisational success and able to enhance their own sense of well-being.

Interviewed for a *People Management* article, MacLeod (2009) also argues that employee engagement goes to 'the heart of the workplace relationship between employer and employee' and that it can be a key to unlocking productivity and transforming the working lives of many people for whom Monday morning is an especially low part of the week. The interest in engagement generated by the MacLeod Report has been continued through the construction of an Engage for Success Task Force in 2011.

More recent research on engagement supports the notion that it is a complex concept. Research from the CIPD (2012) suggests that employees can engage on different levels and that there are two types of engagement. First, **emotional engagement** which is defined as someone who has 'emotional attachment to one or more aspects of their work' and second, transactional engagement which is described as a person who is 'happy to exhibit the behaviour of engagement ... but not committed to the job or the organisation and willing to leave if a better offer appears elsewhere' (CIPD 2012, p3). These definitions imply that emotional engagement happens at a deeper level compared with the more superficial transactional engagement.

For the purposes of this chapter, employee engagement is conceptualised in accordance with Kahn (1990) and the CIPD (2014; 2012) as a three-dimensional concept which is discretionary and can occur on two different levels. The implication of this conceptualisation is that 'one size does not fit all and this means that employers have to understand the different drivers of engagement in different parts of their business' (Purcell 2010, p4).

4.3 WHAT IS DISTINCTIVE ABOUT EMPLOYEE ENGAGEMENT?

One of the concepts closely related to employee engagement is organisational commitment, which loosely refers to an individual's psychological attachment to the organisation. Commitment can be contrasted with other work-related attitudes, such as 'job satisfaction' (the employee's feelings about his or her work) and 'organisational identification' (the degree to which the employee feels a sense of 'oneness' with the organisation, and therefore doesn't see any appreciable difference between his or her own self-interests and the interests of the employer).

There are three 'mindsets' that can characterise an individual's commitment to his or her organisation:

- *affective commitment* – This refers to the employee's positive emotional attachment to the organisation. An employee who is affectively committed strongly identifies with the goals of the business and wishes to remain a part of it (and them). Such employees commit to the organisation because they 'want to', so in that sense this psychological condition is very similar to the CIPD's own definition of employee engagement – that is, it is something that employees have to 'offer', and it cannot therefore be part of the employment contract.

- *continuance commitment* – This kind of commitment is more negative in character, because these individuals commit to the organisation on account of the perceived 'costs' of departure and loss. These 'costs' include straightforward economic costs (such as pension rights) but also embrace social costs (friendship links with work colleagues) and personal costs (fear of insecurity and unemployment). Such committed employees remain members of the organisation because they 'have to'.

- *normative commitment* – These individuals commit to and remain with the organisation because of feelings of obligation and indebtedness. For example, if the employer has invested resources in training and developing the employee, the employee then feels a 'moral' obligation to put forth effort and stay in the organisation at least until the 'debt' is repaid. These employees remain committed to the organisation because they feel they 'ought to'.

It has been shown that engaged workers are characterised by low levels of 'burnout', as well as by low levels of neuroticism and high levels of extraversion when compared with the overall features of a typical workforce. Some researchers go further by suggesting that workers with high levels of engagement also enjoy good mental and physical health, again in comparison with their colleagues.

Engagement may be about behaviour, but ultimately and even more importantly it is about performance, results and outcomes. Harnessing the discretionary effort of people produces better results than if people simply work within the confines of their job descriptions. When individuals 'go the extra mile', it makes sense to believe that teams, divisions, departments and organisations will work more effectively, customers will receive better service, and efficiency will improve.

As always, however, we must keep our feet on the ground. Employee engagement does not follow automatically from feelings of job satisfaction and happiness. A person can be happy at work and satisfied with the job because the tasks being performed are intrinsically challenging – but it may still be the case that no meaningful work is being performed. So job satisfaction and happiness do not in themselves create high performance.

4.4 WHAT ARE THE ENABLERS OF EMPLOYEE ENGAGEMENT?

Purcell (2010) argues that despite the different dimensions of engagement, there are some common factors associated with engagement, described as the building blocks of engagement. These are listed below:

- Employee trust in management
- Satisfaction with the work itself
- Satisfaction with involvement in decision-making at the workplace
- Quality of relationships between management and employees
- Satisfaction with the amount of pay received
- Job challenge
- Satisfaction with the sense of achievement from work

These building blocks can be regarded as prerequisites for engagement and highlight a number of implications for HRM policy and practice. The building blocks emphasise the importance of policies and practices which create and sustain good relationships between management and employees, underpinned by trust and contributing to fulfilment from the job and the terms and conditions of service. Such HRM policies and practices can be constructed in order to encourage employees to exhibit the discretionary effort associated with engagement.

The MacLeod Report (2009) identifies four enablers of engagement which are presented and defined in Table 4.1.

Certainly, the enablers identified by MacLeod and Clarke (2009) described in Table 4.1, along with Purcell's (2010) research, emphasise the role of managers in promoting an engagement culture. This is supported by Robinson and Hayday (2009), who on behalf of the Institute of Employment Studies (IES), have reported on a project designed to understand how managers who inspire and engage their teams to perform. From seven participating organisations the IES identified 25 'engaging managers' who had little in common except their ability to engage their teams through very similar behaviours. Their jobs and roles varied, their spans of control ranged from four people to over 5,000, and they were very different in terms of personality, background and training. But what was spectacular was that their behaviours were broadly the same:

Table 4.1 Enablers of employee engagement

Enabler	Definition
A strategic narrative	A strategic narrative is defined as 'a strong transparent and explicit organisational culture which gives employees a line of sight between their job and the vision and aims of the organisation' (MacLeod and Clarke 2009, p31).
Engaging managers	These are defined as managers 'who offer clarity, appreciation of employees' effort and contribution, who treat their people as individuals and who ensure that work is organised efficiently and effectively so that employees feel they are valued, and equipped and supported to do their job' (MacLeod and Clarke 2009, p80).
Employee voice	This refers to when 'Employees' views are sought out; they are listened to and see that their opinions count and make a difference' (MacLeod and Clarke 2009, p75).
Integrity	Integrity is defined as 'A belief among employees that the organisation lives its values, and that espoused behavioural norms are adhered to, resulting in trust and a sense of integrity' (MacLeod and Clarke 2009, p33).

Source: MacLeod and Clarke 2009

- They communicate and make clear what is expected ('I try to encourage people to think of the wider objectives . . . and how they fit in').
- They listen, value and involve their teams.
- They focus on targets rather than on processes, tasks and procedures.
- They have, and share, a clear strategic vision.
- They show an active interest in others.
- They exercise good leadership skills, especially through positive role-modelling.
- They act with respect, and in turn are respected.

The managers in the sample were put forward by their organisations because their teams had high engagement scores. Yet it soon became apparent that these were also high-performing managers with high-performing teams. It was also noticeable that these managers were good at the difficult stuff, like tackling poor performance quickly and effectively, and breaking bad news.

As well as describing engagement behaviours, respondents to the IES study were also asked to describe the behaviours of managers who were disengaging:

- They lack empathy and any interest in people.
- They fail to listen and communicate.
- They are self-centred.
- They don't motivate or inspire.
- They blame others when mistakes are made, and don't take responsibility for team actions and results.
- They are typically aggressive.
- They lack personal awareness (of how their behaviour impacts on others).
- They don't deliver on promises.

? REFLECTIVE ACTIVITY 4.1

In the IES research discussed here, team members were asked to draw pictures that represented how they saw their managers. Several themes emerged. The most popular picture of all, however, was of a sun or a smiling face.

Try drawing a picture which symbolises how you see a manager you have either worked for or have observed in action. If you are in touch with colleagues who also know the manager you have chosen to draw, ask them to do the same (without showing them your picture first).

1   Analyse the results. To what extent do the pictures reinforce each other?

2   Could you see yourself showing these pictures to the manager? If not, why not?

4.5 WHAT ARE THE BENEFITS OF ENGAGEMENT FOR ORGANISATIONS, THEIR PEOPLE AND THEIR CUSTOMERS?

All sorts of sometimes extravagant claims are made about the organisational results achieved by organisations characterised by high levels of employee engagement throughout their workforces. The extravagance is exemplified by the MacLeod (2009, p6) report which asserts that 'it is our firm belief that (engagement) can be a triple win: for the individual at work, the enterprise or service, and for the country as a whole'. This suggests that engagement is universally beneficial.

CASE STUDY 4.1

TRY SOMETHING NEW TODAY

Gwyn Burr, previously customer service director at supermarket Sainsbury's, has been put in charge of the HR function as well. She points out that 'Colleagues and customers are inextricably linked ... Every touch point that we have between a customer and a colleague is a people interaction.

Therefore I'm a big believer in engaging our colleagues. Having engaged colleagues leads to excellence in customer service.'

This philosophy has led Burr to try something new, by using the principle behind the company's tried and tested customer engagement technique ('universal customer appeal') and applying it to staff ('universal colleague appeal'). The aim is to put the customer and the staff at the heart of everything that Sainsbury's does.

Burr has slightly realigned the reporting relationships in the Sainsbury's HR department so that her team now has three HR directors rather than the previous five: these directors are responsible for retail HR, central HR, and colleague engagement, so engagement has a director all to itself.

That's how important it is in this company.

Source: Churchard (2011)

According to the CIPD (2014), 'Employers want engaged employees because, as well as being happier, healthier and more fulfilled, they deliver improved business performance'. One of the most significant research reports supporting the positive impact of employee engagement is the Towers Perrin 2007/2008 Global Workforce study (2009), which clearly demonstrates the links between high engagement and high performance. Observing 50 global organisations over a one-year period, this investigation found that organisations with high employee engagement levels benefited from a 19% increase in operating income, whereas organisations with low levels of engagement saw a 32% drop. The same report also found that organisations with highly engaged workforces experienced a 28% growth in earnings per share, compared with an 11% decline in earnings per share for organisations with low levels of engagement.

Other research has shown that high levels of employee engagement are positively associated with organisational commitment (Saks 2006), customer satisfaction, employee loyalty, profitability, productivity and even safety (Harter et al 2002).

Those employees who feel themselves to be engaged typically experience greater job satisfaction (irrespective of the specific nature of the jobs they perform) and greater well-being (Schaufeli et al 2008; Alfes et al 2010). It is also claimed that engaged employees are more likely to act as organisational advocates than non-engaged or disengaged employees, and can therefore play a powerful role in promoting their organisation as an employer of choice (employer brand).

In reality, however plausible such claims – about the causal relationships between employee engagement and corporate profits and profitability – may be, in many cases they cannot be verified because crucial information is not made public by the consultancy firms from which many such claims originate. An exception is the Gallup Organization, which has shown in a study based on nearly 8,000 business units of 36 companies that those units in the top 25% on 'work engagement' produced 1% to 4% higher profitability and had, on average, between $80,000 and $120,000 higher monthly revenues or sales than the units in the bottom 25%. This translates into a difference of at least $960,000 per year per business unit.

Indeed, several Gallup studies have demonstrated the massive benefits to be gained when employee engagement and customer engagement are pursued in tandem, especially given the belief that each can feed off the other (either positively or negatively). For an American clothing retailer, Gallup has been able to show that stores that strove to satisfy both customers and employees had significantly better profit margins than stores that focused on just one objective or the other. It is worth noting that similar results have been reported by Hutchinson and Purcell (2003) when comparing four matched Tesco stores in the UK. As in most retailers, performance is measured by something called the conversion rate, which is the percentage of customers who actually buy something. Stores that scored in the top of the Gallup measures in terms of both customer satisfaction and employee engagement had much higher conversion rates than stores scoring at the bottom.

Faced with the undeniable significance of these results, the manager of one low-scoring store in the study made some changes. Ordinarily, a manager might ask a retail employee to check stock, clean up dressing rooms or work at the cash desk.

This top-down system does little to encourage employee engagement and does nothing to enhance the customer's experience – so the manager decided to give staff the freedom to respond to customer needs on their own. When they noticed that the changing rooms were filling up, for example, some employees moved to the cash registers, anticipating that customers who were trying on clothes were about to make purchases. This pleased customers, because they didn't have to wait a long time to pay, and it made employees happy because they were felt they were making a difference (Fleming and Harter 2001).

Other studies, principally involving specialised groups of respondents, have suggested similar positive outcomes linked to employee engagement. Some examples are listed below:

- Where staff in hotels and restaurants are engaged, their actions lead to better service quality as measured by customers – the people who ultimately matter most (Salanova et al 2005a).
- In the USA, evidence among university students shows that the more engaged students produce higher Grade Point Average scores (Salanova et al 2005b).
- The higher the level of engagement among cabin service staff in airlines, the better is their in- and extra-role performance on each flight (Xanthopoulou et al 2008).
- In the US beverage company MolsonCoors, it was found that engaged employees were five times less likely than non-engaged employees to have a safety incident and seven times less likely to have a lost-time safety incident. In fact, the average cost of a safety incident for an engaged employee was $63, compared with an average of $392 for non-engaged employees (Lockwood 2007).

Such evidence appears pretty conclusive. However, we must be cautious and even sceptical before we automatically accept that employee engagement yields superior corporate outcomes. First of all, profits and profitability depend on many complex and complicated considerations, some inside the business and some outside, and to rely on monocausal explanations for a single outcome is notoriously dangerous and potentially very misleading. Second, there may be other factors which produce both high levels of employee engagement and superior levels of profit and profitability, but which give the impression that there is a straightforward relationship between engagement and profit. Thus a small family business (like an Indian restaurant) may employ people who are very 'engaged' with the business – they are, after all, family members – and the business may be highly profitable – especially if the family members, being family members, aren't paid very much. But is employee engagement the cause, the only cause, the only single cause, of the restaurant's profitability?

Another problem concerns assumptions about the direction of causality. It seems to be taken for granted that employee engagement causes profitability to rise, but why shouldn't it be the other way round? After all, people like to be on the winning side, and if their company is doing well, it would make a lot of sense if they became more 'engaged' than if they found themselves unwilling conspirators on a sinking ship.

4.6 WHAT DOES THE RESEARCH INDICATE ABOUT EMPLOYEE ENGAGEMENT LEVELS AMONGST UK EMPLOYEES?

Recent trends from the CIPD Employee Outlook Survey indicate that employee engagement levels amongst UK employees are stable with around 35–39% of employees reporting that they are engaged. In 2009, the CIPD commissioned Kingston University and Ipsos/MORI to undertake a national survey of employee attitudes, in an effort to discover the actual extent of engagement within the UK workforce (see CIPD 2010). The results of this survey constitute a national benchmark against which employers can measure the findings of their own employee attitude surveys. However, it is worth injecting a note of caution here. Merely matching or exceeding the figures in a benchmark survey does not in itself justify any complacency, especially if you want to be a 'world-class' leading-edge business and therefore need to be ahead of the field rather than simply bunched in there with it. Also, you have to bear in mind the possibility that the benchmark may itself be low: as the CIPD (2009) itself concedes in its *Employee Engagement* Factsheet:

> Research confirms ... that there is a significant gap between levels of engagement found among UK employees and those that would produce optimum performance.

Having issued these essential caveats, let's look at the results of the CIPD study.

Overall, the report found that over a third of employees were actively engaged with their work – a rather higher figure than some other investigations have suggested. On looking in more detail at the three dimensions of engagement:

- *emotional engagement*, being very involved emotionally with one's work – this applied to around 60% of those in the CIPD sample
- *cognitive engagement*, focusing very hard while at work – a similar 60% said they were cognitively engaged
- *physical engagement*, being willing to go 'the extra mile' for the employer, and act discretionally to advance the employer's strategic goals – here the figure was somewhat lower, at around 40%.

Other key results from the same research can be briefly outlined thus:

- More women than men were engaged with their work.
- Around a quarter of the under-35 group felt engaged, compared with about 40% among the over-35s.
- Almost half of managers were engaged, compared with around 30% of non-managers.
- Those on flexible contracts tended to be more emotionally engaged, more satisfied with their work, more likely to speak positively about their organisation and less likely to quit than those not employed on flexible contracts.
- Public sector employees were more likely to feel that their senior managers did not have a clear vision (a Big Idea) for the organisation, and, perhaps partly as a result, they had less trust and confidence in their senior managers. They were also less likely to believe the contents of organisational communications.

As with all survey results, especially those with a self-report and self-assessment content, the figures are capable of being interpreted in ways that do not necessarily support the most positive spin placed on them by the CIPD. For example, it is possible –

perhaps even likely – that when employees are asked about the extent of their engagement with their work, they will be motivated to produce positive responses because if they don't, they are exposing themselves to the possibility of cognitive dissonance (that is, doing one thing while saying something different).

Thus if people are asked how they feel about their work and express negative sentiments, they may begin to question their own actions: why stay in a job that you actively dislike? Of course, there are reasons for doing so – often depending on the poverty of the local labour market – but these reasons, brought into the conscious mind, can still make us feel uncomfortable. Much better, it seems, to reduce or eliminate the likelihood of cognitive dissonance by almost literally 'making the best of a bad job' and trying to find psychological and other benefits from a task that was initially entered purely for instrumental reasons.

Clearly, we cannot know for certain whether any of the CIPD respondents actually thought along these lines. It is highly likely that even if they had been asked, they might have denied it or refused to admit it, anyway. What is important is that when evaluating the extent of engagement among employees we must look further than employees' own self-assessments.

A significantly more negative picture of employee engagement in the UK economy emerged from a report by Marcus Buckingham (2001) involving a national sample of the UK working population. The research used the Gallup Q12 Index and produced the following results.

The most important primary finding from the Gallup research was that more than 80% of employees in the UK are not engaged at work. From the data, Gallup identified three distinct categories of employees:

- *engaged employees* – These are loyal, productive, less likely to leave, more inclined to recommend their employer as a place of work (and as a source of products or services, if appropriate) to friends and family
- *non-engaged employees* – These people may be productive, but they are not psychologically bonded to their organisation; they are more likely to defect to other employers
- *disengaged employees* – Such employees are physically present (assuming in fact that they have actually turned up for work in the first place) but psychologically absent; the only thing that enthuses them is the need to share with colleagues all the reasons why the organisation is such a rotten place to work.

Based on this classification, and bearing in mind once again that these results were achieved in 2001 using a particular methodology (although the Gallup Q12 instrument is a very strong device), Gallup found that only 17% of British workers were engaged, 63% were non-engaged and 20% were actively disengaged.

Not surprisingly, engaged employees looked on their employers much more positively than their actively disengaged colleagues did. Woody Allen once said that 80% of success is about showing up, so Gallup investigated attendance and absence figures. At the time, the engaged people in the sample missed, on average, 4.67 days of work a year, whereas actively disengaged employees missed 10.68 days. Gallup was also able to show that turnover levels among the engaged work groups were much lower than those of the actively disengaged groups.

The second most important finding was something that was definitely counterintuitive. It was this: the longer employees stay with you, the less engaged they become. There is no easy explanation for this state of affairs, and it definitely contradicts one of the basic precepts of the human capital advantage model – namely, that human capital is one of the few assets that genuinely appreciates over time. Perhaps people really do become more valuable to the organisation – in terms of their skills, implicit knowledge, experience and so forth – but it is apparent from the Gallup results that these same people don't feel themselves to be more valuable.

As time goes on, and their work experience accumulates, they may encounter fewer opportunities for learning and challenge: so their lives become more predictable, more routinised, and therefore less adventurous and exciting. In such circumstances it would not be surprising if their engagement levels fell away.

The research evidence on engagement levels amongst UK employees, therefore, suggests that engagement is low. This is surprising given the suggested benefits of engagement, as discussed in the next section.

4.7 HOW CAN WE EXPLAIN THE LOW LEVELS OF EMPLOYEE ENGAGEMENT IN THE UK?

One possible explanation for the low levels of engagement amongst UK employees could be due to problems with measuring engagement. As alluded to above, there are some concerns amongst commentators about approaches to measuring employee engagement and the interpretation of results. The engagement survey is the most common method for measuring engagement levels. However, Purcell (2010) highlights three key limitations with engagement surveys:

1   They create a tendency to treat engagement in isolation as an annual tick-box exercise

2   Engagement is articulated through the engagement score (or index) which might be used to punish managers in performance reviews, and

3   Engagement score does not explain reasons for engagement levels.

This suggests that engagement surveys will provide some useful insights into engagement levels within organisations, but as MacLeod and Clarke (2009) comment, 'simply doing a survey and publishing the results is not the same as an engagement strategy'. Indeed, Cattermole (2014, p31) argues that 'many organisations place too much emphasis on external benchmarking, rather than using surveys as tools to meet their specific business needs'. Cattermole (2014, p31) describes these types of surveys as transactional rather than transformational and suggests that in order to overcome the kinds of limitations identified by Purcell (2010), engagement surveys benefit from being interpreted in conjunction with other key organisational indicators such as profitability, productivity, absence and turnover rates. Interestingly, Silverman (2014) suggests that social media offers opportunities for organisations to gain insights into employee engagement in a more open and conversational manner compared with traditional surveys. This could possibly enhance knowledge of employee engagement in organisations in the future.

The other possible explanation for the low levels of engagement amongst UK employees is derived from research evidence which suggests that engagement can have detrimental implications for employees, specifically in relation to the following areas:

1   Burnout

2   Work intensification, and

3   Lack of work–life balance.

First, in relation to burnout, Welbourne (2011, p97) suggested that there was a dark side of engagement associated with 'burnout, health problems and disengagement'. If this is the case, then employees may resist engagement which could explain the low levels amongst UK employees.

Second, in relation to work intensification, Rees et al (2013) associated engagement with work intensification, observing that 'engagement can drive work intensification with employers coming to expect employees to go the extra mile as a matter of course with overtime becoming normalised and probably unpaid'. This implies that engagement could be perceived as exploiting employee's goodwill which could explain why engagement is low amongst UK employees.

Third, in relation to a lack of work–life balance, Halbesleben (2011) observes that not all employees will be willing and/or able to exhibit discretionary efforts due to other commitments in their lives. This could be a factor which explains the low levels of engagement amongst UK employees.

These concerns about engagement raise questions about its desirability and feasibility, which implies that engagement may not be as universally beneficial as suggested by MacLeod and Clarke (2009).

4.8 HOW CAN WE DEVISE AND IMPLEMENT HRM STRATEGIES AND PRACTICES THAT WILL RAISE LEVELS OF EMPLOYEE ENGAGEMENT?

The first essential point to acknowledge is that there has to be a compelling and convincing business case before any organisation should contemplate specific moves to create a genuinely engaged workforce. Merely doing it because it is thought to be 'good' for everyone involved will not work, for the following reasons:

- Not everyone in the organisation will support a principle of positive action for change being initiated merely because it sounds like a 'good' idea and will make everyone feel warm and comfortable inside. Some of those who won't support any such idea will hold very senior positions in the hierarchy and will therefore be in a position to block any engagement initiative that they think (rightly or wrongly) is being promoted for unjustified reasons.
- When organisations consider financial investments, they know that if any investment is to succeed, it must have a clear and unambiguous objective. Certainly the same is true of any organisational 'investment' in people, because if it is undertaken merely because it appears plausible, it sounds like a 'good' idea, or because it makes the organisation feel righteous, then it definitely won't work. So the presence of a business case for employee engagement is critical – and the strength of that business case must ultimately rest on the strong probability that higher levels of employee engagement will produce an investment return in terms of higher productivity, lower turnover, improved customer retention, and so forth. In turn, such evidence has to be persuasive and convincing, not merely founded on wishful thinking or people-focused rhetoric.

A strong business case can be constructed around any one or more of the following outcomes – and research evidence can always be found to bolster them:

- improved profitability and bottom-line results
- improved levels of customer satisfaction, customer loyalty, customer retention and new customer acquisition through the activities of 'advocate' customers
- reduced amounts of employee absence
- lower labour turnover (coupled with transient higher turnover among those who do not appreciate or welcome an engagement culture)
- more impressive degrees of organisational citizenship and corporate social responsibility
- enhanced rates of creativity and innovation.

However, in order to construct a credible and convincing business case for engagement, some consideration of the context within which the organisation is operating is essential. As Purcell (2014, p247) notes, 'The lack of context is a problem with much of the current work and practice in engagement'. Jenkins and Delbridge (2013, p2671) agree that much of the engagement research ignores the organisational context and suggest this oversight 'has generally obscured the degree to which management's ability to deliver engagement is influenced by a number of contingent factors: the wider economy and particular industry sector, specific market conditions, ownership and governance arrangements as well as organisational size and internal structures'. This suggests that HRM policies and strategies designed to increase engagement levels need to be informed by contextual factors.

The current economic context poses a number of challenges to organisations seeking to increase employee engagement levels. Private sector organisations are operating in competitive environments and facing pressures to cut costs and increase efficiencies in order to drive high performance. Public sector organisations have been under pressure to cut costs and increase efficiencies since the Government's Comprehensive Spending Review in 2010. The Workplace Employment Relations Study (WERS 2013) highlighted how the majority of workplaces reported detrimental implications arising from the recession. According to WERS (2013), the main responses by employers to the recession have been to freeze wages and recruitment, and change the organisation of work. These responses could be a barrier to organisations securing discretionary effort from their people and highlight the importance of interpreting engagement within the context of the organisation and external environment. There is a lack of research evidence which investigates engagement within the context of the recession but the limited research evidence which is available suggests that sustaining engagement is problematic within a recessionary context. Teague and Roche (2012) for example, investigated organisational responses to the recession in Ireland. They identified three possible responses. First, transformation through introduction of a harsh new deal with limited concern for engagement. Second, high commitment HRM with an emphasis on engagement. Third, short-term pragmatism with a dual concern for engagement and cost cutting. Their study found evidence that short-term pragmatism was the dominant response. This suggests that engagement is likely to be one of a number of concerns for organisations during difficult economic conditions.

Thus, if organisations are seeking to engage their people or increase engagement levels, then a coherent strategy is vital. Guest (2015) proposes a strategy for promoting engagement which entails the following elements:

- Implementing engagement by managers and leaders promoting engagement values
- Creating and reinforcing a climate for engagement by treating employees with fairness and trust
- Promoting engagement through recruitment of employees who welcome engaging jobs, provision of training and development and design of jobs to provide autonomy
- Monitoring progress towards high engagement through surveys, feedback and action planning

This strategy requires engagement to be integrated into the vision, policies and practices of an organisation.

? REFLECTIVE ACTIVITY 4.2

Critically evaluate Guest's (2015) engagement strategy. What do you think is good about it? What do you think is difficult? Is there anything you would suggest doing differently?

CASE STUDY 4.2

REVOLUTION BY DEVOLUTION

Until the 1980s the Halewood car plant on Merseyside was a dark and dirty old factory with grime on the floor and boxes of car parts cluttering the aisles between the production lines.

Operators used to eat their sandwiches perched on benches, or would sit in the cars once the seats had been installed.

As *The Economist* (2001) stated, 'Managers used to hide in their offices poring over printouts and merged on the shopfloor only to shout at workers to get them to do their job better and faster, or even to do it at all, since work tended to interfere with smoking, sleeping, betting or discussing football.'

Not surprisingly, the factory had a history of poor labour relations, and it was therefore surprising to some that when Ford acquired Jaguar they decided to locate production of the then new X-type at Halewood.

However, this decision was dependent on a massive culture change coupled with equally massive infrastructure reforms. The assembly area now has a white floor, wide aisles (clearly marked with pedestrian and forklift lanes), large rest areas at intervals with tables and refreshments, plus a noticeboard run principally by the workers themselves.

An orange cord runs at head height all the way along the line. Any operator can pull this to stop the line if they feel it is necessary. In other words, this is a factory designed to be as pleasant as possible to work in and to be micromanaged by the employees. 'In the old days, when we could see a quality issue that needed tackling, we were just ignored,' said one of the Halewood workers. 'Now we are asked to give our input. Management listens to what we've got to say.'

David Crisp, corporate affairs manager, says: 'We went from a volume-driven culture where you didn't stop the line ever – and that was right through the organisation – to a culture where you stop the line rather than pass on poor quality. But you are trying to change working practices of 30 or 40 years, and you don't just throw a switch and make it happen.' One of the consultants involved in the change process said: 'I talked to a guy in "trim and final" who had stopped the line seven times in eight months. But the first time he did it, he said, "I was shit scared."'

Question

In what ways do the changes that occurred at Halewood provide evidence of improved employee engagement?

Source: Pickard (2002)

4.9 WHAT ABOUT THE FUTURE FOR EMPLOYEE ENGAGEMENT?

Clearly, the future of employee engagement may be particularly problematic in times of economic uncertainty, characterised by high unemployment and fears about the future. Some naïve observers may believe that surely engagement levels will rise as employees thank their lucky stars they still have jobs and work hard to preserve them – but this is not so, for two reasons:

● As we have seen, employees are not truly engaged simply because they are employees: they may still be there, but they could be non-engaged (indifferent) or even actively disengaged (hostile). 'Employment' is not synonymous with 'engagement'.

- People who still have jobs while all around them are losing theirs are inclined to be preoccupied with themselves and their own security – perversely and paradoxically though it may seem, thoughts of engagement are far from their minds.

Therefore, what is the future for employee engagement? Purcell (2014, p251) asserts that 'It is not sensible to abandon employee engagement and disengage from it'. This suggests that there is merit in further research into engagement. This is supported by Truss et al (2014) who identifies seven key questions for further development in the future:

1 What is engagement?

2 What is the link between engagement and Human Resource Management/ Development?

3 How can employee engagement strategies be evaluated?

4 How is engagement related to its wider internal and external context?

5 How does engagement work at the group or team level?

6 How does engagement interact with diversity?

7 How is engagement understood from a more critical perspective?

It is proposed that these seven questions can enable the development of further insights into engagement in the future.

4.10 CONCLUSION

Employee engagement is here to stay. It has a long way to go – not just because there are many organisations that have not yet come to grips with the tools and drivers of engagement, but also because engagement itself is a movable feast. Just as customer aspirations keep rising (there's no imaginable end to them), so the ingredients for employee engagement also keep evolving. Today's high-engagement culture isn't necessarily tomorrow's competitive winner: you have to keep working at it. What remains the subject of debate is what exactly engagement is and how distinctive it is in comparison with concepts such as commitment, the causes and outcomes of engagement as well as the more critical questions regarding concerns about, barriers to, and unintended consequences of, engagement. These areas will benefit from further scrutiny. In the contemporary context of change and uncertainty, there is arguably more need than ever for employee engagement. Managers and leaders clearly have a key role to play in creating and sustaining engagement as part of their overall approach to managing people although it has to be acknowledged that engagement is likely to be one of a number of priorities for organisations.

What is certain, however, is that the following elements will continue to be key to developing, embedding and benefiting from employee engagement.

- A Big Idea – a vision that is ethical, ambitious and ultimately **transformational**, not merely a collection of vacuous platitudes.
- Coherent, consistent and continuous role-modelling from the top.
- Good-quality management at all levels – managers who lead, who encourage their teams to perform well, who take an interest in their people and who provide opportunities for development.
- Two-way open communications – encouragement for 'employee voice' and also keeping employees informed about things that are relevant to them.
- Collaboration between people, between departments and between functions – a team-working emphasis that avoids any 'silo' practices and stereotypes.
- A customer-centric focus – both customers and people are critical to success.

- Commitment to employee well-being – taking health and safety seriously, avoiding harassment and discrimination.
- A strong, unyielding emphasis on performance and results with challenging and stretching goals that require more than incremental effort.
- Permanent dissatisfaction with the status quo, coupled with improvement and change programmes.
- Learning within the organisation and learning from outside – in a high-engagement organisation, the entire workforce is assumed to be a source of 'talent' and the business regularly surveys the outside world to see what can be learned.
- Clear, accessible HR policies and practices.

CASE STUDY 4.3

B&Q

B&Q was founded in March 1969 in Southampton, by Richard Block and David Quayle. Within 10 years there were 26 stores across the UK, and it subsequently expanded rapidly through a mixture of growth, mergers and acquisitions. It is now owned by parent company Kingfisher plc, and is very active not just in the UK but also in Europe (especially in Poland and France) and further afield. Its store in Beijing is now the largest B&Q store in the world. Today B&Q is the UK's leading do-it-yourself and garden centre retailer and is nearly twice the size of its nearest competitor. It caters for more than 3 million customers a week, through more than 350 stores and with around 23,500 employees.

B&Q was the first retailer in the world, and the only non-US company, to win the Gallup worldwide award for outstanding employee engagement, and has picked up this award every year for the last five years. B&Q has also achieved the *Observer*'s Ethical Business Award, appears on the *Sunday Times* Best Green Companies list and was the first retailer to buy 100% responsibly sourced wood.

Within the context of its Big Idea ('Helping people create homes to be proud of'), B&Q has these five value statements that explain 'how we do things':

- Customer first
- Down to earth
- Respect for people
- We can do it
- Nobody does it better.

These values illustrate what B&Q stands for – both internally and externally. The values are translated into everyday action in various ways.

One is by the deliberate recruitment of a diverse workforce because it makes business sense. B&Q customers come from everywhere, so it helps if B&Q employees also come from everywhere.

In 2006 B&Q was one of only two retailers to make *The Times* Top 50 Places Where Women Want To Work, and it has continued this achievement in subsequent years. The company has also acquired a reputation for employing older workers. This was a strategy first tried in 1989 when the company experimentally staffed an entire store (in Macclesfield) with employees over the age of 50. The results were compelling: productivity increased, sales rose and absenteeism fell. Today, over 26% of B&Q employees are over 50, with ages ranging from 16 to 95.

Speaking at a conference in 2003, B&Q's then personnel director, Mike Cutt, claimed that improved levels of employee engagement in B&Q stores could save the company 'tens of millions of pounds' over the next few years. By bringing all B&Q outlets up to the level of its best stores, the company was likely to save around £3 million a year in absenteeism costs, and around £2.5 million a year in recruitment costs.

B&Q has also significantly reduced the amount of 'shrinkage' – the loss of stock and profits through employee and customer theft.

The results being achieved at B&Q hold out great hope of an improved status for HR leaders: 'Measuring and quantifying employee engagement is a great opportunity for HR to prove its worth,' said Mike Cutt. 'As a result, we have seen an increase in the training budget at B&Q of around 60 per cent.'

This is an aspect of B&Q's personnel and development strategies that has continued to reflect the company's requirement to create an engaged workforce, which will in turn demonstrate a 'world-class people capability'.

The drive towards a significantly improved level of employee engagement received further impetus in 2005, when sales fell by 8 per cent in a single year. Tackling what was regarded as the crucial issue of employee engagement was perceived as essential for the company's recovery, and so B&Q recruited the Gallup Organization, which then administered the Gallup Q12 Index instrument throughout the entire B&Q workforce, including the board, all senior executives and all managers. Everyone was measured on their performance as a leader or manager, and the results published.

They showed that 26% of the company's employees were actively disengaged. At the time, the HR director pointed out that 'We must be a charity – out of a £450 million wage bill, we're spending £120 million on people who don't want to be here. We're paying them to destroy our organisation and make life miserable for all the good, engaged employees.' Some of those who were disengaged were in managerial roles. They were given opportunities to improve, and those who failed to do so, or didn't subscribe to the engagement drive, were asked to leave.

By 2008, the B&Q 'engagement score' (measured by responses to the Gallup Q12 Index instrument) had risen to 60%, compared with a global average of 28% and a UK average of 16%.

Questions

1   B&Q is the only UK retailer to have achieved worldwide recognition for its employee engagement activities. To what extent is it feasible to argue that there are special difficulties in the retail sector so far as employee engagement is concerned?

2   B&Q is well known for its policies about attracting and retaining older workers, and also for its positive reputation for diversity. To what extent might there be a connection between these policies and its employee engagement initiatives?

3   What do you consider to have been the major reasons why the employee engagement score at B&Q has steadily risen over the years since 2005?

The MacLeod Report on employee engagement (MacLeod and Clarke 2009), commissioned by the Department for Business, Innovation and Skills, is available to download free from the Department's website. It provides an excellent and very readable guide to recent research on engagement at work and its potential benefits.

Understanding the people and performance link: unlocking the black box, by John Purcell and his colleagues (2003) deals with issues that go beyond engagement. But it describes a seminal research project that has been very influential on HR practices in this area.

The Towers Watson/Perrin Global Workforce study 2007/2008 (2009) sets out a very coherent and persuasive case for taking employee engagement seriously, also providing good guidance about how it can be enhanced.

REFERENCES

ALFES, K., TRUSS, C., SOANE, E. C., REES, C. I. and GATENBY, M. (2010) *Creating an engaged workforce.* London: Chartered Institute of Personnel and Development.

BUCKINGHAM, M. (2001) What a waste. *People Management.* 11 October. pp19–22.

CATTERMOLE, G. (2014) Key drivers and trends for employee engagement in 2014. *HR Review*, 17 January, [Online] www.hrreview.co.uk/blogs/blogs-hr-strategy-practice/gary-cattermole-key-drivers-and-trends-for-employee-engagement-in-2014/50203

CHURCHARD, C. (2011) Try something new today. *People Management.* 27 January. pp19–21.

CIPD (2009) *Employee engagement.* Factsheet. London: Chartered Institute of Personnel and Development.

CIPD (2010) *Creating an engaged workforce.* London: Chartered Institute of Personnel and Development.

CIPD (2012) *Emotional or Transactional Engagement: Does it Matter?* Research Insight. [Online] www.cipd.co.uk/hr-resources/research/emotional-transactional-engagement.aspx

CIPD (2014) *Developing Managers to manage sustainable employee engagement, health and well-being.* Research Report. [Online] www.cipd.co.uk/hr-resources/research/developing-managers.aspx

FLEMING, J. H. and HARTER, J. K. (2001) Optimize. *Gallup Management Journal.* Vol 1, No 4. pp14–17.

GUEST, D. (2015) Presentation on "Employee Engagement: A Path to Organisational Success?" made at the Lead, Engage, Perform expert meeting on public sector leadership, OECD, 21–22 January 2015.

HALBESLEBEN, J. R. B. (2011) The consequences of engagement: The good, the bad and the ugly *European Journal of Work and Organizational Psychology.* Vol 20, No 1. pp68–73.

HARTER, J. K., SCHMIDT, F. L. and HAYES, T. L. (2002) Business-unit level relationship between employee satisfaction, employee engagement, and business outcomes: a meta-analysis. *Journal of Applied Psychology*. Vol 87. pp268–79.

HUTCHINSON, S. and PURCELL, J. (2003) *Bringing policies to life: the vital role of front-line managers in people management*. London: Chartered Institute of Personnel and Development.

JENKINS, S. and DELBRIDGE, R. (2013) Context matters: Examining 'soft' and 'hard' approaches to employee engagement in two workplaces. *International Journal of Human Resource Management*. Vol 24, No 14. pp2670–2691.

KAHN, W. A. (1990) The psychological conditions of personal engagement and disengagement at work. *Academy of Management Journal*. Vol 33. pp692–724.

LOCKWOOD, N. R. (2007) Leveraging employee engagement for competitive advantage: HR's strategic role. *HR Magazine* (USA). March. pp1–11.

MACLEOD, D. and CLARKE, N. (2009) *Engaging for success: enhancing performance through employee engagement. A report to government*. London: Department for Business, Innovation and Skills.

PICKARD, J. (2002) Top gear. *People Management*. 18 April. pp37–42.

PURCELL, J., HUTCHINSON, S., KINNIE, N., RAYTON, B. and SWART, J. (2003) *Understanding the people and performance link: unlocking the black box*. London: Chartered Institute of Personnel and Development.

PURCELL, J. (2010) 'Building Employee Engagement', ACAS Policy Discussion Paper [Online] www.acas.org.uk/media/pdf/s/1/Building_employee_engagement-accessible-version-Jun-2012.pdf

PURCELL, J. (2014), 'Disengaging from engagement'. Human Resource Management Journal. Vol 24, No 3. pp241–254.

REES, C., ALFES, K. and GATENBY, M. (2013) Employee voice and engagement: connections and consequences, *International Journal of Human Resource Management*. Vol 24, No 14. pp2780–2798.

ROBINSON, D. and HAYDAY, S. (2009) *The engaging manager*. Brighton: Institute for Employment Studies.

SAKS, A. M. (2006) The antecedents and consequences of employee engagement. *Journal of Managerial Psychology*. Vol 21, No 7. pp600–19.

SALANOVA, M., AGUT, S. and PEIRÓ, J. M. (2005a) Linking organisational resources and work engagement to employee performance and customer loyalty: the mediation of service climate. *Journal of Applied Psychology*. Vol 90. pp117–22.

SALANOVA, M., BRESO, E. and SCHAUFELI, W. B. (2005b) Hacia un modelo espiral de las creencias de eficacia en el studio del burnout y del engagement. *Ansiedad y Estres* [Anxiety and Stress]. Vol 11, No 2/3. pp215–31.

SCHAUFELI, W. B. and BAKKER, A. B. (2010) The conceptualization and measurement of work engagement. In: BAKKER, W. B. and LEITER, M. P. (eds). *Work engagement: a handbook of essential theory and research*. New York: Psychology Press.

SCHAUFELI, W. B., TARIS, T. W. and VAN RHENEN, W. (2008) Alcoholism, burnout and engagement: three of a kind or three different kinds of employee well-being. *Applied Psychology: An International Review*. Vol 57. pp173–203.

SILVERMAN, D. (2014) *The Future of Engagement*. Research Report. CIPD [Online] www.cipd.co.uk/hr-resources/research/future-engagement.aspx

TEAGUE, P. and ROCHE, W.K. (2012) Line managers and the management of workplace conflict: Evidence from Ireland. *Human Resource Management Journal*. Vol 22, No 3. pp235–251.

THE ECONOMIST (2001) 'The worst car factory in the world', March 2001. [Online] Available www.economist.com/node/550581

TOWERS PERRIN (2009) *Global Workforce study 2007/2008: closing the engagement gap – a road map for driving superior business performance*. London: Towers Watson.

TRUSS, C., ALFES, K., DELBRIDGE, R. and SOANE, E. (2014) *Employee engagement in theory and practice*. London, Routledge.

WELBOURNE, T.M., 2011. Engaged in what? So what? A role-based perspective for the future of employee engagement. In *The Future of Employment Relations* (pp. 85–100). Palgrave Macmillan UK.

WERS (2013) The 2011 Workplace Employment Relations Study (WERS): first findings – updated May 2013, Available www.gov.uk/government/publications/the-2011-workplace-employment-relations-study-wers

XANTHOPOULOU, D., BAKKER, A. B., HEUVEN, E., DEMEROUTI, E. and SCHAUFELI, W. B. (2008) Working in the sky: a diary study on work engagement among flight attendants. *Journal of Occupational Health Psychology*. Vol 13, No 1. pp345–56.

CHAPTER 5

Contemporary Developments in Employee Relations

CECILIA ELLIS

CHAPTER CONTENTS

This chapter provides the reader with an overview of Employee Relations including:
- Introduction
- Defining employee relations
- Perspectives on employee relationships
- The parties involved in employee relationships
- The labour market context for employee relationships
- The legal framework for employee relations
- Employee voice practices
- Conflict at work
- Conclusion

KEY LEARNING OUTCOMES

By the end of this chapter, you should be able to:

- explain different perspectives on employee relations
- critically discuss the roles of the government, management and trade unions in employee relations
- analyse the contexts of employee relations and the ways in which they shape relationships between employers and employees
- evaluate the impact of the UK and EU legal framework on employee relations
- evaluate employee voice practices with particular reference to the aims, types and benefits of these practices
- analyse different sources and forms of conflict at work, including approaches to resolving disputes.

5.1 INTRODUCTION

Employee relations is traditionally understood to describe the relationship between organisations and trade unions. Although trade unions continue to have an important role to play in employee relations, there are many other features of, and influences on, employee relations in the twenty-first century that merit exploration.

The ways in which employers create and sustain relationships with their employees are complex. These relationships are shaped by the turbulent worlds within and outside of organisations. They are the product of different parties with different interests who hold different levels of power in employee relationships.

Employment relationships are uncertain because there is no guarantee about their duration or outcomes. Contemporary employee relationships are characterised by the need for co-operation, the possibility of conflict and the reality of uncertainty.

Managing effective employee relationships is therefore a relevant challenge for HR professionals that demands attention.

This chapter begins by focusing on definitions of and perspectives on employee relations. Then, labour markets are discussed as the world in which employee relationships begin and evolve, and the impact of UK and EU employee law on employee relations is considered. The roles of management, trade unions and government in relation to employee relations are explored, before attention turns to practices and possible outcomes of employee relations. This covers an analysis of employee voice practices, the possibility of conflict at work and approaches to resolving conflict.

5.2 DEFINING EMPLOYEE RELATIONS

Before exploring contemporary developments in employee relations, it is important to have an understanding of the nature and characteristics of employee relations. Numerous definitions of employee relations are available, and two main types of definitions can be identified. The first type of definition emphasises the regulatory nature of employee relations, and the second type of definition is relationship-based.

Regulatory-focused definitions of employee relations are exemplified by Gennard and Judge (2010, p225), who claim that 'The purpose of employment relations is to establish rules, regulations and agreements to regulate the employment relationship.' This definition highlights the importance of regulation in employee relations. Regulation of the employee relationship is evident within organisations in staff handbooks, policies and agreements between managers and trade unions collectively (for example, relating to pay) and managers and employees individually (for example, regarding flexible working practices). Regulation of the employee relationship can also occur through sources outside of organisations, in particular when derived from employment law. The government develops laws that regulate the employee relationship (for example, the Equality Act 2010). This regulatory focus can be regarded as a traditional definition of employee relations.

The alternative to the traditional regulatory-focused definition is exemplified by the CIPD Factsheet (2015), which states that 'the main focus of employee relations is not on collective machinery but on individual relationships and there is a new emphasis on helping line managers to establish trust based relationships with employees'.

These relationships between employers and employees cover the entire employee cycle, from the point at which an employee joins an organisation to the time when they leave an organisation. Whereas this definition recognises that employee relations occur between people, it does not convey the various influences that have an impact on the relationships between employers and employees (for example, the influences of the economic context in the UK and globally on employee relationships).

For the purpose of this chapter, it is suggested that employee relations in contemporary organisations is about creating and sustaining effective employee relationships between employers and employees within the constraints and opportunities presented by organisational contexts. Different ideas about the approaches available to organisations for creating and sustaining relationships are explored in the next section.

5.3 PERSPECTIVES ON EMPLOYEE RELATIONSHIPS

The traditional perspectives on employee relationships are derived from the work of Fox in the 1960s. Fox (1966) suggested that there are two main ways in which managers view the employee relationship. One view is described as a **unitarist** relationship, and an alternative view is described as a **pluralist** relationship. Fox (1966) suggested that if managers hold a unitarist view of the employee relationship, they may think of the organisation and workers as a united team who pull together behind the authority of the manager in order to pursue the organisation's goals. An analogy can be drawn between unitarism and a successful football team who support each other on and off the pitch and unite behind the authority of their manager in order to help the football club win matches and increase profits. Unitarist perspectives suggest that the employee relationship is characterised by harmony, co-operation and a team ethic.

An alternative way of thinking about the employee relationship can found in pluralist views. According to Fox (1966), pluralism suggests that organisations and workers have both similar and different interests in the employee relationship. For example, it could be claimed that organisations seek to maximise profits whereas workers seek to develop their careers and maximise their incomes. Although there may be areas of overlap and shared interests, these different agendas can result in tensions and conflict, which must be managed (for example, through discipline and grievance procedures). If a manager holds a pluralist view, conflict is an inevitable feature of the employee relationship and systems for managing conflict (including for example, discipline and **grievance procedures**) are essential for sustaining effective employment relationships. This contrasts with a unitarist perspective in which conflict is notably absent.

? REFLECTIVE ACTIVITY 5.1

Two interview candidates are discussing possible responses to interview questions. The candidates are called Katie and Sophie and they both hold CIPD qualifications and have five years' generalist HR experience. This is an extract from their conversation.

Sophie: The main point that I want to make is that all employees need to be committed to what the organisation is trying to achieve. I know that it can be difficult to get everyone on board but if we communicate the business plans in the right way, people will understand where we are trying to get to and understand how they can contribute so that we all move forward together. Do you think that sounds good?

Katie: Well, I suppose it does sound good if you think it is possible.

Sophie: Of course, everyone needs to pull together. That's what our job is all about isn't it – getting people on board with what the organisation is trying to achieve. Why? Don't you think that's possible?

Katie: Well, if I'm really honest with you, I have my doubts about how realistic it is even though I know it is what senior managers like to hear. I think that people should try to pull together but I don't think it's that easy, especially considering all the different needs and wants that people bring into an employment situation.

Clashes and conflicts are bound to happen, and they need to be managed before we can even think about co-operation.

Sophie: Don't talk to me about conflict. I've had enough of it. That's what I spend all my time dealing with in my current job, and I'm sick of it. That's why I want to move jobs to try and get away from it.

Katie: But do you really think you can get away from it? If you ask me, there's bound to be conflict in employee relationships. I don't think we should ignore it. I think we need to understand that it is inevitable given the different interests of managers and employees. We can add value as HR practitioners by managing the conflict in an appropriate way, which involves being honest about differences and trying to find ways which are mutually acceptable to overcome the differences and work together.

Sophie: Maybe we are talking about the same thing but just approaching it differently?

1   Do you think that Katie and Sophie illustrate unitarist or pluralist perspectives on employee relationships?

2   What are the indicators that suggest their perspectives to you?

Hopefully, the reflective activity above enabled you to reflect on the key features of traditional perspectives on employee relationships. In addition to Fox's (1966) unitarist and pluralist perspectives on employee relationships, there are two key alternative views on employee relationships, which highlight features of employee relationships other than conflict. First is the view of employee relationships as an economic exchange in which work is provided in exchange for financial reward.

Under this economic view, the employee relationship is all about money – in other words, a financial transaction. For example, an employee who works for money and works harder for more money could be seen as holding an economic view of the employee relationship. This view has been criticised by some authors as a narrow view of the employee relationship that does not consider the vast array of reasons why people work. Budd (2011, p58), for example, argues that 'work is also undertaken by individuals seeking personal fulfilment and identity', which highlights a limitation of this perspective on the employee relationship.

Second is the **psychological contract** view on the employee relationship, which has increased in popularity since the mid-1990s. Guest and Conway (2002, p22) define the psychological contract as 'the perceptions of the two parties, employee and employer, of what their mutual obligations are towards each other'. This highlights how the psychological contract is based on perceptions and consists of obligations.

This definition suggests that employees perceive that they have obligations to the organisation and that the organisation has obligations towards them. Such perceptions can be concerned with financial aspects of work (such as pay) but also other aspects (such as career development and job security), which is how this perspective differs from an economic view of the employee relationship. These perceptions that employees and employers hold are seen as important because they define the relationship between employees and employers. The perceptions of the parties are influenced by various factors including the age, education and length of service of employees, the business strategy, the labour market and HRM policies and procedures. If the parties perceive that they have fulfilled their obligations to each other then psychological contract theory suggests that there will be positive attitudinal and behavioural consequences. If, however, the parties perceive that they have not met their obligations towards each other, then the psychological contract is perceived to be damaged (referred to as a breach and/or violation in the psychological contract literature) with negative consequences for attitudes and behaviours. For example, in a redundancy situation, employees may perceive that an organisation has breached its obligation to provide them with secure employment and may reduce their performance levels and/or seek alternative employment.

?   REFLECTIVE ACTIVITY 5.2

Imagine that you have been working part-time in a local bar for the last year to help to fund your studies.

1   What are the main things that you think your manager is obliged to do for you?

2   What are the main things that you think that you are obliged to do for your manager?

3   If your manager informed you that the business was closing due to falling profits, which, if any, of the above obligations might you think that your manager had breached?

5.4 THE PARTIES INVOLVED IN EMPLOYEE RELATIONSHIPS

There are three main parties involved in employee relationships. These are:

● management
● employees and their representatives (trade unions)
● the government.

These parties play different roles, which influence employee relations in various ways. This section analyses the role of each of these parties and its influence on employee relations in contemporary organisations.

5.4.1 MANAGEMENT AND EMPLOYEE RELATIONSHIPS

The term 'management' can be used to refer to a process, a system of authority and a group of people. All of these are relevant in influencing an organisation's employee relations. The process of management includes the organisation and delivery of people and work. Management is a system of authority dependent on the power it holds and exercises through the development and administration of rules. Management can operate individually or as a group of people who hold responsibilities for facilitating the smooth operation of organisations.

Management has a key impact on the day-to-day disposition of employee relationships, and the style that it adopts can determine whether it creates and sustains effective employee relationships. Sisson (2010, p235) argues that since the 1980s, management 'ha[s] become the major force for change in the arrangements governing the employee relationship'. This suggests that the role of management in employee relations has increased in comparison with the roles of the government and trade unions. In contemporary organisations, management function as agents of the employer.

Management style is the approach adopted by managers in their interactions with employees. Since the 1980s, a number of summaries or typologies of management styles have been produced. A recent contribution is derived from Kilroy and Dundon's (2015) exploratory study which identified three different types or faces of front-line managers which are presented and described in Table 5.1.

Table 5.1 Different types of front-line managers

Type of front-line manager	Description
Organisational leader	Implements HRM policy into practice selectively
Policy enactor	Implements HRM policy into practice in a rigid way
Employee coach	Implements HRM policy into practice in a tailored way depending on the employee and/or the situation

Source: Kilroy and Dundon 2015

Whilst Table 5.1 identifies three different types of front-line managers, Kilroy and Dundon (2015) found that a dominant type of leader will be identified by employees – in this case, that of organisational leader. Furthermore, they found that the type of management style had implications for employee outcomes. For example, the employee coach style was identified as contributing to employee commitment. This study suggests that the ways in which front-line managers interact with their employees can vary and can have implications for employment relationships.

Typologies of management styles, such as that of Kilroy and Dundon (2015) presented in Table 5.1, can function as a useful tool for managers who want to explore the approaches available to them for managing employee relationships. However, the number of typologies has expanded since the 1980s, which could cause confusion for management seeking to explore its style options. Alternatively, it can be suggested that the numbers of different versions of management styles indicate that a number of different management styles possibly co-exist in contemporary organisations, and that it is possible and perhaps desirable for management to shift between different styles. Management can therefore have an impact on employee relationships through its management style and its use of different styles.

CASE STUDY 5.1

MANAGEMENT STYLES

XCo is a market-leading retail business. Last year, XCo achieved record-breaking profits but the workforce is unhappy about how XCo achieved these great results. In particular, employees are concerned about:

- how they have to work seven days a week and have money deducted from their salary if they take time off sick
- the unachievable sales targets, which mean that they rarely achieve their bonuses
- only getting two short breaks during an eight-hour shift and having to ask permission to leave the shop floor to go to the toilet.

The workforce has tried to raise its concerns with management but got the impression that XCo had no intention of changing while it was so profitable, and that if employees felt unable to meet the required standards, perhaps they ought to consider alternative employment.

Questions

1   Using Kilroy and Dundon's (2015) typology of management style, how would you describe the management style of XCo?

2   What are the advantages and disadvantages of this management style for XCo and the workforce?

3   What alternative management style, if any, might you advise XCo management to consider adopting?

5.4.2 TRADE UNIONS AND EMPLOYEE RELATIONSHIPS

A trade union is defined in law as an organisation which consists of 'workers of one or more description and whose principal purposes include the regulation of relations between workers and employers' (Trade Unions and Labour Relations (Consolidation) Act 1992, Section 1 (TULRCA)). Trade unions are independent from government and management but work with those other parties to regulate employee relationships. The largest trade union in the UK is the UNITE union, which had around 1.42 million members in 2015, the members working in a wide range of sectors across the UK.

The role of trade unions is to represent the interests of their members in pursuit of democracy in the workplace. Nowak (2015, p684) explains that trade unions aim 'to win fairness, justice and equality for working people'. Trade unions can represent their members' interests on an individual basis but rely upon the logic that they can exert more influence on management by operating collectively. They emerged from a desire among working people to re-balance the distribution of power in employee relationships more equally between management and workers. Trade unions have an impact on employee relationships by trying to secure the best possible arrangements for their members, particularly in relation to their salaries. Indeed it is suggested that trade union members receive around 5% higher pay than non-trade union members. In addition, trade unions also seek to enhance the non-financial aspects of employment relationships such as working time and working conditions. In order to achieve this enhancement, trade unions rely heavily upon negotiation and consultation processes. For example, trade unions may negotiate with management about the size of the reward budget available in organisations and then consult with their members before accepting or rejecting a pay deal. In many contemporary organisations, trade unions have been consulting with their members over management proposals to change workers' pension schemes. These proposed changes are the subject of strong resistance from trade unions, who believe that they are unnecessary and detrimental to workers. This example illustrates how trade unions try to have a positive influence on employee relationships for the benefit of their members.

Trade union membership in the UK was at its peak in 1979 when the unions exerted a strong influence on employee relationships. This strong level of influence is evident in the role that trade unions played in high profile disputes such as the miners' strike in the 1980s. The following link is to a YouTube clip which provides an insight into the historical role of trade unions:

www.youtube.com/watch?v=qzwATFfA1Lo

However, the membership levels of trade unions have been in decline since 1979, as illustrated in Table 5.2.

Table 5.2 Trade union membership levels 1980–2014

Year	Membership (millions)
1980	12.6
1985	10.8
1990	9.8
1995	8.0
2000	7.8
2005	7.5
2010	7.4
2014	6.4

Source: Certification Officer's Annual Reports

Table 5.2 illustrates the decline in trade union membership levels and suggests that trade unions have a reduced impact on the management of employee relations in contemporary organisations compared with 30 years ago. Rose (2008) suggests that there are four reasons for the decline in trade union membership levels. These are:

- Employer policies, often influenced by human resource management (HRM), have promoted the individualisation of employee relationships, which runs contrary to the logic of collectivism upon which trade unions rely.
- Membership levels have fallen as unemployment rises in line with business cycles.
- Legislation specifically targeted at reducing the influence of trade unions has led to a drop in membership levels.
- The composition of the workforce has changed. For example, industries such as coalmining and shipbuilding in which union membership levels were high have disappeared. In addition, trade unions have struggled to access members outside of their core membership of male full-time employees (for example, female and temporary workers).

Given the patterns of declining membership levels, the future prospects for trade unions increasing their influence on employee relationships look limited. In addition to the reasons identified by Rose (2008) for declining membership levels, trade unions have contemporary challenges to overcome in order to increase their impact on employee relations. These challenges include organising on a less UK-centric and more global basis, exploring the possibilities for engaging new and existing members through social media, and attracting and retaining younger members from diverse backgrounds. However, the findings from the Workplace Employment Relations Study (WERS 11, p14) indicate that 'since 2004 the prevalence of union workplace representation has continued to fall in small private sector workplaces, but has proved relatively robust in other sectors of the economy'. Trade unions continue to play a dominant role in the UK public sector and there is a need, therefore, to be cautious about dismissing trade unions as irrelevant parties in contemporary organisations. Indeed, Nowak (2015, p688) comments that 'There has plainly never been more need for strong, effective trade unionism than now. The systemic problems now facing workers – stagnant wages and endemic low pay; unfair rewards and spiralling inequality; insecurity at work and a huge imbalance in the employment relationship – demand powerful unions'.

? REFLECTIVE ACTIVITY 5.3

Identify three advantages and three disadvantages for employers and employees of trade union involvement in employee relationships.

How would you advise trade unions to increase their appeal to younger workers?

5.4.3 THE GOVERNMENT AND EMPLOYEE RELATIONSHIPS

'The government' includes both the current Conservative Government, led by David Cameron, and government agencies such as the Advisory, Conciliation and Arbitration Service (Acas) and the Equality and Human Rights Commission (EHRC) who implement the government's employee relations policies. The government has a substantial impact on the management of employee relationships through its roles as an employer in the public sector, as a legislator, and through its agencies, which focus on improving the management of problematic areas of employee relationships.

The government can have a direct impact on the management of employee relationships through its roles as employer and legislator. The government is a major employer in the UK owing to the size of the public sector, which includes central and local government and NHS Trusts. This role as an employer provides the government with the opportunity to influence policy and practice through the terms of its employee relationships. Traditionally, the government used this role as employer to demonstrate good practice in employee relations, which led to its being regarded as a model employer. In the model employer era, public sector employee relationships were associated with high levels of job security, pay levels and pension schemes that compared favourably with the private sector and collective employee relationships with an integral role for trade unions.

This model employer tradition has been challenged as different governments (notably the Conservative Government of 1979–97) have provided alternative views of what it means to be a model employer. Since 1979, successive governments have sought to increase the efficiency of the public sector and looked to the private sector for inspiration to guide their policies and practices.

This has led to the introduction of policies and practices associated with private sector employee relationships – for example, a shift away from promises of a job for life, changes to pension schemes, consideration of the market rate for pay, and the introduction of performance management and individual performance related pay.

Since 2010, the Coalition and Conservative Governments' version of what it means to be a model employer has relied upon policies and practices that are designed to achieve substantial cost savings. These include the introduction of job cuts and pay freezes, which have been the source of resistance from employees and trade unions within the public sector. Within this context of austerity, the government is associated with policies and practices which are regarded as having detrimental implications for employment relationships, rather than being a model employer.

In addition to its role as an employer, the government can also have a direct impact on the management of employee relationships through its role as a legislator. In the UK, the government decides and implements employment laws that originate both from the UK Parliament and from the European Union (EU). There has been a huge growth in employment law over the last 25 years to the point where new legislation is now introduced into the UK on either 6 April or 1 October each year in an attempt to regulate the flow of legislative changes.

When Labour entered government in 1997, the UK signed up to the Social Chapter of the Maastricht Treaty. This committed the UK to adopting a European dimension to its employee policies and practices and to implementing EU law. The European dimension is associated with 'a strong welfare state, a partnership between government, employers and workers, and minimum standards at work' (IRS 1997). This EU influence is evident in government policies that promote partnership and co-operation between management and trade unions. The implementation of EU law is evident in legislation relating to working hours, the National Minimum Wage and parental leave. These employment laws have substantial implications for reward and flexible working, and illustrate how EU law has a direct impact on UK employee relationships.

The UK government can also exert an indirect influence on employee relationships through its agencies, which include Acas and the EHRC. Acas receives funding from the government but describes itself as an independent body whose aim is to 'improve organisations and working life through better employment relations' (Acas website). In order to achieve this aim, Acas provides advice, information, training and assistance with dispute resolution. For example, in 2014, the government introduced a requirement for all Employment Tribunal claims to be lodged with Acas in the first instance in an attempt to resolve disputes informally and reduce the number of claims going to Employment Tribunals. This example illustrates how the government can influence employment relations processes through its agents such as Acas.

The EHRC was formed by the government in 2007 following the merger of three separate specialist equality organisations. The aims of the EHRC are:

- to enforce discrimination legislation

  and

- to promote equal opportunities in society.

The government formed this organisation as a vehicle to deliver its equality agenda. In 2010, the Coalition Government committed to eradicate discrimination from workplaces. This commitment is driven by the socially undesirable nature of discrimination, its legally unacceptable nature and the ways in which discrimination is contrary to creating and sustaining effective employee relationships. Through its enforcement and promotion roles, the EHRC can influence the management of employee relationships to achieve the government's equality commitments.

In summary, there are three main parties to employee relationships, and each makes a different contribution to the management of employee relations.

Management contributes the organisation's agenda while trade unions contribute the employees' agenda. The government contributes the UK's employee agenda and delivers this directly in the public sector as well as through its legislation and agencies such as Acas and EHRC. The varying agendas of these three parties to employee relationships mean that the management of employee relations is often contested. This contest takes place in the arena of labour markets, which are explored in the next section of this chapter.

5.5 THE LABOUR MARKET CONTEXT FOR EMPLOYEE RELATIONSHIPS

Labour markets 'consist of workers who are looking for paid employment and employers who are seeking to fill vacancies' (Claydon and Thompson 2010, p123). Employee relationships are formed in a marketplace where the product being bought and sold is labour (compared with the goods or services that may be traded in other marketplaces). For employees, the labour market is the place where they search for a job. For employers, the labour market is the place where they look for and find someone to do a job for their organisation. However, it is misleading just to think about a single labour market because there are many different types of labour markets for different skills in different locations within which employee relationships are formed.

Let us imagine that you are already working for an organisation but want to develop your career further. You might start by considering job opportunities within your current organisation. This is an example of an *internal* labour market. If your current organisation did not have any suitable vacancies for you to apply for, you might search for job opportunities outside of your organisation in the *external* labour market. Then, in the external labour market, if you are a graduate, you might search for jobs mainly in the *graduate* labour market. Once you have gained sufficient experience in a graduate role, you might thereafter search for job opportunities within *local, national or international* labour markets. Similarly, if you are an employer, depending on the type of vacancy that you have in your organisation, you may search for employees in the *internal* and/or *external* labour markets.

Like all marketplaces, labour markets are affected by the forces of demand and supply. A shop is an example of a marketplace, and is affected by the numbers of customers who want to buy their goods (*demand*) and the amount of goods they stock for sale in their shop (*supply*). Labour markets are affected by the numbers and types of people who are searching for jobs and the numbers and types of vacancies that exist. The *demand* for labour relates to the numbers and types of vacancies that employers are seeking to fill. The *supply* of labour relates to the numbers and types of people who are searching for work. It is rare that the demand for, and supply of, labour, are equal. More frequently, it can be observed that there are more vacancies in labour markets than there are people suitable to fill them (a situation where demand exceeds supply). The likely outcome of this imbalance between demand and supply is a shortage of people and particular skills. Or alternatively, there may be more people searching for jobs than there are vacancies for them to fill (a situation where supply exceeds demand). The likely outcome of this imbalance between supply and demand is unemployment. Considering the supply side of labour markets in more depth, the workforce can be divided into three categories: employed people, unemployed people and economically inactive people (which includes full-time students, carers and disabled people). Table 5.3 illustrates the numbers of people in each of these categories in the UK in 2011 compared with 2015.

Table 5.3 The size of categories of the UK workforce

Category	Numbers of people in the UK (millions) 2011	Numbers of people in the UK (millions) 2015
Employed	29.07	31.03
Unemployed	2.62	1.85
Economically inactive	9.36	8.99

Source: Office for National Statistics

Table 5.3 informs us that the majority of the workforce are in the employed category and that employment has increased whilst unemployment has decreased between 2011 and 2015. This suggests that the labour market is on the road to recovery following the global recession from 2008 and beyond.

The CIPD (2013) *Megatrends* report identifies seven factors which have shaped contemporary labour markets. These are presented and explained in Table 5.4.

As Table 5.4 shows, these trends mean that the external environment has been subject to significant changes which have substantial implications for the spaces within which employment relationships are created and sustained. On the one hand, these trends can be regarded as enhancing employment relationships. For example, technology can be used to facilitate communications in organisations which could have favourable implications for employment relationships because employees might feel more involved and engaged with what is happening in their organisations. However, these factors could also be regarded as having detrimental implications for employment relationships. For example, some commentators argue that globalisation has promoted competition between organisations and a common response has been to cut labour costs to the detriment of labour standards. Therefore, it can be argued that the key trends which have shaped contemporary labour markets have mixed implications for employment relationships.

The CIPD (2013) *Megatrends* report identifies four key future trends for labour markets. These are:

1 Reduced job turnover

2 Restraint on pay increases

3 Lack of trust between organisations and employees

4 Job intensification

These four future trends pose a number of challenges for creating and sustaining employment relationships. If there is reduced job turnover then employees will remain in organisations. This has benefits in terms of their knowledge and capability to perform but could mean that there is a lack of innovation and barriers to engaging people and securing their commitment if they feel they have to remain with an organisation rather than wanting to remain with an organisation. Restraint on pay means that other levers may need to be used in order to engage employees and incentivise them to perform. This may require some creative thinking and practices. Trust is perceived to be a key component of employment relationships. From the perspective of the psychological contract for example, a lack of trust is very damaging and a barrier to sustaining effective employment relationships. This means that organisations need to understand how and why they might have lost the trust of their employees and identify what they can do to restore this trust. Finally, the challenging external context with recruitment freezes and redundancies has meant that, in some organisations, employees feel obliged to perform the same or a bigger job with less resources, leading to a more intense experience with detrimental implications for employment relationships.

Table 5.4 Factors which have shaped contemporary labour markets

Factors shaping contemporary labour markets	Implications for employment relationships
De-industrialisation and the rise of the knowledge worker	Broader composition of the labour market. More variety in the types of employment relationships (eg full-time, part-time, temporary, term-time working, etc).
Technological change and globalisation	Increased size and scope of labour markets. Need to consider global context for employment relationships and scope for technology to enable/constrain.
Demographic change	People are working longer and this extends the duration of employment relationships. May have implications for labour turnover.
Increased female labour market participation	Often associated with a rise in demands for flexibility in employment relationships.
Increased educational participation	Increased the supply of skilled labour but need to ensure graduates have the skills that employers want and that there is sufficient demand.
Decline of collective workplace institutions	Contributed to a shift away from collective to individual employment relationships.
Greater diversity in employment relationships and how we work	Rise of atypical employment relationships (eg homeworking and flexible working practices).

Source: CIPD 2013

? REFLECTIVE ACTIVITY 5.4

Imagine you are an employee relations advisor working for an organisation which is concerned about these future trends for labour markets. How would you advise them to respond in order to minimise the potential for damage to employment relationships?

What, then, are the implications of these contemporary trends in labour markets for employee relationships? Labour markets are the changing worlds within which employee relationships are created and sustained. Labour markets are varied and complex in nature, which implies the need to think of a range of forms of employee relationships that exist in current labour markets. These include employee relationships of a long- and short-term nature, and those of a typical and atypical nature. The complexities of labour market regulation mean that policies and practices that are introduced into employee relationships may have mixed effects for employers and employees and could be a source of conflict in the employee relationship. The research evidence suggests that future labour market trends will pose substantial challenges to creating and sustaining employment relationships.

5.6 THE LEGAL FRAMEWORK FOR EMPLOYEE RELATIONS

Employee relationships are shaped and influenced by a legal framework. This legal framework is designed to promote particular behaviours (for example, work–life balance) and to regulate management behaviour towards employees (for example, protecting employees from harassment). There has been a substantial growth in the legal regulation of employee relationships over the last 40 years, which means that employment law plays a key part in the management of individual and collective employee relationships. For those involved in the management of employee relationships, ensuring legal compliance is essential. Here, the implications of the legal framework for employment relationships is discussed. However, this section should be considered in conjunction with Chapter 2 for a more detailed analysis of employment law.

The legal framework is evident in employee relationships in the form of contracts of employment. In contrast to a psychological contract, which is about employees' expectations, a contract of employment is a legally enforceable agreement between an organisation and an employee. It is formed after an organisation makes an offer of employment to an employee, the employee accepts that offer, and then begins to work in exchange for reward. The idea of a contract of employment as an exchange between employers and employees has some critics, who argue that the exchange between employers and employees is inherently unfair. This is based on the view that employers hold the balance of power in employment relationships and are therefore in a position to determine the terms of the exchange whereas employees hold a subordinate position and are effectively bound to accept the terms offered to them by employers.

Notwithstanding debates on the fairness of the formation of contracts of employment, the content of contracts of employment can either be expressly agreed terms or implied terms. Express terms are explicitly agreed between employers and employees, outline the rights and obligations of both parties, and typically cover the following areas:

- job title
- rate of pay
- when and how payment is to be made
- start date
- hours of work
- place of work
- holiday entitlement/pay
- pension provision
- sickness absence
- notice requirements.

Implied terms, on the other hand, are details that can be inferred as included within contracts of employment. Mutual trust and confidence is an example of an implied term. It is not usually expressly stated within contracts of employment, but it is generally accepted that it is an essential feature of employee relationships.

If an employer cannot trust its employee to do his or her job to a good standard without constant direct supervision, the future of their relationship is limited. If an employee does not trust the employer to pay him or her on a regular basis, the employee may not be able to afford to continue with this employment. Implied terms may provide employees and employers with rights and obligations depending on the circumstances. In the case of mutual trust and confidence, it is usual to consider this implied term as incorporated within contracts, but if other implied terms are unusual, they may not be so incorporated into contracts of employment. If the content of a contract of employment is breached by employers or employees, the other party can seek remedies for such a breach.

Remedies are frequently financial – and this highlights the consequences of not managing (and the incentives to manage) employee relationships within the legal framework.

Keeping up to date with the changing legal framework is a challenge for managers and HR professionals. The legal framework is subject to change through new legislation and amendments to existing legislation emerging from both UK and EU institutions on a regular basis. In the UK, the main source of employment law is legislation or Acts of Parliament. These become law once they are approved by the Houses of Parliament and the sovereign. A recent example of such legislation is the Equality Act 2010 which consolidates and reviews an array of existing discrimination laws and aims to achieve equality of pay between men and women.

In addition to legislation, other sources of employment law include common law and Codes of Practice. Common law is made by judges based on decisions reached on cases considered in the courts. These decisions set precedents or benchmarks, which can be applied to similar cases. For example, there can be uncertainty about whether someone is an employee, and this has implications for his or her ability to make employee tribunal claims against the employer. Over time, a series of tests have been developed by judges hearing similar cases, which are intended to help other judges thereafter reach a decision on employee status.

Such tests can be applied in the context of each case to inform decisions. Codes of Practice do not have legal status but they provide guidance on laws and are expected to be used in the management of employee relationships. For example, the Acas Code of Practice on Discipline at Work outlines the steps that employers and employees are expected to take to ensure the effective handling of disciplinary cases, and is an example of how the legal framework can have a direct impact on employee relationships.

European law has informed UK employment law since the UK joined the European Community in 1973. There are various forms of European law including Regulations and Directives, Regulations being the most important type of EU legislation (for example, the Working Time Regulations). Regulations and Directives are developed in the EU and then implemented in the UK. There has been a notable growth in the EU as a source of law since Labour signed up to the Social Chapter in 1997, leading to legislation in the UK including that relating to the transfer of undertakings, information and consultation, part-time work, agency workers and fixed-term contracts. This source of employment law has contributed a European dimension to the management of employee relationships.

Recent developments in employment law are dominated by the government's Employment Law Review which was undertaken between 2010 and 2015. The aim of this review was to reduce the amount of regulation to which organisations were subjected and to provide increased flexibility.

Key developments in employment law can be broadly categorised into individual and collective laws. Individual developments relate to laws regulating employee relationships, whereas collective developments apply to laws regulating relationships between employers and trade unions, and trade unions and their members. In the area of individual laws, four key developments are summarised below.

- the Equality Act 2010

  The Equality Act 2010 consolidates and reviews a raft of existing discrimination laws and specifically aims to achieve equality of pay between men and women. The impact of this Act on employee relationships is likely to be minimal because there are limited changes included in the Act. Instead, the Equality Act 2010 may encourage employers to enhance their existing approaches to ensuring equality in employee relationships.

- default retirement age (2011)

  The default retirement age of 65 was removed in 2011, and means that employers can no longer require employees to retire at age 65. Employees can continue to work for longer than previously, with no specific end date for employee relationships. This is evident at organisations such as B&Q, who have sought to recruit more mature workers, and potentially increases the open-ended and uncertain nature of employee relationships.

- the Agency Workers Regulations 2010

  The Agency Workers Regulations 2010 mean that temporary agency workers are now eligible for the same treatment as permanent employees. It is intended to provide employees in a precarious position with more rights and protections. This blurs the distinction between permanent and temporary employees, and has the effect of standardising employee relationships and potentially reducing the demand for temporary workers.

- an increase in qualifying service for unfair dismissal (2012)

  In April 2012, the qualifying service required by employees in order to lodge a claim for unfair dismissal at an employee tribunal increased from 12 months to two years. This was intended to reduce the numbers of claims made to employee tribunals and to provide employers with more flexibility to recruit and dismiss employees based on their business needs. It can be argued that it provides employers and employees with more time to create and sustain effective employee relationships. However, the change reduces the protection for employees against being unfairly dismissed and means that employee relationships could become more insecure for employees until they accrue two years' continuous employment.

The main developments in the area of collective law relate to information and consultation provisions, trade union recognition and restrictions on industrial action:

- the Information and Consultation of Employees (ICE) Regulations 2004

  The ICE Regulations were introduced to promote meaningful information and consultation arrangements. In particular, the Regulations require employers to inform and consult with employees and/or their representatives about the likelihood of any business changes that might affect job security. The Regulations offer the potential for employees to be better informed about and consulted upon key business decisions, such as redundancy. However, in practice, the Regulations can be interpreted loosely by employers, meaning that employees can be involved in exchanges of information about business performance and can be involved in consultation exercises over the future plans for a business, but may remain not necessarily any better informed nor able to influence future business plans. These Regulations have not therefore definitively improved the arrangements for information and consultation in employee relationships.

- statutory trade union recognition (2000)
  The Employment Relations Act 1999 means that employers are legally bound to recognise a trade union if the majority of employees vote in favour of trade union recognition. Once a union is recognised, employers have to negotiate with trade union representatives to determine pay and possibly hours of work and holiday entitlements. This recognition introduces a collective flavour to employee relationships, which requires employers and trade unions to jointly regulate employee relationships – which in turn implies some power-sharing between management and trade unions. Potentially, statutory trade union recognition can increase the influence of trade unions on employee relationships. Although reasonably high numbers of trade union recognition agreements have been signed, however, there is no indication of a halt in the overall decline of trade union membership levels. This suggests that trade unions may contribute to the regulation of many employee relationships but that statutory recognition has not necessarily increased the influence of trade unions on employee relationships.

- industrial action
  Although it is not the subject of new developments, the law on industrial action has been highlighted in the last five years through a small number of high-profile strikes, such as the British Airways dispute. Unlike other countries in the European Union, there is no legal right to strike in the UK, and strike action is regarded as undesirable by management and a last resort for trade unions and their members. In order for trade unions and their members to take lawful strike action, a lengthy ballot process must be followed. This requires trade unions to be highly organised and can act as a deterrent to strike action. It also provides employers with time to challenge the planned strike action, to try to resolve the dispute, and to plan for any disruption that may occur during a strike. In the case of the British Airways cabin crew dispute, a flaw in the ballot process adopted by the trade union enabled the management of British Airways to avert a strike planned for Christmas 2009. Notwithstanding the flaws in the ballot process, the British Airways dispute reminds us that employees have a voice – and the different voice practices used in contemporary organisations are explored in the next section.

?   REFLECTIVE ACTIVITY 5.5

In what ways has the UK and EU legal context had an impact in your workplace (or one with which you are familiar)?

5.7 EMPLOYEE VOICE PRACTICES

Employee involvement and participation are forms of employee voice which, according to Benson and Brown (2010, p83), provide employees with the opportunity to express their concerns and to influence the actions of management.

Employee voice is traditionally associated with trade unions on the view that employee voice has to be channelled through trade union representation in order to have any impact. However, in the light of the decline in trade union membership levels, it can no longer be assumed that forms of employee voice will involve trade union input, and that where they do, trade union involvement will enhance the impact of employee voice. Instead, there has been a growth in non-trade-union forms of employee voice by which there is direct communication between management and employees on an individual and/ or collective basis without any input from a third-party trade union representative.

There are two main forms of employee voice. First, there is **employee participation**, which is where employees participate in organisational decision-making through their representatives. Examples of employee participation practices include partnership working, joint consultation committees and employee forums. Employee participation can be contrasted with **employee involvement**, which is where management introduces practices directly with employees in order to gain their ideas and co-operation. Examples of employee involvement practices include email communications, management briefings, problem-solving groups, suggestion schemes and newsletters. Based on data from the Workplace Employment Relations Survey (WERS 2013), it is apparent that downward communication is the most extensively used form of employee voice in contemporary organisations. This is interesting because it constitutes a direct form of communication that does not involve trade unions and exemplifies a growth in non-trade-union forms of voice.

The use of employee voice practices was optional for organisations until 2005 when the Information and Consultation of Employees (ICE) Regulations were implemented in the UK. These Regulations provided employees with a legal right to be informed and consulted with about various employee matters, notably the likelihood of any changes to employee relationships and job security. As well as providing organisations with legal compliance, employee voice practices are believed to have benefits for both employers and employees. According to the CIPD (2011b), the benefits for employers are regarded to be:

- employees' skills and knowledge can be better used, leading to higher productivity
- employees feel more valued, so they are more likely to stay and to contribute more
- the organisation gains a positive reputation, making it easier to recruit good employees
- conflict is reduced and co-operation between employer and employee is based on interdependence.

The CIPD (2011b) highlights the following benefits of voice practices for employees:

- having more influence over their work
- higher job satisfaction
- more opportunity to develop skills
- more job security if their employer is more successful as a result of 'voice initiatives'.

This suggests that as well as being a legally essential feature of employee relationships, employee voice practices can be beneficial to both employers and employees. For example, Chapter 4 discusses how employee voice is an enabler of employee engagement. However, research by Wilkinson et al (2010) suggests that different employee voice practices can have different levels of impact. They argue that voice practices can be evaluated based on factors including their depth and scope. They believe that some voice practices are of deeper importance and are concerned with a broader range of issues than others, which enables employees to have more of an influence on organisational decision-making. For example, they regard practices that provide employees with information as being shallow in depth and narrow in scope, and therefore providing employees with limited opportunities to influence organisational decision-making. In contrast, they evaluate practices that involve consulting with employees and/or their representatives as being of deeper importance and broader scope. This suggests that different employee voice mechanisms have different outcomes and offer employees varying levels of influence and opportunity to contribute to organisational decision-making. Although downward communication has grown in popularity, this employee involvement practice can be evaluated as shallow in depth and narrow in scope, which may limit the power and influence of this type of voice.

In summary, employee voice practices are an essential feature of employee relationships. There are different forms of employee voice practices, and each form has advantages and disadvantages for employers and employees and their representatives.

There has been a growth in non-trade-union forms of employee voice, but there are doubts about the impact of these practices and ultimately, whether it provides employees with an opportunity to influence organisational decision-making.

5.8 CONFLICT AT WORK

In line with a pluralist view of employee relationships, conflict is regarded as inevitable owing to the different interests of parties to employee relationships. What is important for organisations under this approach is to ensure that they have robust systems in place to manage conflict. In contrast, a unitarist view of employee relationships assumes that conflict will not occur owing to the alignment of management and employee interests. Conflict is regarded as the exception rather than the norm under a unitarist approach. According to Sisson (2010, p207), conflict, which can be defined as the discontent arising from a perceived clash of interests, can involve individuals and/or groups and take a number of expressions.

Purcell (2014, p233) recently described what many have known or suspected for some time, that 'line managers are at the heart of most workplace conflict, whether causing it, experiencing it, dealing with it or coping with its consequences'.

Table 5.5 summarises the different forms of conflict that can be evident in contemporary organisations.

Table 5.5 Different forms of conflict

Organised conflict	Unorganised conflict
Strikes	Fiddles/theft
Protests, demonstrations, boycotts	Sabotage
Work-to-rule, go-slow, overtime bans	Absence, resignation

Source: Williams and Adam-Smith 2010, p343

Organised conflict – such as strikes – usually occurs on a collective basis. An example of this type of conflict was evident in October 2015 when NHS workers including nurses went on a four-hour strike for the first time in 30 years. Organised conflict can be official if it has been organised by a trade union, or unofficial if it has not been formally approved by a trade union. There is an expectation that conflict organised by trade unions will be lawful through compliance with the legal framework outlined in TULRCA (1992). Unofficial organised conflict tends to be unlawful although frequently short-term (for example, a group of employees may instigate a go-slow for part of a working day in order to demonstrate their discontent, before returning to normal working practices). In Table 5.5, organised conflict is distinguished from unorganised conflict, or 'misbehaviour' as it is sometimes known. Misbehaviour such as sabotage can occur on an individual and/ or collective basis. For example, if an individual or group of employees is dissatisfied with an organisation's decision to make employees redundant, they could damage property belonging to the organisation as an expression of their discontent.

Conflict at work is traditionally associated with strikes. However, in contemporary organisations, this association is misconceived. Statistics on strike action illustrate that strikes have declined in the UK. At their peak in 1979 there were 29.4 million working days lost from strike action, compared with 788,000 working days lost from strike action during 2014 (Office for National Statistics). A number of reasons have been suggested for the decline in strike action, including the impact of a decline in trade union membership levels over the same period and an increasingly complex legal framework, both of which can be regarded as making it harder for trade unions to conduct lawful and significant strike action. It is plausible to predict an increase in the numbers of days lost from strike action during the implementation of austerity measures in the public sector from 2010 to 2015. It is, however, highly unlikely that any increase will herald a return to the high levels of the 1970s given the deterrents, costs and limited public support for strike action.

In contemporary organisations, conflict is more associated with individual than with collective forms, expressed as grievances, absence, resignations and complaints to employment tribunals. The CIPD's (2011a) *Conflict Management* survey reported that there had been an increase in the mean (average) numbers of grievance per organisation each year from 8 in 2007 to 22.3 in 2011. Data from the Employment Tribunals Service indicates an increase in numbers of employment tribunal claims between 2008/9 and 2009/10, as illustrated in Table 5.6.

Table 5.6 Total numbers of claims made to employment tribunals

Year	Number of claims
2008/9	151,028
2009/10	236,100
2010/11	218,100

Source: Annual Tribunal Statistics

The growth in numbers of employment tribunal claims between 2008/9 and 2009/10 prompted the government to issue proposals for the reform of the employment tribunal system in an attempt to reduce the numbers of claims. For example, the government plans to increase the qualifying length of service for claiming unfair dismissal from one to two years and to introduce fees for those seeking to make an employment tribunal claim. These reforms are intended to reduce the numbers of claims and the impact of these reforms is evident in Table 5.7:

Table 5.7 Reduction in applications to employment tribunals since 2013

Time period	No. of cases
January to March 2013	57,737
April to June 2013	44,335
July to September 2013	39,514
October to December 2013	9,801
January to March 2014	6,054
April to June 2014	4,245
July to September 2014	4,653
October to December 2014	5,008
January to March 2015	4,878

Table 5.7 indicates that the increase in qualifying service and the introduction of fees has significantly reduced the numbers of employment tribunal claims and achieved its purpose. However, this does not necessarily mean that there has been a reduction in conflict in organisations. Although this is a possible explanation, the data in Table 5.7 suggests that there are fewer people pursuing these claims at employment tribunals.

Conflict of whatever form can be regarded as having undesirable effects on employee relationships. Even if managers adopt a pluralist view that conflict is inevitable, there remains a desire to resolve disputes in order to minimise any detrimental impacts on performance, working relationships and organisational reputation. The CIPD's *Conflict Management* survey (2011a) indicates that organisations have increased their investment in training managers to help with conflict resolution, specifically offering help with handling difficult conversations. Although this is an essential skill that may enable managers to resolve disputes more effectively, there is also a need for managers to be aware of and compliant with the legal framework that governs the handling of discipline and grievance cases. Furthermore, the point at which managers are facing difficult conversations may be too late to prevent conflict escalating into strikes or employment tribunal claims. In view of the key role of managers in conflict management, therefore, there is a case for broader investment in supporting managers with conflict prevention and resolution to complement any training provided in dealing with difficult conversations.

The CIPD's *Conflict Management* survey (2011a) reveals that 85% of disciplinary and grievance cases are resolved internally within organisations. However, if all internal options for resolving disputes have been exhausted, organisations can draw upon the services of independent organisations such as Acas to assist with dispute resolution. Acas can assist organisations to resolve disputes through the use of arbitration, conciliation and mediation techniques. Arbitration is an option for resolving disputes relating to unfair dismissal and flexible working by which an independent person (an arbitrator) evaluates the dispute and issues a binding decision. Conciliation attempts to identify a mutually acceptable resolution to a dispute that has resulted or is likely to result in a claim to an employment tribunal. Mediation is essentially the same as conciliation, except that the dispute has not resulted in an employment tribunal claim. Acas identifies mediation as the most commonly appropriate form of conflict resolution, and the technique is likely to broaden as a result of government proposals that highlight the importance of mediation for resolving disputes. Government reforms of the UK conflict resolution system have led to the promotion of informal approaches to resolution, with mediation in particular being encouraged. Mediation is a process which 'involves a neutral third party bringing two sides together with the aim of reaching a mutual agreement' (ACAS/CIPD 2013, p3). Although the CIPD (2011a) *Conflict Management* survey indicates that the use of **mediation** has increased, it is not appropriate for resolving all types of conflict. For example, the CIPD Workplace Mediation Report found that it was most suited to conflict associated with a breakdown in relationships rather than a breach of disciplinary rules. This suggests that there are some limits to the use of mediation in practice and that it cannot be assumed to be a universally applicable approach to conflict resolution.

In summary, various forms of conflict are evident in organisations owing to the different interests of the parties to employee relationships. This undermines the achievability of a unitarist approach to employee relations. In contemporary organisations, conflict is more likely to manifest itself in individual forms such as grievances and employment tribunal claims rather than collective forms, including strikes. Recent reforms of the UK conflict management system have introduced substantial changes and reduced the numbers of claims going to employment tribunals and encourage organisations to resolve conflict more informally. However, we need to be cautious about assuming that this has reduced levels of conflict; instead it is suggested that it has implications for approaches to resolving conflict.

5.9 CONCLUSION

This chapter has highlighted the key features of employee relationships in contemporary organisations. The chapter began by defining employee relationships as the main focus of employee relations and discussed different perspectives on employee relationships. Next, the contribution of management, trade unions and government to the management of employee relationships was explored, the influences of labour market contexts were discussed, and the legal framework on employee relationships was examined. Finally, the practices of employee voice and the realities of conflict at work were analysed.

Looking ahead, it is reasonable to suggest that the business of creating and sustaining employee relationships will continue to be relevant and extremely important over the next five years. The decline in trade union membership shows no signs of abating, which suggests that the role of trade unions in the management of employee relationships will continue to diminish. In line with this decline, the growth of employee involvement rather than employee participation forms of employee voice may be expected to continue. There is, however, an opportunity for the trade union movement to engage with the mediation agenda in the area of dispute resolution and to demonstrate different ways of thinking and acting through its involvement in the public sector reforms. Because the public sector is likely to shrink in size and bear a closer resemblance to the private sector with an emphasis on competition, resistance and conflict are likely to continue to pervade this context. This presents a longer-term challenge for managers and HR practitioners in balancing the need for co-operation with the expectation of conflict, amid the continuing reality of uncertainty. As the UK economy emerges from a recessionary context, organisations should have more scope to invest more resources into creating and sustaining effective employment relationships. It remains to be seen whether organisations will seize these investment opportunities.

FURTHER READING

ACAS (2011) *The future of workplace relations – an Acas view* [Online]. Available at: www.acas.org.uk/media/pdf/n/8/The_Future_ of_Workplace_Relations_- _An_Acas_view.pdf. This report provides some predictions about the future directions for employee relations over the next ten years.

CIPD (2005) *What is employee relations?* [Online]. Available at: www.cipd.co.uk/hr- resources/research/employee-relations.aspx. This report outlined the contemporary focus on employee relations, and prompted debate among academics and practitioners about the changing nature and relevance of employee relations.

CIPD (2011) *Employee relations at capgemini UK*. [Online]. Available at: www.cipd.co.uk/hr-resources/research/employee-relations-capgemini-uk.aspx. This is an interesting case study, which explores contemporary employee relations practices within the context of a global IT services organisation.

CIPD (2012) *Employee relations information page*. [Online]. Available at: www.cipd.co.uk/hr topics/employee-relations.aspx. This website provides factsheets, podcasts and survey reports on the subject of employee relations.

GENNARD, J. and JUDGE, G. (2010) *Managing employment relations*. 5th edition. London: Chartered Institute of Personnel and Development. This CIPD text discusses the contexts of employee relations, explores key theoretical perspectives and discusses employee relations practices in depth.

LEWIS, P., THORNHILL, A. and SAUNDERS, M. (2003) *Employee relations: understanding the employment relationship*. Harlow: Pearson Education. This text focuses on the employee relationship as the central feature of employee relations and provides a comprehensive overview of key areas with practical examples to consolidate learning.

ROSE, E. (2008) *Employment relations*. 3rd edition. Harlow: Pearson Education. This is a useful resource, which provides a comprehensive overview of the theory and practices of employee relations.

REFERENCES

BENSON, J. and BROWN, M. (2010) Employee voice: does union membership matter? *Human Resource Management Journal.* Vol 20, No 1. pp80–99.

BUDD, J. W. (2011) *The thought of work*. New York: Cornell University Press.

CIPD (2011a) *Conflict management*. Survey. London: Chartered Institute of Personnel and Development.

CIPD (2011b) *Employee relations*. Overview Factsheet. July. London: Chartered Institute of Personnel and Development.

ACAS / CIPD (2013) *Mediation: an approach to resolving workplace issues*. 2nd ed. London, Chartered Institute of Personnel and Development.

CIPD (2013) *Megatrends: the trends shaping work and working lives*. London: Chartered Institute of Personnel and Development.

CIPD (2015) *Factsheet: employee relations: an overview*. London, Chartered Institute of Personnel and Development

CLAYDON, T. and THOMPSON, A. (2010) Human resource management and the labour market. In: BEARDWELL, J. and CLAYDON, T. (eds). *Human resource management: a contemporary approach*. 6th ed. Harlow: FT/Prentice Hall.

FOX, A. (1966) *Industrial sociology and industrial relations*. Donovan Commission Research Report, No. 3. London: HMSO.

GENNARD, J. and JUDGE, G. (2010) *Managing employment relations*. 5th ed. London: Chartered Institute of Personnel and Development.

GUEST, D.E. and CONWAY, N., 2002. Communicating the psychological contract: an employer perspective. *Human resource management journal*, *12*(2), pp.22–38.

KILROY, J. and DUNDON, T. (2015) www.emeraldinsight.com/doi/abs/10.1108/ER-06-2014-0071 The multiple faces of front line managers: A preliminary examination of FLM styles and reciprocated employee outcomes Employee Relations, 37:4, 410–427.

NOWAK, P. (2015), "The past and future of trade unionism", Employee Relations, Vol. 37 Iss 6 pp. 683–691.

PURCELL, J. and SISSON, K. (1983) Strategies and practices in industrial relations. In: BAIN, G. S. (ed.). *Industrial relations in Britain*. Oxford: Blackwell.

PURCELL, J. (2014), 'Disengaging from engagement'. Human Resource Management Journal, 24:3, 241–254.

ROSE, E. (2008) *Employment relations*. 3rd ed. Harlow: Pearson Education.

SISSON, K. (2010) *Employment relations matters*. Available at: www2.warwick.ac.uk/ac/soc/wbs/research/irru/ [accessed 2015].

WERS (2013) The 2011 Workplace Employment Relations Study (WERS): first findings – updated May 2013, Available https://www.gov.uk/government/publications/the-2011-workplace-employment-relations-study-wers

WILLIAMS, S. and ADAM-SMITH, D. (2010) *Contemporary employment relations: a critical introduction*. 2nd ed. Oxford: Oxford University Press.

WILKINSON, A., GOLLAN, P., MARCHINGTON, M. and LEWIN, D. (eds) (2010) *The Oxford handbook of participation in organisations*. Oxford, Oxford University Press.

CHAPTER 6

Reward Management

GRAHAM PERKINS AND CAROL WOODHAMS

CHAPTER CONTENTS

- Introduction
- Defining reward management
- The business context of reward management
- Internal and external factors that shape reward management
- Gathering and analysing reward intelligence
- Theories of reward management
- The concept of 'total reward'
- Reward initiatives and practices
- Line managers and reward management
- Evaluating the impact of reward management

KEY LEARNING OUTCOMES

By the end of this chapter, you should be able to:

- analyse the context of reward management highlighting key internal and external factors that influence reward processes and systems
- critically discuss the most appropriate methods of gathering and analysing data relating to reward management
- analyse the various theories and perspectives which underpin the reward management field
- evaluate the concept of 'total reward' highlighting its overall aims and key benefits
- analyse various reward management practices including grade/pay structures, job evaluation and the idea of 'contingent' reward
- critically discuss the role the line managers play in reward management systems and processes.

6.1 INTRODUCTION

When **reward management** is discussed and analysed within organisations cash pay is often the first thing that comes to mind. It is very important to remember that cash pay is only one part of reward management and that there are many other factors and variables which must be considered.

The way in which employees are rewarded can provoke a great deal of controversy both within and outside organisations. The methods and reasons which sit behind reward decisions have strategic, practical and symbolic implications; so it is crucial to recognise that if firms stop paying people in ways that broadly match their economic value and expectations they are unlikely to successfully recruit and retain staff. On the other side of the argument paying in excess of market norms can significantly impact the financial performance of organisations. HR professionals have a delicate balance to achieve.

This chapter begins by focusing on the business context of reward management, considering relevant trends and factors that can impact on reward decisions. Following this section attention turns to the various ways in which reward 'intelligence' (ie data) can be gathered and analysed. As we analyse reward at a deeper level in the chapter, various reward perspectives, theories and principles are covered including the concept of '**total reward**', before specific reward incentives and practices are evaluated. Towards the end of the chapter there is a section dedicated to the role of line managers in reward management, and a final section evaluating the impact of reward management.

6.2 DEFINING REWARD MANAGEMENT

The logical place to begin this chapter is by defining the term 'reward management'. There are countless definitions available, each with a slightly different slant or approach. One of the more comprehensive definitions is from Armstrong and Taylor (2014, p370), who suggest that:

> Reward management is concerned with the strategies, policies and practices required to ensure that the value of people and the contribution they make to achieving organizational, departmental and team goals is recognized and rewarded. It is about the design, implementation and maintenance of reward systems that aim to satisfy the needs of both the organization and its stakeholders and to operate fairly, equitably and consistently. Reward management deals with non-financial rewards such as recognition, learning and development opportunities and increased job responsibility, as well as financial rewards.

This definition highlights the intricacies of reward management and demonstrates that it is not solely concerned with financial issues. Armstrong and Taylor (2014) specifically state that reward management involves both financial and non-financial elements and that the overall objective of reward management is to reward people fairly, equitably and consistently.

It is notable that Armstrong and Taylor suggest that reward management aims to meet the needs of both the organisation and its stakeholders. This is a point that is sometimes missed. It is important to remember that the territory of reward management is as concerned with the needs of organisational stakeholders (such as shareholders and line managers) as it is with the needs of employees. Imagine a situation where an HR professional managed to put through a 20% pay increase for all workers at a particular company site. No doubt the employees affected would be delighted – but shareholders on the other hand might be very disappointed because their earnings from organisational profits would drop. It is crucial to recognise that HR professionals have a delicate balance to achieve in order to satisfy the many different stakeholders of reward.

6.2.1 THE PRINCIPLES OF REWARD MANAGEMENT

Now that the basic concept of reward management has been defined, its underlying principles must be briefly discussed before the concept as a whole can be related to the wider business environment.

As hinted at in the previous section, a key principle of reward management is that individuals in organisations are rewarded for their contributions fairly, consistently and transparently. It is important to recognise that pay itself is a very emotive issue – that is to say, that individuals can have very strong feelings about what is 'right' and what is

The Coalition Government

During 2010 the ongoing recession and presence of a large budget deficit divided electoral opinion on economic policy. The election held in 2010 reflected these divisions in that no one party was clearly re-elected. A change of government took place and a coalition was formed between the Conservatives and the Liberal Democrats. Once elected, the Coalition took action to reduce public borrowing and imposed strict cuts in government spending. In essence, the parties argued for a much reduced role for government and an increased role for ordinary citizens, particularly in the delivery of public services.

What implications did this shift in policy have for reward management? The government argued for a reduction in regulation, built on its position that this constrained business and economic growth. Examples of this were the delaying of the implementation of certain provisions in the Equalities Act (2010) and extending the qualifying period for unfair dismissal to two years. The government committed to keeping the National Minimum Wage, increasing it from £5.93 per hour in 2010 to £6.50 per hour in 2014. Collective bargaining continued in the public sector, but was constrained in the face of the challenging employment position. In the private sector, market forces continued to be the prevailing factor in determining pay.

The 2015 Conservative Government

The 2015 general election returned the first Conservative majority administration for almost 20 years. Still dealing with a budget deficit, during his first budget speech in July 2015 the Chancellor, George Osborne, announced plans to create a new national living wage of £7.20 per hour in 2016, rising to £9 per hour in 2020. The chancellor also made changes to welfare spending and continued with pensions reforms, with the aim of reducing the welfare bill but enabling people to keep more of the money that they earned through increases in personal tax allowances.

6.3.3 THE CORPORATE CONTEXT

The CIPD's (2015b) *Reward Management* survey highlighted a number of key findings regarding organisational attitudes to reward in the UK. Some of the important findings include:

- Almost half of organisations questioned said that 'ability to pay' was the most important factor in determining pay levels
- Individual bonuses and pay rises are the most common performance-related reward schemes among organisations offering such schemes
- Most organisations favour pay confidentiality over transparency
- Most organisations position total cash earnings at, or close to the market median.

More generally, we also have to remember that there are a number of significant aspects of the corporate environment that affect reward management (Armstrong 2002) including the impact of change programmes, employee and employer expectations, organisational culture and, finally, corporate values. Importantly, the CIPD's (2015b) survey also highlights issues connected with organisational justice and the individualisation of salaries in the private sector, whilst also emphasising the importance of communicating reward management decisions in a clear and effective manner.

Many of the factors listed above are internal to organisations but nevertheless have a substantial impact on reward. It is important to understand that these internal factors are also influenced by the external context. Employee expectations, for example, are formed within the organisation but are influenced by external variables such as education levels and comparisons that are made with family and friends who work in other organisations. If perceptions of unfairness arise during these comparisons, this can impact upon the psychological contract. It is important to recognise that even at the corporate level, the range of influences brought to bear on reward constrains the ability of management to determine outcomes (such as final pay settlements, and so on) on their own terms.

?   REFLECTIVE ACTIVITY 6.1

In what ways does the corporate context inside your organisation (or in one with which you are familiar) shape reward management practices or systems?

Hopefully, the reflective activity caused you to reflect on the specific elements of corporate context that impact on reward management. Perhaps your chosen organisation has developed a reward system that encourages specific behaviours or attitudes. Alternatively, you may have highlighted that your chosen organisation is trying to minimise costs and find efficiencies, in which case you may feel that pay systems are being tightened up or reward packages are becoming less generous overall.

REWARD IN THE PUBLIC SECTOR

CASE STUDY 6.1

There are often substantial differences in reward practices between public and private sector organisations – not least because governments of whatever political persuasion have a role as a model employer and thus attempt to offer favourable terms and conditions of employment. This has also led to most of the public sector continuing to recognise trade unions and to collective bargaining being dominant in wage determination. We continue to see, for example, incremental pay scales, a limited emphasis on contingent pay and generous benefits in the form of flexible working, holiday entitlements and final salary pension schemes. While the *quid pro quo* for this was often argued to be lower base salaries and higher job security than the private sector, economic recession and government spending programmes have led to the erosion of salary differentials. Indeed, there have been claims that public sector salaries are in many instances now comparable with or superior to private sector equivalents. This has led to

considerable hostility around the issue of public sector reward. Gillian Hibberd (2010), however, argues that much of this hostility is based around myths on levels of reward in the sector.

Reward in the public sector: fiction or reality?

Hibberd (2010) sets about exploding some of the myths she believes have arisen about public sector pay in recent years. She includes:

Myth 1: public sector pensions are gold plated. Final salary pension schemes do still exist but take-home payments from these are not, in most cases, excessive. Average salary is £13,000 and average pension £4,000.

Myth 2: the tax payer meets the cost of all public sector pensions. There are both funded and unfunded schemes in the public sector. For example, the Local Government Scheme is funded, employer and employee contributions are invested, and pensions paid from the returns – not by the tax payer. Employee contribution rates also vary widely – eg 0% for the armed forces and 11% for the police.

Myth 3: public sector workers are paid more than their private sector equivalents. An Institute for Fiscal Studies (IFS) report has concluded that public sector workers are paid in line with their private sector counterparts. Raw data may not indicate this, but it needs to be adjusted to account for the often highly skilled labour that is employed in the public sector – for example, in the NHS.

Myth 4: the public sector has grown out of all control. A perception has emerged that the public sector has expanded hugely in the past decade. The IFS report suggests that public administration jobs

rose by 1% and other public sector jobs by 4% in the period 2000–2005. These figures are now predicted to decline sharply.

Myth 5: many public sector workers are paid more than the prime minister. Around 300 senior public sector executives earned more than the prime minister out of a workforce of over 5 million. Hibberd argues the salaries of chief executives of public bodies are commensurate with the responsibilities they take, and less than those of most private sector senior executives.

Source: Hibberd, G. (2010) HR column 'fiction or reality?'. *People Management*. 12 August.

6.4 INTERNAL AND EXTERNAL FACTORS THAT SHAPE REWARD MANAGEMENT

Many sources, including Hatchet (2008), outline a number of pressures on reward management including inflation, rates of economic growth, labour market issues and increases in individual domestic expenditure, such as Council Tax. Alongside these issues there are a number of other factors that HR professionals need to keep in mind when setting reward strategies including:

- *the desire to maintain purchasing power*: this is eroded by inflation, and workers will seek pay increases to compensate for it in order to maintain or improve their living standards
- *talent management*: there has been a long period of tight labour markets in the UK, and skills shortages continue even in labour markets where there are larger numbers of unemployed individuals
- *transparent pay structures*: there is a greater demand both legally and socially for transparency and equity both internally and externally, and reward practices must respond to this
- *equal pay issues*: there have been a number of successful claims in the public sector with substantial financial implications. There is consequently a need for reward processes to support equal pay structures
- *market-related comparisons*: economic difficulties mean that there will be modest (or no) rises for some while others will receive higher rises in the face of skills shortages. This can create tensions within the workforce and highlights the need for transparency in pay decisions.

Alongside the issues outlined above it is important to understand that employers have a range of mechanisms for establishing job and grading systems – for example, job evaluation systems and internal labour markets – to which they attach pay structures. All of these terms are explored later in this chapter, but at the moment the key point to keep in mind is that a key justification for imposing pay and **grade structures** is to ensure that pay processes are seen to be fair. At the same time, HR professionals need to ensure that issues surrounding equality of opportunity and diversity are attended to. Pay scales and structures seen to be discriminatory could have serious consequences for an organisation, both in terms of legal action and damage to the psychological contract.

Despite the points made above, the external labour market can create problems for attempts to standardise internal systems, especially where they are applied at a national level. The price of labour in the external market may, for example, vary by geographic location. Living costs and thus wage expectations are very different in the north-east from what they are in the south-east of the UK. Similarly, there tend to be surpluses of labour in the north-east and skills shortages in the south-east. Such factors have implications for the way that pay levels are set within organisations. This discussion introduces the issue of how pay is determined in organisations. The following subsection defines the term '**pay determination**' and briefly considers how organisations go about setting pay levels in practice.

6.4.1 PAY DETERMINATION

'Pay determination' may appear to be a complex term at first glance but the concept is a relatively simple one. Pay determination is simply the process of making decisions about how much employees should be paid for their work. White and Druker (2008, p23) believe that:

> the method and level at which decisions are taken and criteria used to determine pay levels are key issues in reward management.

This statement highlights crucial components of pay determination – the level at which decisions are made and the criteria used. Some organisations devolve pay decisions to individual managers whereas others keep control at higher levels. In the public sector, for example, salaries are often pegged against national frameworks and there is little, if any, room for manoeuvre. In the same way, different organisations use different criteria to determine pay levels. In some settings skills and competencies are used as ways to set pay levels while in other environments pay may be set by reference to specific achievements against set objectives. These issues are debated in more detail a little later in this chapter.

A key external factor that impacts on the reward management decisions made by employers is legislation – notably the national minimum wage and equal pay.

6.4.2 THE NATIONAL MINIMUM WAGE (NMW)

The National Minimum Wage Act was passed in 1998 by the Labour Government in office at the time. It marked a shift away from a reliance on market forces to determine wages effectively, and established the first national pay rate in UK history.

From April 1999 all employers in the UK have had to pay at least the national minimum wage to their employees. When it was introduced, the NMW was set at £3.60 per hour (£3.00 for 18 to 21 year olds). Opponents of the legislation argued that a NMW would lead to higher unemployment because employers could no longer afford to employ as many staff. Opponents also suggested that inflation would increase as higher wages fed through into the economy. There is, however, very little evidence that the NMW has led to increased unemployment and inflation. Indeed, employment in traditionally low-wage sectors such as hospitality and retail has continued to grow since the introduction of the NMW. Table 6.1 shows the progression of the NMW since 2010.

In his summer 2015 budget, George Osborne announced the creation of a 'National Living Wage' of £7.20 per hour for those aged over 25 in 2016, rising to £9 per hour by 2020.

Alongside the introduction of the NMW, employers also have to contend with equal pay legislation.

Table 6.1 National Minimum Wage rates (2010–2015)

Year	21 and over	18–20	Under 18	Apprentice
2015	£6.70	£5.30	£3.87	£3.30
2014	£6.50	£5.13	£3.79	£2.73
2013	£6.31	£5.03	£3.72	£2.68
2012	£6.19	£4.98	£3.68	£2.65
2011	£6.08	£4.98	£3.68	£2.60
2010	£5.93	£4.92	£3.64	£2.50

6.4.3 EQUAL PAY

There are several pieces of legislation that impact on reward decisions, including those around equal pay and discrimination. The Equal Pay Act 1970 (as amended by the Equal Pay (Amendment) Regulations 1983) now incorporated into the Equality Act 2010 was needed to address pay discrimination on the grounds of gender. For example, as noted by Perkins and White (2011, p77), until the passing of the Equal Pay Act in 1970 it was perfectly legal to pay women less than men for doing the same job. Legislation now prevents this from occurring.

Equal pay legislation defines pay as wages and all other contractual entitlements, including holiday and sick pay, for example, as well as any discounts offered by the employer and 'benefits in kind'. The specific provisions of the legislation around equal pay now provide for the right for men and women to be paid the same in the following three circumstances:

- for like work (where two employees are doing exactly the same or very similar work)
- for work rated as equivalent (how this rating should be arrived at is not specified in law but is often informed by **job evaluation**)
- for work of equal value (where jobs are very different in terms of their skills and abilities but contribute a similar amount of 'value' to the organisation).

Interestingly, in a leading equal pay case, *Hayward v Cammell Laird* (Lewis and Sargeant 2013), it was found that employers could not defend equal pay claims by arguing that other, favourable, employment terms balance issues of pay discrimination. In this particular case, the Supreme Court decided that a female canteen chef was entitled to the same basic pay as her male comparators, despite the presence of other contractual terms (sickness benefits, meal breaks, holidays) that were favourable to her.

 EQUAL PAY, OR MORE-THAN-EQUAL PAY?

CASE STUDY 6.2

Gemma Cartwright and Steven Garth work in the same organisation doing work of equal value. At present she earns £20,000 and Steven earns £21,000. A job evaluation exercise is conducted, but the results are not communicated because they are considered too politically sensitive. No changes are made to salaries. Gemma learns via the organisational grapevine that her post was evaluated 25% above Steven's. She takes the organisation to an employment tribunal and wins her case. What should her new salary be?

- £25,000?
- £26,000?

or

- £21,000?

6.5 GATHERING AND ANALYSING REWARD INTELLIGENCE

There are many sources of reward management data that HR practitioners can take advantage of. The CIPD, for instance, produces an annual reward management survey, which examines issues such as pay positioning, pensions and benefits and performance-related bonuses. Alongside reports produced by professional institutions such as the CIPD there are also various industry benchmarking reports and surveys, including those produced by the local government group for the public sector and private sector organisations such as Croner (www.cronersolutions.co.uk) and Incomes Data Services (www.incomesdata.co.uk).

Together with the data sources listed above, national statistics also have relevance within reward management. Before making pay decisions HR professionals often need to take account of the following factors:

- inflation
- unemployment rates
- the number of vacancies
- average working hours
- average earnings.

Information relating to factors such as inflation, unemployment rates and average earnings/working hours can be found from government websites such as www.statistics. gov.uk. By examining these sorts of data sources HR professionals can quickly identify trends in particular areas and can adapt their reward management strategies and decisions as a result. When thinking about the number of vacancies it is important to recognise that positions that are particularly difficult to fill generally command higher reward packages. Vacancies that attract many applicants, by contrast, can usually be given lower reward packages – although this is not always the case.

When examining reward management data it is important to recognise that statistics can be influenced by issues occurring at a variety of different levels. The previous section of this chapter considered the international, national and corporate contexts of reward management, and it is important to understand that these factors shape the ways in which organisations make their final decisions. Alongside these considerations, as we saw above, HR professionals must also take the effect of legislation into account when gathering and analysing reward data.

Before moving on to examine the various theories of reward management, it is important to consider the ways in which reward data may be presented to various stakeholder groups. The primary consideration here is the level and type of data that is going to be relevant to each group. Whereas senior managers might want to see detailed benchmarking data from comparable organisations or data that allows them to gauge how factors such as inflation or the number of vacancies are affecting reward management, other stakeholders may have different requirements. Employees, for example, are unlikely to be concerned with specific comparisons between particular roles but they are likely to want to know how their earnings compare to the average across an industry. It is important that HR professionals can provide appropriate information for each specific stakeholder group.

From the discussions in this section it should be clear that there are a variety of internal and external factors that influence reward management in organisations. To add greater complexity to the lives of HR practitioners there are also several underpinning theories that inform the reward management field. These theories shed more light on reward management decisions. However, their positions frequently contradict. It is important to understand that there is not necessarily one theory that is 'right' or one theory that is 'wrong' – they are simply different interpretations that may or may not be relevant in given contexts.

6.6 THEORIES OF REWARD MANAGEMENT

It is important to understand that there are a variety of perspectives and theories that exist within the reward management field. This part of the chapter outlines and discusses the main theories and perspectives:

- economic theory
- institutional theories of reward
- human capital theory.

Please do not be put off by the terminology in the bullet list above. The theories are relatively straightforward and the key principles of each are explained in detail.

6.6.1 ECONOMIC THEORY

Economic theories broadly consider wage rates to be determined by a combination of the supply of labour and the demand for that labour from employers. Wage rates are therefore arrived at to try to achieve a balance between supply and demand. If labour is in short supply, the value of the labour increases and wages go up. Conversely, where labour is plentiful, its value drops. Key assumptions of economic theories are firstly that both employers and employees are rational actors who have all the information they need to make informed choices, and secondly that employees are fully mobile – that is, they will move to where there are jobs available.

There are, however, complexities within these theories. Firstly, of course, not many employees are really 'fully mobile' because they are constrained by family and social circumstances. So the opportunity to maximise their reward is limited. Secondly, economic theories focus only on forms of financial reward to attract labour and achieve organisational goals. Within these theories the 'worth' of the potential employee and the state of the labour market are the features that determine wage rates. A criticism of these assumptions has been provided by individuals who are more disposed towards what are termed social psychological theories. Social psychologists emphasise, instead, the long-term nature of the employment relationship and suggest that economic theories that focus only on pay rates do not accurately reflect reality. They suggest that it is more important for employees to experience job satisfaction and a sense of fairness in relation to reward. It is important to understand that tensions in the employment relationship can lead to the adoption of different perspectives on reward.

6.6.2 INSTITUTIONAL THEORIES OF REWARD

Perhaps unsurprisingly, given all the above criticism of economic theories, there are a number of other theories that seek to explain how wage rates are established. These have all influenced thinking in different ways, rather than one being superior to or replacing another theory. This is an important point to keep in mind.

Institutional theories of reward introduce a more 'open systems' approach to setting wage levels. They recognise the role of institutions within reward systems – in other words, contextual or environmental factors are recognised as influencing wage levels. An open systems approach allows for the possibility of an employer's actions in the use of wages to influence employee attitudes and behaviours. An example of an employer action might be if an employer offered a wage premium in order to attract labour. Such a decision might motivate workers to focus their efforts on achieving organisational strategy. In addition to this point it is important to remember that workers do not necessarily 'sell' their labour as individuals: they may act collectively (most obviously through a trade union) and such activity will affect wages. The sizes of organisations or of industry sectors are also thought to influence pay-setting.

Institutional theorists argue that recognition of these factors helps to explain why wage levels rarely appear to fall. Classical economic labour market theories such as those explored above suggest that wages will be lower when there is a surplus of labour, but in reality wages are often described as 'sticky' – that is, they are resistant to being reduced. It can certainly be argued that trade union activity may well achieve this outcome, because workers operating collectively often prevent any reduction in their pay. There are a number of competing explanations for the 'stickiness' of wages, and it is important to understand that this issue is not generally well understood.

6.6.3 HUMAN CAPITAL THEORY

Human capital theory (Becker 1975) is one of the founding theories in understanding reward. This theory suggests that workers 'invest' in themselves via education, training and development to increase their own capital (or value to employers). Different levels of reward are used to attract workers dependent upon their skills, experience and qualifications. In other words, the higher an individual's capital, the higher is the return on it in terms of pay and benefits as organisations compete for skilled labour.

? REFLECTIVE ACTIVITY 6.2

Which of the theoretical approaches outlined here do you think best fits with the reward management practices and systems inside your organisation (or one that you know well)?

6.7 THE CONCEPT OF 'TOTAL REWARD'

The term 'total reward' is often used in modern reward management systems, but what does it actually mean? The CIPD (2015a) state that total reward:

> encompasses all aspects of work that are valued by employees, including elements such as learning and development opportunities and/or an attractive working environment, in addition to the wider pay and benefits package.

This definition demonstrates that total reward considers far more than just base pay. It highlights the holistic nature of total reward, and this is a key point to keep in mind. Within this interpretation the basic elements of a total reward package include:

- financial compensation
- benefits
- work–life balance
- performance and recognition
- development and career opportunities.

The key learning point in this section, then, is that a total reward approach involves both extrinsic and intrinsic elements. An example in practice can be seen in the case study below, which has been taken from *People Management*.

CASE STUDY 6.3

CHARITIES USE TOTAL REWARD TO MAKE WORK STAFF'S OWN EDEN

Third-sector organisations can achieve success with a total reward approach to make up for their inability to offer high salaries, delegates at this month's CIPD Reward Forum heard.

Leah Brewer, organisational development manager at the Eden Trust, explained how the environmental charity had pioneered a range of innovative benefits, including on-site yoga, podiatry and massages. High-performing employees are nominated for one-off bonuses, vouchers for the Eden Project shop, or a one-to-one lunch with Tim Smit, Eden's chief executive. Workers are also entered into a draw to take an extra week's annual leave.

'Working for Eden is rewarding, and not only for the pay packet,' said Brewer. 'It's important to make sure it works for the organisation as well as the individual.'

Firms should not be afraid to try new things when it comes to reward, and

while pilot schemes are a good way of getting management buy-in, not everything will work, she said.

'Sometimes knock-backs can be good – you have a reason why [a scheme didn't work] and you can deal with that,' Brewer told PM.

Joe Bennett, HR director at Scope, told delegates that performance-related pay had proved a success at the charity, although it concentrated on senior staff.

'HR can add value by focusing its attention on that particular group of people and really getting them to excel,' said Bennett. 'To help get a feeling of clarity and consistency, you have to get the messages right. You need the top team banging out those messages.'

Source: Chubb, L. (2007) Charities use total reward to make work staff's own Eden. *People Management*. 29 November.

? REFLECTIVE ACTIVITY 6.3

Does your organisation (or one that you are familiar with) use a 'total reward' approach? Do you think that this has/would have any effect on your level of engagement with your organisation?

6.7.1 THE AIMS OF TOTAL REWARD

Although there are many different models of total reward that organisations can adopt, the CIPD states that 'the principle of viewing a range of non-financial factors as part of the rewards package' is the same. Many organisations are now looking at the experience they offer in a more holistic manner when deciding how best to attract, retain and engage existing and potential employees. The broad aim of a total reward approach is to achieve a better balance between the needs of the employee and the needs of the organisation.

Looking at the fundamental purpose of total reward a little more closely, Armstrong and Taylor (2014, p365) believe the central aim 'emphasizes the need to consider all aspects of the work experience of value to employees, not just a few such as pay and employee benefits.' There is a broad view that total reward should aim to increase employee satisfaction and ultimately business performance. To this end the CIPD (2015a) maintains that the aims of total reward include 'the desire to enhance recruitment, retention and performance levels'. This statement adds to the view that total reward aims to balance the needs of the employee with the needs of the employer. Having now understood the broad aim of total reward, let us consider its benefits in an organisational setting.

6.7.2 THE BENEFITS OF TOTAL REWARD

The CIPD factsheet on total reward (2015a) states that total reward 'has a particularly strong potential to enhance the reputation of an organisation as an employer of choice through its capacity to place a value on the non-basic pay or wider non-financial benefits of working for an organisation'.

Whereas the above statement may seem appropriate from a theoretical stance, how might it translate to operational practice? Empirical evidence gathered from Buckinghamshire County Council, where total reward was introduced in 2006, displays evidence of the benefits listed in section 6.7 being realised in practice (Hibberd 2009). The results from this particular study included the following findings:

- Confidence in the leadership of the authority had risen by 21%.
- 80% of staff felt 'well recognised' for the work they did (an increase of 3%).
- Those who felt 'valued' increased by 7%.
- 91% of employees enjoyed being part of a team (a rise of 13%).
- 76% of staff enjoyed working for the Council.

Hibberd (2009) believes that total reward sends a strong message to the workforce. The findings above arguably demonstrate that the organisation in question is perceived to *care* about its employees, which is an important factor when using reward to foster engagement. Hibberd (2009) suggested at a later conference that the public sector needed to communicate the value of total reward in a more effective way in order to retain top talent. Hibberd pointed out that if this could not be done, talented members of staff might be tempted to move to the private sector once it emerged from recession and started to create large numbers of jobs once again.

6.8 REWARD INITIATIVES AND PRACTICES

The focus of this part of the chapter is on specific reward initiatives and practices. In broad terms this territory incorporates:

- grade and pay structures
- job evaluation
- market rate analysis
- 'contingent' reward.

Please do not be put off by the terminology above. The text explains and discusses the concepts in detail in order to convey a detailed understanding of reward initiatives and practices.

6.8.1 GRADE AND PAY STRUCTURES

Grade and pay structures are important parts of reward management. When they are designed properly and fit effectively within the wider context of the organisation, they provide a logical framework within which an organisation's pay policies can be implemented. Grade and pay structures help HR professionals work out where jobs should be placed in a hierarchy, define appropriate pay levels and demonstrate how pay can be progressed over time.

In simple terms, a grade structure is made up of a number of grades, bands or levels into which groups of comparable jobs can be placed. Organisations may choose to operate a single-grade structure into which all jobs are placed, or they may choose to group jobs into job or career 'families'. Either approach can be appropriate: suitability is determined by contextual variables such as the size and complexity of the organisation.

Along similar lines to the thoughts outlined above, a pay structure defines the different levels of pay for jobs or groups of jobs by reference to their relative value to the organisation. Relative value can be determined in a number of ways including job evaluation and market rate analysis (both of these concepts are discussed shortly). As with grade structures, an organisation may decide to implement one pay structure for all employees or it may choose to operate different structures within different occupational groups.

Broadly, there are several different types of grade and pay structures that organisations may choose to operate. The most common are:

- narrow-graded
- broad-graded
- job family
- career family
- pay spines.

As you may imagine narrow-graded structures have many different pay and grade levels (more than 10 and sometimes as many as 18) while broad-graded structures have fewer levels. It is important to understand that within broad-graded structures there may be reference points placed within each grade or level, perhaps splitting each into two or three segments.

By contrast to the approaches above, job family structures seek to group jobs functionally or operationally – in other words, splitting the IT roles from the finance roles or production roles from research roles. Along similar lines, career family structures seek to split roles into different career paths but try to ensure comparability between different families. In other words a 'junior' finance role is pegged at the same level as a 'junior' administration role, and so on.

Armstrong and Taylor (2014) tell us that pay spines are often found in the public sector and in organisations that have adopted a public sector approach to reward management. These systems consist of a number of different pay 'points' extending from the lowest- to the highest-paid positions in an organisation. Increments can be placed at regular intervals – perhaps 2% or 3% of salary – or organisations may choose to widen the gaps between jobs towards the top of the hierarchy. It is very important to understand that there is no 'one best way' to set up a grade or pay structure. An approach that may be appropriate in one organisation may be unworkable in another, and *vice versa*.

6.8.2 JOB EVALUATION

At its most simple, a job evaluation scheme is a systematic process for defining the relative worth or size of jobs within an organisation. The main reason why HR professionals undertake job evaluations is to assess which jobs in an organisation are similar in order to plot their position within grade or pay structures. Job evaluation schemes aim to:

- establish where jobs in an organisation are of similar size or value
- allow for the development of equitable and defendable pay and grade structures
- help practitioners make market comparisons about specific roles
- provide internal transparency to all stakeholders
- ensure that organisations meet equal pay obligations.

Broadly, job evaluation schemes can be either 'analytical' or 'non-analytical'. Analytical job evaluation is by far the more common approach and revolves around analysing specific factors such as competencies and making objective decisions about the relative value of specific roles. Whereas analytical job evaluation seeks to compare and contrast different factors within roles, non-analytical job evaluation seeks to compare whole jobs and place them into a grade or rank order. It is important to understand that non-analytical job evaluation schemes do not meet the requirements of equal value legislation although they can still be useful exercises to broadly assess jobs within an organisation.

Although job evaluation can be a useful method of comparing jobs internally, it is not suitable for making comparisons between organisations. In order to make comparisons of jobs or grades between organisations, a process known as market rate analysis must be used.

6.8.3 MARKET RATE ANALYSIS

It is very important to understand that pay levels within organisations are subject to external as well as internal pressures. Whereas job evaluation schemes can be used to determine internal relativities, HR professionals can only determine external relativities by using a technique called market rate analysis.

Armstrong and Taylor (2014) note that the concept of the market rate is imprecise. They argue that there is no such thing as *the* market rate, and that there are a variety of rates paid by employers even where jobs appear to be identical. Organisations do this for a number of reasons – perhaps a skill shortage in a particular geographical location has pushed up the salary for a particular position, or maybe an organisation has adopted a cost-minimisation model and consequently pays below the market average.

In order to conduct a market rate analysis HR professionals must gather and analyse data related to the salaries and reward packages offered by similar organisations. It is very important to understand that data can often be misleading or incomplete, and HR professionals have to be very careful to make accurate comparisons. When making market comparisons the aim should be to:

- acquire accurate data that correctly details base pay, bonuses and benefits, as was analysed above
- compare like with like – in other words, compare rewards attached to jobs of similar size and importance
- ensure that collected information is up to date
- interpret the information with an eye on the organisation's current needs and circumstances
- collate and present the information in such a way that actions become clear.

6.8.4 CONTINGENT REWARD

At first glance the concept of **contingent reward** looks confusing, but it is essentially focused around two basic questions: what do we value, and what are we prepared to pay for? Armstrong and Taylor (2014) point out that there are many different contingent reward strategies that firms can adopt, including performance-related pay, competence-related pay, skill-based pay and team-based pay. All of these approaches link pay to some form of variable (such as job performance or personal competence) but organisations can take different approaches to the structure of their reward offering.

Most firms that operate some form of contingent reward strategy provide employees with an element of base pay and a bonus related to whatever factor they deem to be important. Within performance-related pay systems this might be individual performance against a set of objectives, whereas within skill-based pay a bonus might be linked to the acquisition of new skills. There are many terms for this bonus element, including 'variable' pay or 'pay at risk'.

Contingent pay systems are popular in organisations because many individuals see them as the best way to motivate people. They assume that linking an element of pay to the achievement of a particular goal will encourage employees to achieve that goal. Having considered the topic of total reward at an earlier point of this chapter, it can be argued that this view of contingent pay is perhaps a little simplistic. Within total reward systems individuals are thought to be motivated by intrinsic factors as well as extrinsic factors. It is important to remember that pay itself is an extrinsic motivator whereas the satisfaction derived from work can often be an intrinsic motivator. HR professionals must ensure that they strike the right balance between extrinsic and intrinsic motivators in their policy frameworks. Additionally, HR professionals must ensure that any system of contingent reward does not discriminate, either directly or indirectly against any particular group of individuals. Considering issues of equal opportunities and diversity when formulating such policies and frameworks will ensure that the resulting pay systems are fair and consistent.

? REFLECTIVE ACTIVITY 6.4

What benefits might contingent reward offer organisations? Do you think the use of contingent reward improves organisational performance?

The reflective activity should have made you think about the applicability of contingent reward. In broad terms it may be argued that contingent reward systems can help to support improved organisational performance because they focus individuals on certain activities and can be used to highlight particularly important goals or targets. But you may think that they are potentially divisive and too subjective in their measurement. Both would be partly true. The use of contingent pay has to be carefully managed and fit with the organisation's goals and culture. The following case study illustrates how an organisation made changes to its contingent reward scheme on the basis that the scheme did not match its strategy.

 NATIONWIDE

CASE STUDY 6.4

Nationwide Building Society operates over 700 branches, within which there are around 450 senior financial consultants (SFCs). They sell many products that are regulated by the Financial Services Authority. The pay and bonus scheme for SFCs required an overhaul for several reasons: it focused on volume rather than value; it was not cost-effective; and it didn't differentiate sufficiently between low and high performers. Because any changes to the reward schemes were contractual, they required full union negotiation. As a result a new total reward package that

met all the outlined criteria was launched four months after the project was started in January 2009. Following a comprehensive communication programme asking SFCs how they should be rewarded, the reward team gained full union support. Staff feedback was also positive. Sales performance in the quarter following launch increased to 184% of target.

Source: *People Management* (2010) CIPD People Management Awards 2010: Performance and reward category. 12 August.

6.9 LINE MANAGERS AND REWARD MANAGEMENT

As with many areas of HR practice, line managers play an important role in reward management systems and processes. Line managers are the individuals who have most contact with employees and are normally responsible for making pay decisions within the frameworks set out by HR professionals. For this reason line managers have a crucial role in maintaining fairness, consistency and transparency across organisations. It is important to understand that these individuals need to be trained in how reward systems work and how decisions should be arrived at.

Towards the beginning of this chapter the fact that reward management consists of both extrinsic factors (such as pay and benefits) and intrinsic factors (such as work itself being meaningful) was highlighted. Line managers have a crucial role to play in enhancing intrinsic rewards and can do it by designing jobs so that employees can feel a sense of purpose at work and by providing praise as and when necessary. Reward management does not revolve solely around monetary pay and benefits, as was shown earlier in this chapter when the concept of total reward was investigated.

Despite the points outlined above, line managers often do not feel involved in reward management – and this can consequently affect employee commitment and engagement. HR professionals must take time to ensure that line managers are consulted about reward management decisions and must make sure that their views are taken into consideration. HR professionals must explain grade and pay structures to line managers and indicate where and when rewards, whether financial or non-financial, might be distributed. If organisations operate some form of contingent pay system, line managers are a vital source of information regarding performance, competence and/or employee skill. Again, it is vital that HR practitioners provide line managers with the necessary training so that they can make objective judgements about relative levels of performance, competence and/or skill – otherwise, final reward decisions may not be consistent or even fair. HR has a responsibility to ensure that line managers do not unfairly discriminate in the distribution of rewards, failing to recognise issues surrounding equality and diversity can quickly erode the psychological contract.

Throughout this chapter it has been shown that reward management is an area of practice that is deeply affected by both external and internal variables, including the business context as a whole, legislative decisions and organisational strategies. If line managers are not supported in making effective reward decisions, reward systems and processes will be redundant. No matter how much thought has gone into grade or pay structures, if line managers do not know how they apply in practical ways, there will be no consistency of reward across the organisation.

6.10 EVALUATING THE IMPACT OF REWARD MANAGEMENT

Organisations must take time to assess the impact of reward management to ensure that strategic decisions are having the desired effect. Evaluation is often an overlooked area but it is important to understand that it need not be a laborious process.

In previous sections it was noted that HR professionals might benchmark their reward strategies or packages against those of their competitors. Although this might be an easier task in public sector environments where information is perhaps more freely available, there are surveys such as those conducted by the CIPD that HR professionals might find useful. By analysing organisational performance against these benchmarks broad trends can be found and reported back to senior managers. In addition to external benchmarks HR professionals can also make use of tools such as staff surveys to attempt to spot any correlations between reward management and both employee commitment and engagement. By examining trends over several surveys HR professionals may be able to highlight the impacts of certain decisions and policies, and produce convincing evidence to support their business cases or proposals.

In addition to the measures outlined above, it is quite possible that HR professionals will be able to link employee performance with reward decisions. By taking time to analyse data emerging from staff appraisals or performance management processes, HR professionals will be able to indicate where specific reward practices are having an impact. Perhaps a team-based bonus might be found to be contributing to more effective team working in a particular department, or perhaps a higher starting salary in another department might have attracted a more skilled workforce. Of course, findings always differ between organisations, but if accurate data is collected, HR professionals should be able to make a judgement about the effectiveness of reward strategies and policies.

 MERIT-BASED PAY VERSUS YEARLY RISES FOR ALL

CASE STUDY 6.5

Please take some time to carefully read through the article from *People Management* presented below, which discusses the idea that organisations prefer 'merit-based' pay increases as opposed to yearly rises for everyone. Once you are happy that you understand the key points from the article, see if you can answer the three questions that appear at the end.

Firms prefer merit-based pay to yearly rises for all

Almost half (46%) of organisations no longer award employees an across-the-board annual rise or cost-of-living adjustment, the Reward Management 2008 survey has revealed. Manufacturing, production and private-sector firms were the least likely to provide such a pay rise. An increasingly popular alternative is to allocate pay budgets to departmental heads to distribute among staff based on their contribution, the survey of 603 organisations found. 'The decline in the yearly traditional pay rise seems to be spreading throughout employment sectors,' said Charles Cotton, CIPD adviser, reward and employment conditions. [. . .]

David Conroy, principal of the human capital business at HR consultancy Mercer, said that 20% of pay deals now have a long-term nature. 'While this helps employers by making planning more predictable, sweeteners are often needed

to overcome union reservations', said Conroy. 'Sometimes there are other benefits bundled in as a way of encouraging the workforce to agree to a deal, such as improvements to annual leave and to maternity and paternity provision,' he said.

Cotton warned that any changes to pay and benefits needed to be effectively communicated by line managers to their teams to avoid leaving staff 'confused, demotivated and in the dark about what they need to do to achieve reward and recognition'.

Paul Ryan, HR operations manager at consumer brands firm Henkel, told PM that across-the-board pay increases in the private sector run counter to the principle of basing rises on merit.

'High-potential staff won't find it motivating if they are told their pay will progress at a mediocre rate whatever they do,' he said. Ryan, who is responsible for compensation and benefits for the company's 1,150 UK staff, added that most people in the private sector were 'conditioned to be more flexible' but admitted that multi-year pay deals might be more commonplace in highly unionised environments.

Meanwhile, unions in the public sector have expressed concern that the government's new longer-term pay deals, which will initially focus on teachers, nurses and the police, may amount to pay cuts in real terms. They have demanded 'escape clauses' if economic conditions change during the three-year period.

Questions

1 Why might firms prefer merit-based pay increases rather than standard annual pay rises for all?

2 Evaluate the role that line managers play in communicating

pay decisions to employees. Why are they such important individuals in this process?

3 In what ways might the external context facing organisations influence decisions related to pay increases?

Source: Phillips, L. (2008) Firms prefer merit-based pay to yearly rises for all. *People Management*. 24 January.

6.11 CONCLUSION

Reward management is a far-reaching subject. There are various theories that underpin the concept and various contextual issues that impact on an organisation's reward decisions. Legislation introduced by the government can influence the approach adopted by an organisation, as can the prevailing culture that exists within the firm. Although there are various methods to determining the practice of reward management inside organisations, HR professionals must ensure that their chosen approach fits with both the wider HR strategy and the organisation's broader goals. Mismatches between strategies and approaches can have significant consequences for employee attraction and retention.

FURTHER READING

ARMSTRONG, M. (2012) *Armstrong's handbook of reward management practice: improving performance through reward*. 4th ed. London: Kogan Page. This is a useful resource which covers both theory and best practice in the reward management field.

CHURCHARD, C. (2010) Reward professionals go 'back to the drawing board'. *People Management*. 23 February. This *People Management* article discusses reward strategies and priorities in the wake of the recent recession.

CHURCHARD, C. (2011) Creative non-cash rewards 'drive key staff behaviours'. *People Management*. 1 November. This *People Management* article discusses how employers might be able to get more value for their money by investing in 'non-cash' rewards.

CIPD (2015) *Reward Management Information Page* [Online]. Available at: www.cipd.co.uk/hr-topics/reward-management.aspx. This website provides factsheets, podcasts and survey reports on the subject of reward management.

E-REWARD (2015) *E-Reward* [Online]. Available at: www.e-reward.co.uk/. This website provides practical guidance, 'top tips' and links to other websites which contain reward management content.

HALL, J. (2012) Hundreds of gold-plated final salary pension schemes close. The *Telegraph*. 31 January. This article discusses the move from final salary to 'defined contribution' pension schemes.

PERKINS, S. and WHITE, G. (2011) *Reward management*. 2nd ed. London: Chartered Institute of Personnel and Development. This CIPD text discusses the overall context of reward management, explores key conceptual frameworks and discusses the various elements of pay- and benefit-setting in detail.

REFERENCES

ARMSTRONG, M. (2002) *Employee reward*. London: Chartered Institute of Personnel and Development.

ARMSTRONG, M. and TAYLOR, S. (2014) *Armstrong's handbook of human resource management practice*. 13th ed. London: Kogan Page.

BBC (2015) UK interest rates held at 0.5% after 8–1 bank vote [Online]. Available at: www.bbc.co.uk/news/business-34473146 [Accessed: 13 November 2015].

BECKER, G (1975) *Human capital: a theoretical and empirical analysis, with special reference to education*. 2nd ed. Chicago: University of Chicago Press.

BROOKS, I., WEATHERSTON, J. and WILKINSON, G. (2011) *The international business environment: challenges and changes*. 2nd ed. Pearson Education Limited: Harlow.

CIPD (2015a) *Strategic reward and total reward*. Factsheet. May. London: Chartered Institute of Personnel and Development.

CIPD (2015b) *Reward management 2014–15*. Annual survey report. London: Chartered Institute of Personnel and Development.

CRONER (2015) *Croner* [Online]. Available at: www.cronersolutions.co.uk [Accessed: 21 July 2015].

HATCHET, A. (2008) Area of high pressure as cold front approaches. *People Management*. 10 January.

HIBBERD, G. (2009) Engage staff through total reward. *Employee Benefits*. 16 January.

HIBBERD, G. (2010) HR column: fiction or reality? *People Management*. 12 August.

IDS (2015) *Thomson Reuters: IDS* [Online]. Available at: www.incomesdata.co.uk [Accessed: 21 July 2015].

LEWIS, D. and SARGEANT, M. (2013) *Employment law*. 12th ed. London: Chartered Institute of Personnel and Development.

PERKINS, S. J. and WHITE, G. (2011) *Reward management*. 2nd ed. London: Chartered Institute of Personnel and Development.

PHILLIPS, L. (2008) Firms prefer merit-based pay to yearly rises for all. *People Management*. 24 January.

TAYLOR, S. (2011) *Contemporary issues in human resource management*. London: Chartered Institute of Personnel and Development.

TORRINGTON, D., HALL, L., TAYLOR, S. and ATKINSON, C. (2014) *Human resource management*. 9th ed. Harlow: Pearson.

WHITE, G. and DRUKER, J. (2008) *Reward management: a critical text*. 2nd ed. London: Routledge.

CHAPTER 7

Human Resource Development

GRAHAM PERKINS

CHAPTER CONTENTS

- Introduction
- What is human resource development?
- The organisational context of HRD
- The links between HRD and corporate strategy
- Engaging stakeholders with HRD
- How people learn
- New technologies and their impact on learning
- The design and delivery of learning events
- Developing a business case for HRD

KEY LEARNING OUTCOMES

By the end of this chapter you should be able to:

- understand and define the concept of human resource development (HRD)
- discuss the organisational context of HRD and how HRD functions are typically structured
- explain how HRD links to both corporate and HRM strategies
- understand the various groups of learning theories and how they inform the development of learning events
- discuss the role of new technologies in facilitating HRD activity, exploring their impact on learning
- understand how learning events can be successfully designed and delivered
- develop effective business cases arguing for investment in HRD activities.

7.1 INTRODUCTION

The core purpose of this chapter is to introduce you to the subject of human resource development (HRD). By encouraging you to think carefully about the role that HR professionals have with respect to the development of their workforces, and subsequently their organisations, this chapter will illuminate key debates and important theories from the HRD field. In order to provide you with a succinct and logical introduction to the subject area, this chapter first defines the term 'HRD' before considering the links between HRD and organisational strategy and how HR professionals might engage others with HRD activity. From a practical perspective, a considerable portion of this chapter is devoted to understanding how people learn, and how HR professionals might be able to apply new technologies within their HRD strategies and learning events. Of course, it is also important to consider the justification and rationale behind HRD activity and, to this end, the chapter will also consider how HR professionals might build business cases to support their HRD plans and strategies.

7.2 WHAT IS HUMAN RESOURCE DEVELOPMENT?

Change is ever present in society and, if anything, the pace of this change appears to have accelerated in recent times. Organisations of all shapes and sizes continue to evolve in many ways with changes occurring to their fundamental strategic goals, sizes, structures and visions. This pace of change has been remarked on by many authors (Brooks et al 2011), with Kempster and Cope (2010) arguing that the business environment is likely to become increasingly competitive and turbulent in the coming years.

In keeping with the theme of change, the HRD function has also itself changed substantially in recent times. There is no longer a focus on 'training' delivered by a 'teacher' (Reid et al 2004), but a wider focus on learning and **continuing professional development**. This change aligns very much with the growing understanding that **human capital**, and the development of that human capital, underpins much of the competitive advantage enjoyed by our organisations (Lawler 2009; Jin et al 2010; Campbell et al 2012). This therefore brings about an increasing focus on learning within the workplace.

Like 'human resource management' as a whole, the term 'human resource development' originated initially in the United States. As is the case with HRM, HRD is generally considered to have a more strategic outlook than previous incarnations of the 'training' or 'learning' function. McGuire (2014) does, however, highlight that there is currently significant debate as to whether HRD should be considered a discipline in its own right, or whether it exists solely as a subset of HRM. While there are many competing definitions of HRD perhaps one of the clearest was produced by Nadler and Nadler (1989, p4), who suggest that HRD is:

> Organized learning experiences provided by employers, within a specified period of time, to bring about the possibility of performance improvement and/or personal growth.

In the same way that debates exist about the nature of HRD, Gold et al (2013) note that this definition is also a source of controversy. This controversy arises because the definition implies that HRD has a dual focus, being responsible for performance improvement on the one hand, whilst also bringing about personal growth on the other. It is important to remember that the first focus of this definition, performance improvement, is associated with what is known as the 'performative' focus for HRD, while the second is relevant to those ascribing to a 'learning' focus (Rigg et al 2007).

While there are undoubtedly many definitions and views of HRD as a concept, a key learning point to take from this introductory discussion is that HRD is not solely concerned with 'training'. While HRD, as a function, is responsible for the provision of 'learning' events inside organisations, its reach extends beyond this, which is why it is important to understand HRD as it is situated within its broader organisational context.

7.3 THE ORGANISATIONAL CONTEXT OF HRD

Previous discussions have noted the changes that have, and continue, to affect organisations and HRD functions in particular. McGuire (2014) argues that organisations must adopt strategic approaches to HRD in order to respond effectively to the challenges posed by globalisation and other rapid changes occurring in the external environment. In short, organisations can be affected by a variety of political, economic, social and technological forces. It is therefore important for HR professionals to be aware of the impact that these can have on businesses of all shapes and sizes and, consequently the impact that these external forces also have on the HRD function.

?   REFLECTIVE ACTIVITY 7.1

Consider an organisation with which you are familiar. What political, economic, social and technological changes can you identify, and how might they impact HRD activities inside that firm?

At a more immediate and local level, organisations can be directly affected by changing consumer demands and tastes, competition from other firms, the general health of the economy (Brooks et al 2011) and, internally, strategic visions, levels of employee engagement and the 'value' that is placed on learning. While the purpose of this chapter is not to consider the strategic context of the organisation, HR professionals must develop an appreciation for how approaches to HRD can be impacted by various factors and issues. For instance, where an organisation's strategy means that a focus is put onto cost minimisation, this will have a consequential impact on the resources that are available for HRD activity. In these situations, HR professionals may have to develop more efficient ways of delivering learning activity, or, alternatively reduce the scope of learning activity. Alternatively, where an organisation places focus on growing its own leaders, the HRD function will be expected to prioritise and implement leadership and management development activity. The key learning point to draw from this is that the organisational context can, and does, have a significant impact on HRD.

7.3.1 HRD IN LARGE AND INTERNATIONAL ORGANISATIONS

Large organisations generally have extensive, sophisticated HRM and HRD functions alongside highly developed policy frameworks. HR professionals must recognise that HRD is fundamentally integrated with other HR activity such as **performance appraisal** and reward (particularly total reward). In large organisations, the HRD function can tap into relevant information flows to better assess **learning needs** and evaluate learning activities through performance data and other key metrics. While large organisations can sometimes be inflexible and slow to change, they also command significant resources and can invest heavily in learning activities. Some large organisations such as Unipart, BAE Systems, McDonald's and Hilton Hotels have developed their own '**corporate universities**', demonstrating their commitment to learning and their desire to invest in HRD activity.

In the public sector, Gold et al (2013) note that austerity measures brought in during 2010 mean that these organisations are under pressure to reduce costs and become more efficient. The drive to reduce costs has led to these organisations reducing the numbers of people that they employ, with functions such as HRD being a particular focus of efficiency measures. This reinforces the need for HRD, as a function, to demonstrate how it adds value to an organisation.

HRD at an international level is well discussed by a number of writers and thinkers including McGuire (2014). He notes that while **multinational organisations** can be structured and controlled in a number of different ways, HRD functions and activities encounter very similar problems. HR professionals must recognise that when operating at an international level issues concerning cultural diversity, language skills, differences in education and institutional frameworks, amongst other factors can affect HRD plans and interventions. In this context we cannot assume that a UK-centric approach will be effective. In other words, we cannot expect to develop HRD events and plans for a UK-based workforce and then apply them indiscriminately across various other contexts. As an example of this, consider a multinational organisation (MNC) with bases in the USA, UK, France and China which is seeking to ensure that all line managers have thorough knowledge of employment law. Employment law in each of these countries is very different; as a result HRD professionals could not develop and implement a 'one size fits all' learning event. Each country would need a tailored learning programme, relevant to their context.

In order to develop effective HRD strategies and interventions at the international level, McGuire (2014) argues that we must:

- understand the audience and their needs
- ensure that learning materials are culturally sensitive
- ensure examples and case studies are appropriate to the cultural context
- think cross-culturally
- ensure compliance with legal frameworks
- create various versions of learning programmes
- test learning programmes before delivery
- use local translators where necessary.

By keeping these points in mind, McGuire (2014) suggests that learning plans and events will be significantly more effective in international organisations.

7.3.2 HRD IN SMALL ORGANISATIONS

Small-medium enterprises (SMEs) are very important to the economy of the United Kingdom. In 2014 the Federation of Small Businesses (FSB) noted that there were 5.2 million SMEs in the UK (FSB 2014). In 2014, these organisations employed 25.2 million people and had a combined turnover of over £3,500 billion. It is important to recognise that SMEs can be very diverse. The term covers every type of business from the very small to the comparatively large, from businesses employing only a handful of people, to those employing up to 250 individuals. For this reason, commentary presented here is necessarily general in nature.

In terms of their approach to HRD, SMEs are generally limited by a range of resource constraints including financial, human and physical (Pissarides et al 2003; Hessels and Parker 2013). Furthermore Beardwell et al (2004) note that a number of factors can impact an SME's approach to HRD including the aforementioned lack of time and money, a lack of previous formal education, concerns about return on investment and, more generally, not knowing where or how to access advice or assistance. Because smaller organisations typically tend to be cash-poor, HRD generally takes a less formal approach in these settings, with employees learning 'on the job' rather than attending formal, external courses. Constraints, however, can also be a spur to creativity and innovation (Mayer 2006), with some SMEs developing highly innovative HRD offerings despite their relative lack of resources.

HR professionals working in SMEs will need to present business relevant arguments for investing in HRD, this is where it becomes important to develop strong business cases for learning activity, covered later in this chapter. An advantage that small organisations have is that they are typically more flexible than their larger counterparts. This means that they can switch strategic direction quickly in order to take advantage of opportunities. HRD strategies must therefore be somewhat fluid, supporting rather than stifling change.

Perhaps a key to success for HRD in small organisations is the accurate assessment of learning needs. Due to these organisations being constrained monetarily, it becomes increasingly important for HR professionals to ensure that their interventions present 'value for money'. It is arguably by targeting specific development 'gaps' with well-defined learning events that HR professionals will maximise the impact of HRD in these settings.

7.3.3 THE HRD FUNCTION

Like HRM as a whole, there are a number of ways in which firms can organise their HRD functions. Most basically, HRD can exist as a central team, combined or separate from the HRM department, providing learning and development services as required. Interestingly, Gold et al (2013) argue that the last decade has seen a shift in the significance of the HRD function. Drawing on Sloman's thoughts about the shift from 'training' to 'learning', they argue that with an increasing emphasis on efficiency, the HRD function is expected to be increasingly organisation and business focused. This increasingly brings change management and **organisational development** (OD) under the remit of the HRD function.

Organisations can also choose to structure their HRD functions in line with the business partner model. As with the idea of the HR business partner, here the HRD function is expected to operate as a partner to the various business units, facilitating change within the organisation. When structured in the form of a business partner, the HRD function becomes responsible for aligning HRD strategy and activity with the organisation's strategy. Gold et al (2013, pp38–9) indicate that under a business partner model, HRD has three sub-functions, including:

- *shared services:* Routine transactional services across the organisation, for example the provision of standard training programmes.
- *centres of excellence:* Small, expert teams with specialist knowledge of cutting-edge HRD solutions, for example knowledge management or mentoring.
- *strategic partners:* HRD professionals working closely with business leaders influencing strategy and steering its implementation.

Some organisations may choose to outsource their HRD functions entirely, purchasing services as and when required. The reasoning behind the decision to outsource can be complex, including issues of cost, competence and capacity. It is important to recognise, however, that while difficulties surrounding administration and operational issues can be overcome relatively easily, it can be much more difficult to overcome issues around strategic integration. This said, an outsourced approach can be appropriate in certain circumstances.

An organisation's approach to the structuring and remit of the HRD function will depend on many factors including its strategic goals, size, sector of operation and purpose. While there is no single best approach, organisations do need to consider the role of the HRD function and how it contributes to the achievement of strategic goals.

? REFLECTIVE ACTIVITY 7.2

Consider an organisation with which you are familiar. How does your chosen organisation structure its HRD function? Do you believe this is an effective approach? Please justify your response.

7.4 THE LINKS BETWEEN HRD AND CORPORATE STRATEGY

Upon first inspection it may appear relatively simple to ensure alignment between HRD and corporate strategy. Organisations first set down their vision and purpose, developing that into a strategy, then HR professionals assess the strategic plan and convert it into a set of policies, including learning and development, to enable the achievement of organisational goals. While this is arguably a somewhat simplistic view, the fundamental mechanics are generally the same irrespective of organisational context. Having said this, research indicates that there can be significant problems translating organisational strategy into HRD plans and activity. Lin et al (2001), for instance, found that almost half of all organisations questioned said that they found it difficult to translate business strategy into a strategy for their training department. Why is this?

Arguably the first reason why it is difficult to translate corporate strategy into an operational HRD strategy and set of activities is that the external context is constantly changing. Consider the changes in technology that have occurred in recent times, or the global recession of 2008, these events have profound impacts on organisations and consequently their strategies. Additionally Reid et al (2004), amongst others, note that organisational cultures, structures and budgets have significant impacts on HRD activity. These are all considerations that can influence the ability of HR professionals to distil corporate strategy into a series of actionable steps and events to enable the achievement of organisational goals.

Turning the core argument somewhat on its head, Stewart and McGoldrick (1996) argue for a different model which allows for a proactive contribution from HRD. They suggest that there can be differences in strategic direction and what was initially planned by top managers and leaders. Stewart and McGoldrick argue that HRD contributes to strategic direction by influencing the shaping of organisational culture, involvement with the development of current and future leaders, building commitment among organisational members and how the organisation anticipates and manages responses to changed conditions. Therefore they argue that HRD is a strategic function as it has a significant impact on the long-term survival of an organisation. This view is supported by others including Fredericks and Stewart (1996), who have argued that there are clear links between organisational structure, organisational strategy and the actions and behaviour of organisational members, together with management styles and the substance of HRD policies and practices. In essence business strategy under this line of thinking is co-created by all organisational **stakeholders**.

In addition to the links with corporate strategy, HR professionals need to consider how HRD strategy links into the broader HRM strategy. Derived from corporate strategy, HRM strategy considers all aspects of people management inside the organisation. Clear links exist between aspects of this strategy, such as issues related to performance appraisal, succession planning and leadership development on the one hand, and HRD on the other. Without thorough consideration, it is unlikely that HRD strategies (and consequently HRD events) will be sufficiently 'in tune' with the broader HRM strategy. If this is the case, HR professionals will struggle to present a unified approach to people management within their organisations.

Importantly, HR professionals must remember that the process of strategy formulation is ongoing and must respond to changes in the external and internal contexts. Where changes occur in corporate strategy, these must feed through to the strategies and operational plans developed for HRM and HRD activity. If this link is broken, HR professionals will very quickly find that their events, plans and interventions are not sufficiently aligned with corporate goals and objectives.

7.5 ENGAGING STAKEHOLDERS WITH HRD

HR professionals must recognise that HRD, as a function, has numerous stakeholders. Without the support of stakeholder groups it is unlikely that HR professionals will secure the necessary resources and commitment needed for HRD activities. The stakeholders that HR professionals need to be aware of include:

- company owners and shareholders
- senior managers/leaders
- middle or line managers
- learners
- customers and suppliers
- trade unions
- government.

By considering the needs and requirements of different stakeholder groups at the planning stage, HR professionals will be able to anticipate reactions to HRD strategies and activities, amending their proposals as necessary. It is important that HR professionals can gain support from powerful stakeholders in order to secure resources for their activities. For example, failing to gain the commitment of senior managers or leaders will inevitably curtail HRD activity, restricting the scope of planned activities. HR professionals must recognise that the various stakeholder groups may, at times, have very different expectations of HRD and it is the role of the HR professional to understand these expectations, ensuring that stakeholders are fully engaged with HRD activity.

While all of the groups mentioned above have a 'stake' in HRD as a whole, HR professionals need to recognise that their expectations may be somewhat different. As an illustration of this, consider the case of an organisation looking to improve its customer service skills by requiring front-line employees to complete a National Vocational Qualification (NVQ) in customer service. Table 7.1 illustrates the different expectations that various stakeholder groups may have in this situation.

Table 7.1 Stakeholder expectations for customer service training

Stakeholder	Possible expectations
Individual employee	Obtain new knowledge and a formal qualification that will aid future employability
Line manager	Raising the skill levels of the department as a whole/improved performance of the team
HR manager	Consistency of learning across team(s) and ensuring an adequate supply of skilled labour for the organisation
Finance department	Achieving a positive financial return on the investment made
Customers	An improved experience when engaging with the organisation
Senior management team	Improved customer satisfaction scores, as evidenced through surveys and industry reports

While all of the stakeholder groups may agree, in this situation, that customer service training would benefit the organisation, Table 7.1 illustrates the differences between their expectations. Individual employees themselves, in other words, the front-line employees undertaking the training, may expect to improve their knowledge levels and gain a formal qualification that will benefit their future employment, either within or outside the organisation. By contrast to this, the senior management team may, logically, expect to see improvements in customer satisfaction scores. While these expectations are undoubtedly linked, there are key differences in emphasis that HRD professionals must be aware of. Without a consideration of stakeholder expectations, HRD events are unlikely to provide an appropriate return on expectation (ROE) (Gold et al 2013), and therefore fail to meet the needs of stakeholder groups.

In order to understand stakeholder expectations, HR professionals should engage relevant groups and individuals early in the process. By working with key groups such as senior managers, learners themselves and trade unions when identifying learning needs and planning learning events, there is a greater likelihood that the resultant learning events will meet stakeholders' expectations. How can this be done?

Initially, HR professionals may choose to interview relevant members of stakeholder groups to understand more about their needs and expectations. In larger organisations, HR professionals may utilise focus groups or other such data-gathering techniques to develop a broad understanding of stakeholder needs. Once this data has been gathered, HR professionals can then develop their learning plans and events. After plans and events have been drafted, HR professionals should gather stakeholder views on their decisions and whether their proposed actions will likely meet the identified expectations. At this stage it is possible to modify learning plans and events in light of stakeholder feedback, thus ensuring that HRD activity is as closely aligned to business and stakeholder needs as possible. After the learning events and activities have concluded, HR professionals should engage with relevant stakeholder groups as part of the evaluation process. Considering the return on expectation (ROE), in other words, the extent to which stakeholder groups feel that their expectations have been met through HRD activity, will enable HR professionals to better evaluate the impact of their learning activities.

7.6 HOW PEOPLE LEARN

In light of the commentary presented so far, it is perhaps easy to lose sight of what is at the core of HRD: learning. If organisations are to grow and develop, it is the individuals connected with them that need to engage with learning experiences (McGuire 2014). Without individual growth and development there can be no organisational growth and development.

Over the past century, or more, various philosophers, academics and practitioners have developed theories as to how individuals learn. These theories can be broadly divided into four categories (Stewart and Rigg 2011).

- *Behaviourist:* Learning as behaviour change or conditioning
- *Cognitivist:* Learning as understanding
- *Constructivist:* Learning as construction or creation of knowledge
- *Social:* Learning as social practice

While learning theories can be grouped into these categories, it is important to recognise that these are not distinct 'groups' as such, but rather points on a continuum.

7.6.1 BEHAVIOURISM

The so-called 'behaviourist' school of thought developed during the early to mid twentieth century. Theorists including Pavlov (1927) and Skinner (1950) argued that learning is a result of reinforcement from an individual's prior experience. Pavlov, one of the earliest proponents of behaviourism, conducted experiments on dogs which suggested that physiological reflexes could be conditioned. Pavlov discovered that he could train a dog to associate food with a ringing bell, so much so that upon ringing the bell the dog would begin to salivate, in expectation of food being given. Skinner (1950) built on this foundation and developed the notion of 'operant conditioning', which operates from the premise that learning can be enhanced by rewarding good performance and punishing bad performance. As a result of this the underlying purpose of behaviourist learning practices is to adapt behaviour in a particular direction to serve a specific purpose. Stewart and Rigg (2011, p144) note that there are four key principles to behaviourism. These are as follows:

1 Observable changed behaviour is the sign that learning has occurred.

2 Learning is triggered by external stimulus from the environment. This could be the prospect of promotion or the threat of redundancy.

3 Repetition: On the grounds that 'practice makes perfect', repeated stimulus is given to produce the desired response.

4 Reinforcement of new behaviours is necessary to establish them as new habits; for example, by positive reinforcers such as performance-related financial reward, a manager's praise, kudos with colleagues, or a personal sense of achievement. Negative reinforcers can also produce a learned response; for example, through personal sense of embarrassment at making a mistake or negative customer feedback.

To illustrate this, consider an organisation that is attempting to ensure employee knowledge of health and safety processes. Recognising that previous learning events have not been successful due to employee apathy and disengagement, the HR Manager decides to offer a £100 reward for each employee obtaining a 100% result for the final test. As a result of offering this positive reinforcement, the tutor notes that individuals are substantially more engaged during classroom discussions, they appear keen to learn and do well. Following the test, the HR Manager finds that that the average mark has risen by 15% across the group, with a number of employees successfully achieving the 100% goal.

A key advantage of behaviourism is therefore the belief that learning events can be standardised. Additionally, the outputs of learning events built from behaviourist principles can be clearly measured and this can arguably save an organisation both time and money in the design and administration of such programs. Supporters of behaviourist learning theories also argue that learning occurs rapidly under such conditions, and that this is a useful approach for instructing individuals in basic tasks. Critics of behaviourist theories counter these advantages by arguing that the approach tends to assume that everyone has the same learning capacity. Essentially behaviourist learning theories argue that individuals can be 'programmed'.

7.6.2 COGNITIVISM

Appearing somewhat more recently than behaviourism, cognitivism seeks to explore patterns rather than specific events in order to understand how individuals learn. Key advocates of cognitivist learning theories include Piaget (1950) and Bruner (1961), who argue that cognitivist learning theories seek to go beyond behaviour by attempting to explain how internal memory processes work to promote learning. Stewart and Rigg (2011, p145) define these theories as those which 'view learning as the mental processing of new pieces of information into existing knowledge through assimilation and accommodation'. As a result of this, cognitivism is therefore based on two key assumptions:

1 The memory system is an active organised processor of information.

2 Prior knowledge plays an important role in learning.

Those promoting cognitivist learning theories argue that they are beneficial because they take into consideration the differing mental approaches and abilities that individuals have. They argue that this in turn means that HRD professionals can ensure that there is a consistent approach to learning across a group. Drawbacks to cognitivist learning theories include, as with behaviourism, the HRD professional (or other nominated facilitator) still playing a central role in the learning process. Additionally, it has been argued that cognitivist approaches to learning can lack practical application.

An example of a cognitivist learning technique would be the use of a problem-solving task within a learning session; this could be connected to a case study or a role-play exercise. Suppose a learning session seeks to develop the skills associated with project management. Following an explanation of core principles and key theories, the facilitator then presents the learners with a case study depicting a situation in which a project has encountered some sort of problem or issue. Allowing the learners to work through and solve the problem, with guidance where necessary, means that they can apply their new knowledge individually, testing out ideas and processing the information that they have been given.

7.6.3 CONSTRUCTIVISM

Unlike behaviourism and cognitivism, the key principle underlying constructivism is that individuals 'construct' personal meaning through a process of integrating new ideas and experiences with what they already know (Stewart and Rigg 2011). As a result of this, learning events built around constructivist principles may include active elements such as discovery or action learning and knowledge building. Learning under constructivism is inherently centred on the individual and open in its approach. In other words, there is no defined 'start' or 'end' to the learning process. Due to the fact that learners may approach subjects with differing perspectives, constructivist learning may have multiple outcomes.

Given the points expressed above, it is important to understand that the learning provider under constructivist methods takes on the role of 'facilitator' rather than 'tutor' or 'teacher'. Whereas behaviourist methods, in particular, require the classic 'teacher–student' relationship, leading constructivist learning events requires the use of different skills. Under constructivism, learning providers must be able to set the stage for learning and encourage the learner to interpret and construct from within. As a result of this, constructivist learning events may incorporate activities such as reflective discussion sessions or problem-solving activities.

The keeping of a reflective log or journal is a good example of constructionist learning. While a facilitator may provide some initial guidance on the practice of reflective writing or how such a log could be structured, each individual will inevitably produce a very different final 'product'. This is a very personal process, with no defined 'answer'; the quality of learning is determined by the level of engagement with the task rather than the skill and ability of the facilitator themselves.

An advantage of constructivist learning methods is that they place learners at the heart of the learning process, enabling individuals to apply new learning quickly, encouraging creativity and innovation as a result. Having said this, placing the learner at the heart of the process can mean that learning is inconsistent across a group of individuals, causing any subsequent assessment of knowledge or skill to be, potentially, unreasonably positive or negative.

7.6.4 SOCIAL AND SITUATIONAL LEARNING

Championed by individuals such as Bandura (1977), Lave and Wenger (1998) and Sadler-Smith (2006), social and situational theories emphasise the social aspects of the learning process. Stewart and Rigg (2011) highlight that social learning theories argue that individuals give meaning to new ideas and understandings through their dialogue with others. Along similar lines, situational learning is thought to be built around individuals participating in 'communities of practice', making use of shared resources. An example of this could be HR professionals meeting together after a CIPD branch event to share their experiences of managing redundancy processes or performance appraisal meetings.

Due to their very nature, it is argued that learning under social and situational theories is very easily transferred between contexts. This ease of learning transfer is born from the way in which these forms of learning assist individuals in developing complex, situation-specific knowledge. On the other side of the debate, critics argue that social and situational learning lacks transferability and that it can be very difficult to measure the outcome of these learning events. Critics therefore argue that social and situational learning theories are unsuitable in many contexts.

Picking up on an important idea introduced at the start of this section, HR professionals must recognise that these groups of learning theories exist along a continuum. This continuum of learning theories is shown in Figure 7.1.

Figure 7.1 A continuum of learning theories

While behaviourist and cognitivist learning theories are considered more formal in nature, constructivist and, to an even greater extent, social and situational theories are considered to be more informal. The approach that HR professionals adopt for their learning events will inevitably vary depending on the type of content that is to be delivered and the desired learning outcomes. While some learning events may call for an approach rooted in behaviourist traditions, others may require a different theoretical approach.

7.7 NEW TECHNOLOGIES AND THEIR IMPACT ON LEARNING

The evolution of new technology is certainly impressive with organisations such as Apple, Google and Facebook introducing a wealth of new products and services that can support learning activity. The advent of technology such as the Internet and, increasingly, social media platforms, provides significant opportunities for HR professionals, although 'technology' must not be seen as a catch-all solution for HRD.

Utilising technology within HRD activities certainly offers significant advantages. In an era where more and more learning activity is delivered through a 'just in time' philosophy, with learners able to engage in self-directed learning activity, at a time and place that suits them, making best use of technological systems is vital. Having said this, however, the CIPD's (2013) *Learning and Talent Development* survey reported that while nearly three-quarters of organisations use some form of **e-learning**, only 15% of respondents reported that it was one of the 'most effective' learning practices available. In commenting on the report, Dr John McGurk (CIPD 2013) suggested that organisations were not taking full advantage of the flexibility that e-learning offers. He suggested that participant completion rates on e-learning courses were low and that there were also low take-up rates in the use of mobile learning packages.

Despite the arguably rather troubling statistics noted above, it is important to recognise that technology can help HRD activity to be delivered in a timely and efficient manner. By developing bespoke e-learning programmes organisations can quickly deliver learning content to employees, saving both the time and costs associated with traditional classroom-based activity. Additionally, by enabling individuals to access learning 'on demand' it can be argued that engagement with learning should, theoretically, be maximised. Furthermore, technology can assist not only in the delivery of HRD events, but in the assessment of learning needs and the evaluation of HRD activity. In large organisations operating over many dispersed sites, utilising technology such as online appraisals and learning records will enable HR professionals to efficiently identify learning needs and, thus, target their HRD activity more effectively. Similarly, HR professionals could develop online questionnaires to gather data about the effectiveness of learning events and utilise electronic development records and performance data to assess the outcomes of learning events.

Perhaps the key point, however, is that technology must not be seen as the solution in and of itself. Technology can be a facilitator for HRD, but HR professionals must not assume that investing in technological systems will be the solution for all situations. Sadler-Smith (2006) reinforces this point emphasising that HR professionals should not force technology upon learners and other stakeholders without appropriate support. He further notes that differences in learning styles may mean that while some individuals engage effectively with e-learning methods, other individuals may prefer more traditional approaches. In each case, the choice of approach has to be carefully thought through, with HR professionals ensuring that there is a fit between learning content and the method of delivery. The following case study provides an example of where technology was effectively utilised to support HRD activity.

 MET POLICE EMBRACES INTERACTIVE TRAINING TECHNOLOGY

CASE STUDY 7.1

The Metropolitan Police Service (MPS) has revolutionised constable foundation training with its immersive L&D project, Hydra, delegates at the CIPD's HRD conference were told.

The interactive project, which blends IT with traditional training methods, has cut classroom-based training time from 30 days per student to 15, without compromising on quality. Classroom sessions are now running at 90 per cent capacity, where previously they had been 60 per cent full, making training more economical and requiring fewer staff.

The project consists of groups of students placed in 'pods' where they view a scenario of a potential situation they may come across and respond by recording real-time decisions as the setting develops. Panoramic 360-degree scenarios are provided and students can interact by moving objects and exploring the scene.

Liz Wells, police sergeant at MPS and head of the Hydra development and support team, said it caters for the next generation of officers who are more aware of technology.

'It's a radical change in the way training is delivered,' she said. 'It's a cost-effective programme that allows officers to reach their full potential while

challenging underlying beliefs and values.'

The project was introduced in an attempt to move away from the 'spoon-fed, tick-box culture' of exams and to focus on real-life assessment and students' previous experience, she said.

Trainers also control the scenario and monitor the students' reactions with audio and video equipment remotely with data logged on a computer. The groups then combine to reflect and discuss the scenario while the trainer reinforces key learning points.

The scenarios allow students to view the situation in a broader sense and 'enables students to not only think about the legislation and what it means, but to realise the impact on the community, the person breaking the law and why they are doing it,' added Wells.

'It was an intensive programme to build – there were scripts, storyboards, audio recording and filming, plus other different processes. It was initially costly but is now more efficient and the training continues to be at a high level,' she said.

Source: Booth (2010) HRD 2010: Met policy embraces interactive training technology. *People Management*. 23 April.

What is clear from the ideas presented in this section is that while technology is advancing very rapidly, providing HR professionals with considerable opportunities, care must still be taken in the design and planning of learning events. Technology must not be seen as an answer to all HRD related problems, with e-learning solutions applied even when they are not best suited to the given situation or problem. Applied properly, however, technology can facilitate HRD activity, enabling HR professionals to deliver learning events more efficiently and effectively than before.

7.8 THE DESIGN AND DELIVERY OF LEARNING EVENTS

While the design and delivery of learning events is undoubtedly a large topic in its own right, and would require much more space than is available here to explain thoroughly, this chapter can introduce you to some core ideas and components of learning events. HR professionals must recognise that even though learning events can be incredibly different and diverse, they are essentially built from the same foundations. In general all learning events will include:

- an assessment of the core learning need
- development and agreement of purpose and objectives
- planning and implementation of the learning event
- evaluation of the learning intervention.

7.8.1 ASSESSING LEARNING NEEDS

Developing and delivering learning events without first assessing the underlying need is problematic. Brown (2002) highlights that without first establishing needs and priorities, learning events will likely be rendered meaningless. By assessing learning needs and framing events around the identified development gaps, HR professionals will be better able to target their resources and avoid any potential duplication of input. Stewart and Rigg (2011) note that learning events can exist at a number of separate, but linked, levels including the individual, the department/team and the organisation.

Learning needs existing at the organisational level can result from changes in strategic decisions, such as the desire to develop a new product or service. In order to understand learning needs at this level Stewart and Rigg (2011) suggest that HR professionals can total up the respective department/team and individual learning needs to arrive at an organisation-wide assessment. Learning needs existing at the team or department level can be established in much the same way. HR professionals can sum together the respective individual learning needs, arriving at a total for the given group of individuals. Having said this, HR professionals also need to keep any changes in team priorities, outputs and workflows in mind in order to ensure that future skill and knowledge requirements are addressed.

At the level of the individual, a number of authors have discussed the identification of learning needs (Reid et al 2004; Sadler-Smith 2006; Harrison 2009). In essence, learning needs will concern the requirement to develop one or more of the following:

- knowledge
- skill
- attitude.

A key task for HR professionals is to establish, with a good level of certainty, the nature of the 'development' gap and in order to do this a number of tools are available. Depending on the situation, HR professionals may look to utilise performance appraisal data, key task analysis, competency-based analysis and information contained in job descriptions and person specifications in order to identify learning needs. Irrespective of the chosen method, HR professionals need to understand the existing state of skills, knowledge and attitudes and the desired state of skills, knowledge and attitudes. By plotting the difference between the two, HR professionals will identify the state of the 'development gap', and will then be able to accurately target their subsequent learning and development resources.

7.8.2 AGREEING PURPOSE AND OBJECTIVES

Once an assessment of the core learning need has been completed, HR professionals must turn attention to the precise purpose of the learning event. While *objectives* focus specifically on the expected outcomes from learning, *purpose* explores the reason why the learning event is taking place (Harrison 2009). While, as explained previously in this chapter, stakeholder engagement is key to effective HRD, it is perhaps here where stakeholder needs and expectations come into sharpest relief. In order to identify firstly an appropriate purpose, and subsequently clear objectives, HR professionals need to work closely with relevant stakeholder groups including trade unions, line managers, senior managers and, perhaps most importantly employees themselves.

In order to develop clear, unambiguous objectives, which assist the planning and subsequent evaluation of learning events, Reid et al (2004) argue that HR professionals must consider the following:

- The behaviour/knowledge/skill that the learner is required to demonstrate.
- Important conditions in which the behaviour/knowledge/skill must be demonstrated.
- The standard to which the learner must perform.

Effective learning objectives will be very specific in their nature. It is arguably through the development of these very specific goals for the learning event that HR professionals will be able to ensure the efficacy of their plans. Indeed noted writers within the HRD field such as Gold et al (2013) and Sadler-Smith (2006), argue that without proper objectives, it is very difficult to evaluate the HRD contribution. Generally speaking effective objectives will follow the **SMART** model. In other words objectives must be:

- Specific
- Measurable
- Achievable
- Realistic
- Time bound.

An example of such an objective developed under the SMART method is:

Upon completion of this learning event, participants will understand the principles by which food safety is maintained in Company XYZ's manufacturing facility, and be able to correctly identify safety critical areas on the main production line.

It can certainly be argued that this objective is time bound, realistic and specific. HR professionals could additionally measure the results, potentially by testing whether participants could identify the 'safety critical areas on the main production line'. While more information would be required to determine if the objective was 'achievable', it could certainly be argued that this objective would not be unreasonable as an outcome of a learning event in a food manufacturing facility.

7.8.3 PLANNING AND IMPLEMENTING LEARNING EVENTS

It is widely known that poor planning can significantly impede the effectiveness of HRD events (Sadler-Smith 2006). Once a need has been identified, and appropriate objectives formulated, HR professionals must think carefully about the physical planning and delivery process. Keeping in mind the learning theories covered earlier, HR professionals must consider what they (or another nominated individual) will deliver, and the methods through which information will be passed. As noted earlier in this chapter, some learning events will need to take a 'behaviourist' stance, while others may benefit from the application of social or situational learning theories.

Additionally, there are a number of methods or techniques which HR professionals may need to consider. Some situations may call for lecture-style delivery, while in other instances HR professionals may want to incorporate the use of case study material or role-play activities. Other potentially beneficial methods may include the application of coaching or mentoring techniques and other, less formal learning methods such as work shadowing may also be appropriate in some situations. In all cases, HR professionals must ensure that their chosen delivery method suits both the content that has been identified, the specific learning needs and, perhaps most importantly, the demographics of their audience, as evidenced in the following case study.

CASE STUDY 7.2

MOCK TUBE STATION GIVES LONDON UNDERGROUND STAFF REAL-LIFE TRAINING

A new mock tube station has revolutionised training at London Underground, giving staff preparation for a range of real-life situations before going out into the field.

The simulation suite – a fake station called West Ashfield – is being used to train new London Underground (LU) drivers, gate operators and apprentices, and to retrain staff moving between operational fields. Opened in October at a cost of £800,000, it is anticipated that 20,000 people will use the facility in its first five years.

'Normally we would have to close a tube line on a Sunday for an evacuation exercise, but there is no impact on the front-line railway when training in this way,' said Jim Sitch, LU's development manager, operational learning. 'We have replicated an arena that does everything we do on the front line, and makes staff

much more confident about dealing with a live situation.'

The centre, in Kensington, includes a station platform with a PA system, a tube carriage complete with a driver's cab and a station entrance with an Oyster card reader. A signal training room equipped with a sophisticated model railway and signalling system operates in conjunction with a control room next door. The different room components at the suite are all interactive in order to create authentic scenarios.

Kevin Hafter, head of operational learning at LU, told PM that the centre allowed a move away from traditional classroom teaching to practical training that did not have to either take place out of office hours or involve a disruption to the tube service.

'Hands-on experience is an integral part of training to equip staff with the skills and confidence they need. With simulations we can replicate the pressure of a real workplace and the need to respond quickly, safely and confidently to a situation. We can really test and refine skills,' Hafter said.

Source: Stevens, M. (2010) Mock tube station gives London Underground staff real-life training. *People Management*. 18 January.

? REFLECTIVE ACTIVITY 7.4

What reasons would London Underground have for utilising this sort of practical approach to learning? How could they justify the cost of such a programme?

From a more practical perspective, Reid et al (2004) point out that HR professionals must consider the timetabling of activities whilst also ensuring that the learning 'spaces' are appropriate. In other words are there sufficient tables and chairs? Is the lighting and ventilation adequate? Do any necessary IT systems work properly? These may appear minor considerations, but they can significantly impact the level of learning, and learning transfer that occurs. In many learning situations, HR professionals will require participants to undertake some form of pre-reading or preparation for a learning event. Any such preparatory work must be communicated clearly, and in good time, thus ensuring that all participants in the learning event are properly prepared and briefed (Harrison 2009).

When implementing learning events, HR professionals must ensure that information is conveyed as clearly as possible, effective presentation skills are therefore vital. Information must be pitched at a level that is appropriate to the audience, and the individuals delivering the learning event should allow time for questions and clarification. It is also good practice to demonstrate how the learning content links directly with operational roles and responsibilities to ensure that learning transfer (that is, that participants can apply learning in the workplace) takes place. Without the ability to transfer learning to the workplace, resources invested into HRD activities will inevitably show a poor return on investment.

7.8.4 EVALUATING THE LEARNING EVENT

The evaluation of learning events can take many forms, and should be considered during the development of the learning event. It is at that stage where formal objectives are set which HR professionals can subsequently evaluate their interventions against. The CIPD (2015) highlight the following ways of evaluating learning and development events:

- 'Happy sheets' – that is, post-training questionnaires asking course participants to rate how satisfied they feel with the standard of provision.
- Testimonies of individuals and direct observation.
- Return on expected outcomes (for example, whether line managers testify during performance reviews that individuals are able to demonstrate those new or enhanced competencies that the learning intervention was anticipated to deliver).
- The impact on business key performance indicators.
- Return on investment (the financial or economic benefit that is attributable to the learning intervention in relation to the cost of the investment in learning programmes).
- Development metrics (such as psychometrics or 360-degree feedback).
- Quantitative survey methods to assess behaviour change.

HR professionals must recognise that without evaluation there is no basis for knowing how successful a learning event was. A number of commentators within the HRD field have made this observation including Reid et al (2004), Sadler-Smith (2006), Harrison (2009) and McGuire (2014). While the choice of specific evaluation methods will depend on a number of factors including the underlying purpose of the learning event, the reason that evaluation is required and the identified learning needs, all learning events must include some form of evaluation. One of the most popular frameworks through which HR professionals evaluate learning events is the Kirkpatrick framework (Kirkpatrick 1959).

Figure 7.2 The Kirkpatrick evaluation framework

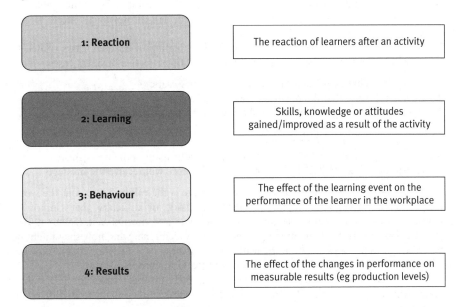

As shown in Figure 7.2, the Kirkpatrick evaluation framework contains four distinct levels: reaction, learning, behaviour and results. The most basic of these, reaction, essentially seeks to gauge opinion of a learning event from the participants, in other words what was their 'reaction' to the learning input? A little more deeply than this, the second level, learning, seeks to understand whether the required skills, knowledge or attitudes have been modified by the learning event. In other words, has the learning event successfully brought about the anticipated changes? Stewart and Rigg (2011) argue that this is where most evaluative activities stop. Organisations and HR professionals, constrained by a lack of resources, often do not have the ability to evaluate learning events in any more detail than this. Kirkpatrick (1959), however, details two further, deeper levels to which the evaluation of HRD activities can theoretically go.

At level three, behaviour, HR professionals are seeking to understand the extent to which learning has transferred to the workplace. This can be done by observing on-the-job behaviour or examining performance appraisal data for signs of change. Finally, at level four, results, HR professionals are seeking to assess the impact that learning activities have had on key organisational metrics, such as customer satisfaction scores, employee productivity or potential profitability. By making connections at this level, HR professionals will be able to demonstrate the impact of HRD activities and identify the effect that their interventions have had on the organisation as a whole. In order to evaluate at levels three and four, ie the deeper parts of the Kirkpatrick framework, Sadler-

Smith (2006) argues that HR professionals must ensure that learning interventions are designed with the key strategic goals of the organisation in mind.

7.9 DEVELOPING A BUSINESS CASE FOR HRD

The contents of business cases will vary depending on the size of a given organisation, to whom the case is being presented and the scale of potential costs. Where HR professionals are seeking large-scale investment in HRD activity, it is likely that relevant stakeholders, such as senior managers, will expect significant justification. A key aspect that HR professionals need to consider when formulating their business cases for HRD is the balancing of costs and benefits. As the benefits of HRD can sometimes be intangible, for instance, how can 'better' management be quantified, HR professionals need to put forward convincing justifications for the plans.

Taylor (2010) provides very useful tips for the formulation of business cases related to HR activity. He argues that there are several keys to writing effective business cases:

- *Think bigger:* What does the proposal do for the organisation?
- *Don't go on:* Ensure that the business case is concise
- *Start with what you want:* Be explicit about what the proposal calls for
- *Cut the HR speak:* Avoid jargon
- *Think heart, not just head:* Show enthusiasm, not just a logical case for the argument
- *Talk about the worst thing:* What problems might your plans come up against?
- *When will they read it?:* Think about how your audience will receive the message

Arguably the most interesting point in the list above is the call to 'talk about the worst thing'. Generally when encountering a significant issue or difficulty that cannot be obviously addressed, a natural reaction is to either avoid or downplay it. Taylor (2010) argues the opposite. Instead, opening up to possible problems, showing how they might be dealt with, communicates an honesty within the business case (Taylor 2010), showing stakeholders that significant thought has been devoted to the proposed plan.

Above all, HR professionals should ensure that their business cases for HRD align strongly with corporate and HR strategy. Without strategic alignment, it is difficult to demonstrate how investment in HRD activity will benefit an organisation or enable it to achieve its stated goals.

 HRD AT ABC INDUSTRIES

CASE STUDY 7.3

Angela is the Human Resources Manager at ABC Industries, a firm that operates in the manufacturing sector, producing all manner of industrial piping and water distribution systems for organisations around the UK. Starting in 1964, ABC has gradually developed itself over the decades, growing organically and by taking over competing firms. It now employs close to 825 individuals at bases in Glasgow, Sheffield, Harlow and its head office in Cardiff. In the main, employees work on the various production lines although a large number of engineers work remotely at customer sites. In short, ABC operates with a relatively dispersed workforce, with effective communication sometimes proving somewhat of a problem for the firm.

As part of her remit, Angela is responsible for all Human Resource Development activity within the organisation. She drafts the 'learning strategy' and, with the help of her team, designs, delivers and evaluates learning activity. One problem that the team have found it very hard to deal with is the fact that when they ask employees about their reactions to learning events, a number say 'well, I already knew that' or 'that was a complete waste of time'. Nigel, the Chief Executive, is becoming increasingly frustrated with this and has said that he will soon stop funding learning activity if something is not done about it. For their part, Angela and the HR team feel that the problem lies with the managers. The HR team ask managers to nominate employees for learning events, working from the assumption that the managers work with employees most closely, and therefore know what knowledge or skills are lacking. This approach, however, appears not to be working.

Angela has also found that key line managers within the organisation, Sally, Geoff and Gordon, who each run sizeable teams, have become increasingly hostile to learning activity. In the past, all three were passionate supporters of HRD events within ABC Industries, but recently Angela has found that they have been obstructive and refuse to let members of their teams attend events. Despite attempts to 'smooth the ground' with all three, Angela has found that they have become increasingly difficult to deal with, accusing her of not 'putting the business first'. Understandably Angela is concerned by the situation and wants to resolve things amicably to ensure continued support for HRD activity inside the firm.

In the recent past, Angela and her team attended an external event run by the CIPD looking into how technology can support learning activity inside organisations. During the event they listened to various speakers, including one talking about the benefits of delivering content through an online portal. This immediately piqued Angela's interest as she had often found difficulty in delivering learning events on budget, as facilitator fees and the cost of booking suitable locations had increased dramatically in recent times. As she listened intently to the speaker, she felt that an online solution would be considerably more cost-effective, given the dispersed nature of ABC's workforce. Having said this, she knew that it would be a challenge to convince Nigel as to the benefits of such an approach.

Questions

1   Why is it important to have an accurate understanding of learning needs? In what ways do you think Angela and the HR team could better assess learning needs within ABC Industries?

2   Please list the stakeholder groups that are mentioned in the case study.

  (a) What expectations would each group have from HRD activity?

  (b) How would Angela better engage the line managers mentioned?

3   What advantages and disadvantages would there be to introducing an online learning system at ABC Industries? How might Angela develop a business case to support her idea?

7.10 CONCLUSION

Human resource development is becoming an increasingly important topic for organisations of all shapes and sizes. With organisational and environmental change occurring at a faster pace, the development of human capital is vital to the continuing success of all firms. While it may be a contested domain, there is recognition that HRD involves bringing about learning experiences which improve performance and allow for personal growth. By considering the strategic alignment of HRD activity, HR professionals will best align this learning activity with corporate goals and objectives.

It is known that individuals learn in different ways and this must be taken into account during the design and delivery of learning events. HR professionals who do not consider the situational and human context of learning, failing to adapt their learning approaches as necessary, will struggle to achieve their ultimate goals. While technological changes do provide for opportunities within HRD, 'technology' must not be seen as a catch-all solution for learning events. The very best HRD plans and interventions will carefully consider stakeholder expectations, be aligned with corporate and HR strategy and be designed in such a way that learners engage effectively with the content presented.

FURTHER READING

ACADEMY OF HUMAN RESOURCE DEVELOPMENT (2015) *Academy of human resource development* [Online]. Available at: www.ahrd.org/. A useful website which includes links to various HRD journals, webcasts and HRD related events.

CIPD (2015) *Learning and development survey* [Online]. Available at: www.cipd.co.uk/research/learning-development-survey.aspx. Includes coverage of the latest CIPD learning and development survey.

CIPD (2015) *Learning and development: HR topic page* [Online]. Available at: www.cipd.co.uk/hr-topics/learning-development.aspx. This area of the CIPD site provides access to various research reports, factsheets and policy reports related to HRD.

CLEGG, A. (2014) L&D leaders urged to embrace technology at CIPD roundtable. *People Management* [Online]. Available at: www.cipd.co.uk/pm/peoplemanagement/b/weblog/archive/2014/07/19/l-amp-d-leaders-urged-to-embrace-technology-at-cipd-roundtable.aspx. An interesting article in which the future of technology in HRD, and the need for HR professionals to get up to speed with new technologies is debated

GOLD, J., HOLDEN, R., STEWART, J., ILES, P. and BEARDWELL, J. (2013) *Human resource development: theory and practice.* 2nd ed. Basingstoke: Palgrave Macmillan. A useful resource which covers a range of debates and theories within the HRD field including learning theories and strategic HRD.

MCGUIRE, D. (2014) *Human resource development.* 2nd ed. London: Sage. A comprehensive textbook which covers a range of issues and debates within the HRD field, looking specifically at HRD at individual, organisational and societal levels.

REFERENCES

BANDURA, A. (1977) *Social learning theory.* New York: General Learning Press.

BEARDWELL, I., HOLDEN, L. and CLAYDON, T. (2004) *Human resource management: a contemporary approach.* 4th ed. Harlow: FT/Prentice Hall.

BOOTH (2010) HRD 2010: Met policy embraces interactive training technology. *People Management.* 23 April.

BROOKS, I., WEATHERSTON, J. and WILKINSON, G. (2011) *The international business environment: challenges and changes.* 2nd ed. Harlow: Pearson Education Limited.

BROWN, J. (2002) Training needs assessment: a must for developing an effective training program. *Public Personnel Management.* Vol 31, No 4. pp569–78.

BRUNER, J. S. (1961) The act of discovery. *Harvard Educational Review.* Vol 31, No 1. pp21–32.

CAMPBELL, B. A., COFF, R. and KRYSCYNSKI, D. (2012) Rethinking sustained competitive advantage from human capital. *Academy of Management Review.* Vol 37, No 1. pp376–95.

CIPD (2013) *Learning and talent development: annual survey report 2013.* London: CIPD.

CIPD (2013) *UK businesses are yet to realise the full potential of modern technology to develop their workforce* [Online]. Available at: www.cipd.co.uk/pressoffice/press-releases/uk-businesses-full-potential-modern-technology-develop-workforce-240413.aspx [Accessed 29 September 2015].

CIPD (2015) *Evaluating learning and development.* CIPD Factsheet: April 2015. London: CIPD.

FEDERATION OF SMALL BUSINESSES (2014) *Small business statistics* [Online]. Available at: www.fsb.org.uk/stats [Accessed 29 September 2015].

FREDERICKS, J. and STEWART, J. (1996) The strategy-HRD connection. In: STEWART, J. and MCGOLDRICK, J. (eds). *Human resource development: perspectives, strategies and practice.* London: Pitman.

GOLD, J., HOLDEN, R., STEWART, J., ILES, P. and BEARDWELL, J. (2013) *Human resource development: theory and practice.* 2nd ed. London: CIPD.

HARRISON, R. (2009) *Learning and development.* 5th ed. London: CIPD.

HESSELS, J. and PARKER, S. C. (2013) Constraints, internationalization and growth: a cross-country analysis of European SMEs. *Journal of World Business.* Vol 48, No 1. pp137–48.

JIN, Y., HOPKINS, M. M. and WITTMER, J. L. S. (2010) Linking human capital to competitive advantages: flexibility in a manufacturing firm's supply chain. *Human Resource Management.* Vol 49, No 5. pp939–63.

KEMPSTER, S. and COPE, J. (2010) Learning to lead in the entrepreneurial context. *International Journal of Entrepreneurial Behaviour and Research.* Vol 16, No 1. pp5–34.

KIRKPATRICK, D. (1959) Techniques for evaluating training programs. *Journal of the American Society of Training Directors.* November 1959.

LAVE, J. and WENGER, E. (1998) *Communities of practice: learning, meaning, and identity.* Cambridge: Cambridge University Press.

LAWLER, E. E. (2009) Make human capital a source of competitive advantage. *Organizational Dynamics.* Vol 38, No 1. pp1–7.

LIN, J., HITCHENS, S. and DAVENPORT, T. O. (2001) Fast learning: aligning learning and development with business strategies. *Employment Relations Today.* Autumn 2001. pp43–57.

MAYER, M. A. (2006) Creativity loves constraints. *Business Week.* Issue 3971. p102.

MCGUIRE, D. (2014) *Human resource development.* 2nd ed. London: Sage.

NADLER, L. and NADLER, Z. (1989) *Developing human resources.* Jossey-Bass, CA: San Francisco.

PAVLOV, I. P. (1927) *Conditioned reflexes: an investigation of the physiological activity of the cerebral cortex.* Oxford: Oxford University Press.

PIAGET, J. (1950) *The psychology of intelligence.* New York: Routledge.

PISSARIDES, F., SINGER, M. and SVEJNAR, J. (2003) Objectives and constraints of entrepreneurs: evidence from small and medium size enterprises in Russia and Bulgaria. *Journal of Comparative Economics.* Vol 31, No 3. pp503–31.

REID, M. A., BARRINGTON, H. and BROWN, M. (2004) *Human resource development: beyond training interventions.* 7th ed. London: CIPD.

RIGG, C., STEWART, J. and TREHAN, K. (2007) *Critical human resource development: beyond orthodoxy.* Harlow: FT/Pearson Education Limited.

SADLER-SMITH, E. (2006) *Learning and development for managers.* Oxford: Blackwell Publishing.

SKINNER, B.F. (1950). Are theories of learning necessary? *Psychological Review.* Vol 57, No 4. pp193–216.

STEVENS, M. (2010) Mock tube station gives London Underground staff real-life training. *People Management.* 18 January.

STEWART, J. and McGOLDRICK, J. (1996) *Human resource development: perspectives, strategies and practice.* London: Pitman.

STEWART, J. and RIGG, C. (2011) *Learning and talent development.* London: CIPD.

TAYLOR, N. (2010) How to write a business case. *People Management.* 2 September. p31.

CHAPTER 8

Organisation Design and Organisation Development

Claire Roberts

CHAPTER CONTENTS

- Introduction
- Part 1: Organisation design
- Part 2: Organisation development
- The future context for organisation design and development

KEY LEARNING OUTCOMES

By the end of this chapter, you should be able to:

- understand the historical and theoretical basis of organisation design and the relationship between organisational elements and the business strategy
- explore the key factors to be considered in the design of organisations and the implications for the management and development of people and resources
- analyse the organisation development process from a historical, theoretical and practical perspective
- explore various organisation development practices, models, and approaches
- understand the value of organisation development interventions to business performance and productivity.

8.1 INTRODUCTION

Organisation design and development both have an overarching goal of improving organisational performance and ensuring this is sustainable. At first glance, this may sound rather similar to Chapter 9 of this book, 'Improving organisational performance', which examines high performance work systems. These are bundles of HR practices and policies which aim to optimise the performance of individuals in the organisation, which are introduced at the same time, and which are mutually reinforcing.

So how do organisation design and development differ from this? Organisation design sets out to improve organisation performance and ensure this is sustainable by addressing the organisation's structure and key elements linked to this (for example, its processes). Organisation development has rather more overlap with the concept of high performance work systems, and sets out to achieve these goals through the involvement of an organisation's people and their behaviour. It addresses this at a system level, is quite strongly linked to change management, and draws on behavioural science. These are vast oversimplifications of two highly complex and strategic areas of HR practice, each of which have entire books and many academic works dedicated to them.

Throughout this chapter we shall explore them both – by examining more detailed definitions, their history and theoretical basis, how each one is put into practice, and some current and future trends and challenges they are subject to.

A few words on terminology: organisation design and development can (and do) go by the abbreviation 'OD'. For the purposes of this chapter, we'll use the abbreviations 'OD' for design, and 'ODV' for development.

Many definitions of the term 'organisation' exist, and we won't explore these in any great detail here. Connor et al (2012) provide a good overview of these, settling on one by Daft (2007, p10) who describes organisations as '(1) social entities that (2) are goal-directed, (3) are designed as deliberately structured and co-ordinated activities systems, and (4) are linked to the external environment'. Buchanan and Huczynski (2010) use a working definition of 'social arrangements for the controlled performance of collective goals'. Most definitions typically contain some of the same reference points – that organisations contain people who are performing defined roles within a hierarchy or structure of authority, and all roles added together help the organisation to achieve a collective goal (Campbell and Craig 2005).

Before we go into more detail on OD and ODV, let's look at a quick definition of each area, and the headlines of their differences and similarities.

Organisation Design is defined by the CIPD as 'the process and the outcome of shaping an organisational structure, to align it with the purpose of the business and the context in which the organisation exists' (CIPD 2015a). Marsh et al (2009) liken OD to creating an 'architect's blueprint' – which provides the structure of the building and specifications to the builders on how to bring it to life.

As well as the organisation's structure, OD must consider several other important elements that must exist and operate within this – for example systems (such as IT systems), processes (such as how customer orders are processed and fulfilled), people, performance measures, communication, and culture. Various OD models exist that tie these elements together in different ways, and OD must ensure that they fit in the most efficient way possible, in order to optimise the organisation's performance and maximise its ability to achieve its goals. This has to take place not only in the current environment, in the short term, but also in the long term. As OD aligns organisational structure with organisational goals, successful OD relies heavily on a truly robust and future-proof organisational strategy.

Organisation Development aims to take 'a planned and systematic approach to enabling sustained organisation performance through the involvement of its people' (CIPD 2015b). If OD addresses an organisation's structure and processes, ODV casts its net much wider, and consequently is rather harder to define. It is distinct from OD in several other important ways.

For example, it is an ongoing, long-term activity, rather than a stand-alone review followed by change management. ODV aims to 'institutionalise change' (CIPD 2015a), embedding a number of interventions which may or may not include OD. ODV is focused on the more dynamic aspect of people – how they are motivated; how they perform; how they develop new skills, capabilities and knowledge to meet the future needs of the organisation; what kind of culture people are working in; and how teams and groups within the organisation relate to each other.

Despite their distinct approaches to improving organisational performance, OD and ODV have some elements in common:

- Both create a framework for aligning people and organisation with business strategy – either through the structure and systems they operate within (OD) or the culture they work in and how they are motivated, rewarded and developed (ODV). Both areas must have the organisation's strategy and goals as a foundation.
- Both aim to drive and sustain organisational performance, and take into account current and future internal and external environmental factors specific to that organisation, for example the economy, regulatory activity, planned business growth.
- Both can take place in the public or private sector, and in organisations that are national or multinational, large or small.
- Both are considered as 'transformational HR', rather than transactional.
- Despite the fact that together they make up 20% of the CIPD's Profession Map (2015d) (the framework that defines what the best HR and L&D professionals and organisations must do, know and understand in order to really drive the performance of their organisation), not all organisations and HR teams have the capability to do this in-house, and OD and ODV are often outsourced to consultants (Marsh et al 2009).
- The border between OD and ODV isn't clear-cut and they can overlap on some areas and interventions. For example, 'culture' can be referred to as part of OD (for example Connor et al 2012), and OD is frequently included as one of a range of activities in ODV (CIPD 2015b).

Before getting started, it is worth considering the current and future context for OD and ODV (something that the conclusion to this chapter also addresses). It is a very interesting time to be studying and/or practising OD and ODV, and there are a couple of key context factors that HR, OD and ODV practitioners (established or aspiring) should bear in mind throughout this chapter, and of course in real life.

As already stated, the ultimate goal of OD and ODV is to improve and sustain an organisation's performance, therefore any changes in an organisation's strategy or the environment that it operates in should impact the way in which these are planned and carried out. In recent years there has been much change in the external environment that organisations operate in, both within the UK and internationally. The global financial crisis, austerity, changes in customer demand and expectations, and technology are just a few.

It is not hugely surprising that 'organisational agility', an organisation's ability to swiftly and effectively respond to change, is of increasing importance in today's complex, fast-paced and rapidly changing world (see, for example CIPD 2013a and CIPD 2014).

Global research carried out by the Economist Intelligence Unit in 2009 (EIU 2009) showed that 90% of executives surveyed believe that organisational agility is critical for business success; however, over a quarter (27%) said that their organisation was at a competitive disadvantage due to its lack of agility. Although 80% said they had undertaken a change initiative aimed at improving agility in the last three years, over a third of these said this had failed to deliver the intended benefits.

Why should this be of concern to practitioners of HR, OD and ODV? The EIU research also showed that the main obstacles to improving agility included slow decision-making, conflicting departmental goals and priorities, cultural issues (such as avoiding risk taking) and working in silos, which also slows down the flow of information. These are all issues which fall within the remit of OD and/or ODV, as we shall explore throughout this chapter.

The CIPD has also highlighted the importance of organisational agility (CIPD 2013a, 2014). Its own research highlights several 'enemies of adaptability', including hierarchy, rigid structures and centralisation (corresponding with OD) and skills deficit, insufficient experimentation, short-term thinking and fear (corresponding with ODV) – all underpinned by a lack of purpose (corresponding with the organisation's strategy) (CIPD 2013a).

This research also suggests that HR can play a hugely positive role in making companies more adaptable, including building more fluid structures that change continuously, re-engineering overly controlling management processes (OD), creating company-wide dialogue around change, giving employees new and conceptual skills (for example values-driven thinking), and fostering a high-trust, low-fear environment (ODV).

With some research suggesting that profits in 'agile' firms can be up to 30% higher (EIU 2009), there is clearly scope for OD and ODV to make a significant contribution to organisational performance, and for practitioners of HR, OD and ODV to establish themselves as strategic partners in this respect.

More recent research suggests that the need for agility is only increasing, with trends such as the seismic evolution of social media, and the need for ever-faster innovation and speed to market already established (for example. PWC Technology Institute 2015).

The CIPD has also identified various other 'megatrends' that will affect workplaces, and may be of more specific concern to HR practitioners when shaping their response to the agility challenge. These include demographic change (both population ageing and migration), greater diversity in employment relationships (such as working patterns, how people are employed), low-trust cultures evolving in many sectors, and employees feeling that they are working harder than ever before (CIPD 2013b).

As this chapter progresses, think back to the CIPD definitions of OD ('the process and the outcome of shaping an organisational structure, to align it with the purpose of the business and the context in which the organisation exists') (CIPD 2015a) and ODV ('a planned and systematic approach to enabling sustained organisation performance through the involvement of its people') (CIPD 2015b), as well as the challenge of organisational agility. Both can help organisations to change and evolve to meet current and future challenges, and there is an essential (and potentially very rewarding role) for HR practitioners in leading this.

8.2 PART 1: ORGANISATION DESIGN

8.2.1 THE HISTORY AND THEORY OF OD

We'll begin by looking at OD and its theoretical roots. These lie in the mid-1800s, with Weber's theory of bureaucracy. Weber advocated 'authority structures' (Campbell and Craig 2005); he maintained that robust processes and hierarchical structures, with strong management control and supervision, were the most effective and efficient way to structure an organisation (CIPD 2015a). The term 'bureaucracy' is now often used in everyday parlance in a pejorative sense, to describe an organisation which is perceived as slow, inefficient or bloated – although in reality, a majority of organisations still operate with a bureaucratic structure at their core.

Although organisation structures had existed for centuries (think for example of the Roman army, or the feudal system of the Middle Ages), Weber was one of the earlier thinkers to study organisation structure and efficiency, and to put forward a philosophy around it.

Another theory which has informed OD as we know it today, and which complements Weber's bureaucracy is *scientific management*, a theory created by Frederick Winslow Taylor (and hence referred to as *Taylorism*) some years after Weber in the late 1800s. With the industrial revolution in full swing on both sides of the Atlantic, production (and therefore organisations and work) had already gone through a major transition, from an agrarian to an industrial economy, with significant proportions of workers moving from small, self-directed agrarian or craft organisations, to large, centrally controlled ones.

Sometimes hailed as one of the first ever management consultants, Taylor applied scientific rigour to the study of work and productivity, identifying and precisely defining the specific tasks required to complete a particular production task (he famously studied shovelling coal), and then measuring elements of each task in order to establish how it could be performed at optimum efficiency, identifying the best way to carry it out, and the type of person best suited to do it (Buchanan and Huczynski 2010). These were the earliest 'time and motion' studies.

Taylorism is often mentioned in the same breath as Fordism – a well-known and revolutionary approach to changing the way that motor cars were produced, enabling rapid mass production on a scale not seen before, created by Henry Ford in the 1920s. Taylor had focused on job design to maximise productivity, creating specialised tasks focusing on one element of the production chain, with precise parameters for how to do this, how long it should take and who should do it. He did not question the production process itself, and did not consider motivational factors which may affect how the work was carried out.

Ford took scientific management several steps further. As well as looking at job design and how each task was performed, he made changes to the organisation's processes – most notably, establishing a moving production line, which moved the vehicles at a pre-defined speed and at varying stages of assembly along to the next team of production workers. He also slightly reduced working hours, and paid workers $5 per day, double the going rate at that time, to help recruit the best mechanics and reduce what had been significant absenteeism and turnover, both of which maximised productivity and thereby profitability (Buchanan and Huczynski 2010).

Readers with an interest in reward may wish to look into this $5 rate further; different accounts of it exist, and it is sometimes referred to in debates around a minimum and/or living wage on both sides of the Atlantic. The $5 was a combination of pay and bonus, and the bonus depended on some rather paternalistic conditions (amongst others), such as living in an 'American way', for example, no gambling or drinking, wives staying home with family and not going out to work (Worstall 2012).

Certain themes emerge from these theories that remain elements of OD practice as we know it today, for example:

- Management control – whether through the traditional authority of a hierarchy, or management setting the speed of a moving production line.
- The structure of the organisation, the hierarchy of management and supervision.
- How the tasks required for the organisation to meet its goals are organised into job roles (job design) and chains of production.
- Processes and how employees interact with them (the examples here occurred in a manufacturing environment, but processes can exist in all types of organisation).
- An early (though fairly minimal) consideration of factors that motivate employees.

Although scientific management may have increased organisation efficiency at that time, and allowed each component task to be carried out with the utmost skill and experience, this approach to job and organisation design arguably led to repetitive and relentless job roles, which could not have provided much motivation to workers operating within it. By the 1960s, theories of organisation behaviour and behavioural science were beginning to take hold, examining the link between motivation and performance, and we'll look at these later in the context of organisation development (ODV).

The majority of early theory on OD was developed in an industrial age. However, in 2015 manufacturing accounted for just 10% of GDP in the UK (Rhodes 2015). With other European countries in the same ballpark (World Bank 2015), most Western economies have seen their service sector grow significantly, and many commentators talk about the knowledge and digital economy that a growing number of nations are moving towards, which rely more on human capital and knowledge than production efficiency.

In this context, it is interesting to consider two types of structure: *mechanistic* and *organic*. These structures each sit on opposite ends of various axes.

Bureaucracy and scientific management can both be characterised as **mechanistic** (Burns 1963), a structure with strongly defined management levels and hierarchy, where roles are specialised, departments and functions are clearly delineated, spans of control are narrow (that is, each manager has a small number of direct reports) and where power and authority is 'centralised' in a clear centre (for example an individual leader, an executive team, head office) (Campbell and Craig 2005).

Organic organisation structures, by contrast, are less hierarchical and more fluid, with less division between different layers of the organisation and teams or functions within it, and altogether more informal. Organic organisations have more cross-functional teams and teamworking, departments or functions with looser and wider 'borders'; a greater flow of communication between different functions and levels of the hierarchy; managers with higher numbers of direct reports (that is, a wide span of control) meaning less supervision and direct intervention into the way roles are carried out; and power and authority is decentralised (for example, managers have the authority to take decisions, authority and control granted to cross-functional team leads) (Campbell and Craig 2005).

Mechanistic structures are typically more suited to stable environments and are slower to change and adapt. They suit some types of business very well, for example manufacturing where it is essential that components are consistently assembled in the same way. However, once in place it may be hard to change, for example due to the infrastructure of a factory, or the pattern of relationships that build up around the existing structure (this is more a concern of ODV). Organic organisations are typically better suited to dynamic environments (which arguably most organisations today are operating in), and are more agile and able to quickly react to changes in the external and internal environment.

In the 1960s, the *contingency approach* to organisation structure also emerged. The contingency approach emphasised the significance of external, situational factors in determining the best structure for an organisation, rather than relying on one best-practice model (as Taylor had advocated, for example). Perhaps more closely aligned with organic structures than mechanistic ones, the contingency approach could be seen as emerging at the time that many Western economies saw growth in other sectors, perhaps signalling the drop in reliance on manufacturing and industry that lay ahead for many of them. In the twenty-first century, intuitively the contingency approach appears very relevant to OD, and also ODV, both of which aim to optimise the organisation's performance, helping it to achieve its goals in the current and future organisational environment.

While certain structures may be better suited to different sectors, and many organisations do still adhere to a bureaucratic, hierarchical structure, the idea that one organisational model fits all does not hold sway, and an analysis of the internal and external environment is central to both OD and ODV.

In the following sections we will go further, looking at the specific types of organisation structure, the factors that should shape the choice of structure, the wider OD models that structure must fit with, and the practical steps to make OD happen.

8.2.2 WHAT IS OD?

We defined OD in the previous section above as 'the process and the outcome of shaping an organisational structure, to align it with the purpose of the business and the context in which the organisation exists' (CIPD 2015a). OD aims to ensure that the structure of an organisation and its aligned key elements enable the organisation to achieve its own goals and to sustain its performance.

Readers will have varying levels of experience of OD – but trying to explain the details of how OD works and why to someone who hasn't experienced it, is like explaining all the parts of a car and how they work together to someone that hasn't seen a car before! So before going into detail on OD and how and why it happens, and its theoretical history, it may be helpful to look at a very top-level, illustrative example of the potential drivers and outcomes of an OD exercise.

CASE STUDY 8.1

FROM REGIONAL TO NATIONAL

Over its 30-year history, a UK-based fashion retail organisation had evolved into a structure with five regions. Each region had its own functional structure, with small teams for finance, HR, marketing, and so on supporting retail operations (that is, the running of the shops and the line managers responsible for this). Each region was quite autonomous, with a regional director responsible for its performance. Very few functions were centralised (only where this was absolutely necessary, such as buying, design, production). This had led to different management practices in all five regions – some had very engaged employees and great service levels, and others had high turnover and poor employee relations.

The organisation was facing increased competition from competitors on the high street and also online – and these trends in particular meant it had to significantly improve the in-store experience that customers had, and it also wanted to develop sales through its own online business. It was slow to get new products into the stores and couldn't react quickly to new trends and customer preferences.

After redefining the organisational strategy, an OD review centralised this structure, with regional operations supported by much larger finance, HR, marketing, and communications teams working out of a head office in Birmingham. An Operations Manager for each region was appointed, reporting into a national Operations Director in Head Office. New KPIs which clarified the required improvements to organisational performance were set and effectively communicated across the business, and were also linked to reward and recognition practices. A new online business team was established, and an external specialised consultancy was appointed to support them. Over the following two years, this led to increased sales and several benefits, including:

- substantial cost savings and economies of scale
- higher levels of expertise within each function, as bigger teams allowed for specialists, rather than a regional generalist
- improved customer experience through greater consistency across all retail outlets, such as merchandising, service levels
- improved and more efficient communications, with far fewer confused or diluted messages from head office reaching staff in the retail outlets
- better and more consistent HR and line management practices, with fewer regional variations, and more transformative HR practices introduced.

This case study also helps to illustrate the fact that OD is a stand-alone activity, in the sense of being a one-off intervention with very specific aims. It may take weeks or months (in rare and no doubt painful cases, years), but in contrast with ODV, it is not a continuous, ongoing process of review. It can lead to wide-scale organisational change, as in the case study above, or fewer changes that impact only part of the organisation.

8.2.3 WHY OD HAPPENS

The overall goal of OD is improving organisation performance and to help the business to achieve its own goals or strategy, and it is frequently initiated within the organisation specifically to achieve this. Several more specific triggers for OD also exist. The list below is by no means exhaustive, but gives some examples of the circumstances or decisions which may trigger an OD review and intervention:

- External demand, for example shareholders requiring organisational efficiency and cost-saving
- Changes in the political, legal or regulatory environment, for example financial service firms after global financial crisis
- Organisational growth, for example small, owner-run organisations increasing sales and setting up a management team, more specific functions and processes
- Economic pressures, for example need to downsize and save costs
- Response to customer demand, for example creating telephone and Internet banking services, extending opening hours in retail.

8.2.4 HOW OD HAPPENS: MODELS OF OD

At various stages, we have referred to other 'organisation elements' which must be aligned with organisation structure and the organisation's goals and strategy. Strategy is the 'articulation of the vision, mission and competitive position of a business' and must form the foundations of OD. Connor et al (2012) provide a clear explanation of how a business strategy is realised.

Over the past decades, many OD models have been developed, which have different perspectives on exactly which elements must be aligned with structure and strategy, and how they should fit together. Identifying the right OD model will depend on the needs and structure of each organisation, and must be one of the earliest activities in any OD process. It determines the areas of focus for the analysis and assessment that should kick-start OD, and also facilitates project and change management, communications about OD and monitoring and evaluation.

Connor et al (2012) highlight some common themes in these models – strategy and structure prevail, but also processes, systems, performance measures, technology, and physical and psychological aspects of the organisation.

It is beyond the scope of this chapter to provide a detailed explanation of how these models are implemented in practice. However, the reader is encouraged to keep in mind firstly, that organisation strategy forms the basis of the majority of these models (and features heavily in the rest), and secondly that there must be congruence between all the elements represented in the model. It is also very clear that OD cannot be a stand-alone HR process, and the specific OD and ODV activities in the CIPD Profession Map also reflect this (CIPD 2015d).

Connor et al (2012) also helpfully distinguish between 'static' and 'dynamic' models.

Static models   (Figure 8.1) enable an overview of the organisation from an OD perspective, and then diagnostic tools can be used on each of the individual elements in order to implement change. For example:

- *McKinsey 7S model*: developed by the well-established McKinsey consulting firm, this model links strategy, structure, systems, style, staff and skills around a core of shared values
- *Galbraith Star*: aligns strategy and structure with processes, reward and people practices.

Figure 8.1 A typical static organisation design model (Connor et al 2012)

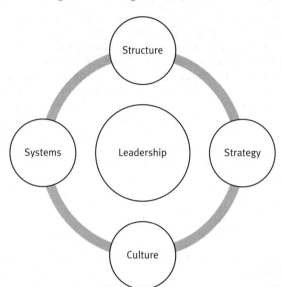

Dynamic models (Figure 8.2) treat OD as a more dynamic process. Although they may incorporate many of the same elements, dynamic models create more of a causal chain, positioning strategy at the start and organisation performance as the output. For example:

- *Weissbord's 6 Box model:* aligns structure with purpose, reward, helpful mechanisms, relationships, all centring around leadership and all in the context of the organisation's environment
- *Burke-Litwin Causal Model:* is particularly comprehensive. Within the context of environment, with ongoing feedback, it aligns mission and strategy, leadership and organisational culture, with structure, management practices, policy/procedure, team climate, tasks and skills, motivation and individual needs and values. This is also considered as an organisation development model.

Figure 8.2 An outline dynamic model of OD (Connor et al 2012)

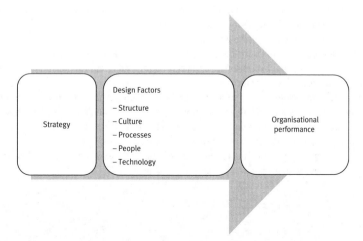

8.2.5 HOW OD HAPPENS: ORGANISATION STRUCTURES

Putting in place an organisation structure that best equips an organisation to achieve its goals and strategy in the current and future environment, is the main end goal of OD and the common feature in all the OD models described above. Choosing a structure is a critical but by no means straightforward task. There are multiple factors to consider and these are highly variable and dynamic, not static (Campbell and Craig 2005, p457). This is in line with the contingency approach to organisation structure that we will look at later.

Campbell and Craig (2005, p454) provide a clear definition of organisation structure, stating this represents 'the pattern of relationships of the workforce and their relative positions in the organisation', and provides 'the framework for order and control whereby the organisation's activities can be planned, organised, directed and monitored'. Although few organisations are structured in exactly the same way, most will resemble one of the models outlined below.

ORGANISATION STRUCTURE: KEY VARIABLES

As organisation structure is a relatively abstract concept. Buchanan and Huczynski (2010) define 7 variables that it is concerned with, and which senior management should carefully consider. As you read about the different structures described below, consider these concepts and characteristics and how they feature in each one:

– **Work specialisation:** the degree to which tasks in organisations are divided into separate job roles. Are employees specialised or generalist? When is specialisation motivating (for example, a lawyer recognised for expertise in one area of the law) and when is it demotivating (for example a factory worker repeatedly welding the same two pieces of a car together, day in day out)?
– **Hierarchy:** how many levels of management are there in the organisation? What is the impact on communication, staff motivation and cost? Is it 'tall' or 'short' (Campbell and Craig 2005)? A *tall* organisation has more layers of management and is more hierarchical. Managers are likely to be more specialised and have smaller numbers of direct reports. A *short* organisation is flatter; managers have broader remits and more direct reports. Two important related terms are:
  (a) *Spans of control*: the number of direct reports a manager has. A narrow span means fewer reports, greater specialisation, and is more common in a tall organisation (and vice versa in a short one)
  (b) *Chain and Unity of command*: who each employee reports into, and the concept that each employee should report into only one manager (this is not the case in all organisation structures as we'll see below).
– *Departmentalisation:* should jobs be grouped together into departments where employees all have the same functional expertise? Or according to their geographical location, the customer group they service, or another factor?
– *Formalisation:* should lots of written rules and regulations exist to control and co-ordinate employees, or should their activities and interactions be more fluid and less prescribed?
– *Centralisation:* this determines where power and authority sits. In a centralised organisation, decision-making power is very concentrated in one place or person, for example head office, a business owner, an executive team, whereas in a decentralised organisation this would be delegated or devolved to teams and less senior managers.

Buchanan and Huczynski (2010) along with many others also distinguish between *line and staff employees:* line employees are responsible for the activities that are the organisation's key purpose, such as delivering front-line services in a hospital, working on a production line, working in or managing the outlets of a coffee chain. Staff employees work in the functions that exist to support these operations, such as finance, HR, IT.

? REFLECTIVE ACTIVITY 8.1

OD and your organisation

- How many levels of management are there in your organisation – is it short or tall?
- How wide are the spans of control? How specialised are managers and employees in their roles?
- How are the various job roles organised into groups? By function? By geography? Does this help or hinder teams in carrying out their work?
- Where are decisions made? Is this centralised (for example by an executive board) or is it devolved (for example, to functional heads or line managers)? How fast is decision-making?
- How 'rule driven' is your organisation? Are there clear policies and processes or can employees/teams carry out their work as they choose to? What is the impact of this on the final product/service? What is the impact on how employees feel?
- Do you think your organisation's structure is mechanistic or organic?
- What would you change about any of these aspects (for example, levels of management, job specialisation, decision-making, overall structure) to help your organisation to perform better? Why?
- What would you/the HR team need to do in order to lead and implement these changes?

Detailed descriptions of organisational structures can be found in many works on the topic of OD, such as Connor et al (2012), Cannon et al (2010) and Campbell and Craig (2005), who helpfully divide the structures into two categories – hierarchical and functional – and whose organisation types we draw on below. Buchanan and Huczynski (2010) provide a particularly light-hearted and well-illustrated overview of organisational structures.

Most organisations have documents showing their structure in varying degrees of detail, for example, divisions, function names, job titles, name of position holder, even photographs. These are used as OD tools, but are often widely available within the business, on an intranet for example. We'll examine the factors that influence the choice of structure in the next section on OD process, but first we'll take a look at the principal types of organisational structure

8.2.6 HIERARCHICAL STRUCTURES

Campbell and Craig (2005) refer to these as 'M form' structures, due to the shape made by the various divisions reporting into the CEO. The different types of hierarchical structure are distinguished by how the parts of the organisation are divided up, for example by function, geography, customer base.

Functional structure: Most readers will have experienced working life in a functional structure at some point (Figure 8.3). Connor et al (2012) refer to this as the most logical and common option, and Wagner and Hollenbeck (2014) describe it as the most basic kind of bureaucratic structure. It can create the risk of functional silos, but allows a clear chain of command and relatively smooth communication. Other factors, such as spans of control, and how many layers of management exist, will determine how reactive and dynamic it is.

Figure 8.3 Functional structure

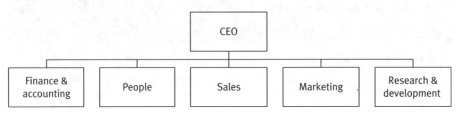

Geographical structure: This can be a regional structure within one country or market, with several regional offices (each potentially with its own regional manager or director) supported by a head office with support functions. Alternatively, it could be an international structure with various national markets or areas of the world reporting to a Global CEO. These structures have the advantage of being close to the regional or national customer base, but require high levels of control, and can potentially create duplication of costs where each geographical branch has its own support functions.

Organisation by product: In this structure, the organisation is divided into areas differentiated by product type. Campbell and Craig (2005) observe that this model is particularly suited to businesses that require very high levels of specialisation, such as chemical or pharmaceutical companies. Here, the degree of specialisation required to carry out a role reduces scope for staff and managers moving across the business, and requires very specialised units in order to carry out the organisation's work. Support functions (such as HR, finance) may be centralised and serve all product divisions (allowing for greater consistency and economy of scale) or within each product division.

Organisation by customer group: The organisation is divided into areas according to the customer group that each one serves, for example retail organisations may have in-store and online divisions, and a transport and distribution company may have divisions for logistics, general freight and courier services. This structure enables the organisation to more effectively meet and react to the needs of specific customer groups.

8.2.7 NON-HIERARCHICAL STRUCTURES

In the introduction to this chapter, we looked at the growing need for organisational agility, and the ability to respond swiftly in changes in the external environment, customer demand, and so on. Non-hierarchical structures have the potential to provide greater flexibility, and therefore greater organisational agility, than hierarchical ones, and we'll look at this in more detail below.

Matrix organisation: This is a more contemporary and non-hierarchical structure, which joins the needs for customer responsiveness and high levels of control. This structure is popular in project heavy organisations, such as a marketing agency. Employees have a functional chain of command into their functional lead (or a manager below them), and a chain of command into a project lead (who may or may not be from their own function). Whilst it is good for organisational agility, the experience of having multiple bosses with different priorities is a potentially stressful one for employees, and it relies on the project team leaders having strong team management and leadership skills.

The example below (Figure 8.4) illustrates a framework through which members of each functional team (headed up by a director), can be assigned to various specific projects. These specific projects may be set up to tackle specific business goals or challenges, such as the launch of a new product. The employees participating in the project teams would continue to report to their 'regular' line manager, whilst also having deliverables and responsibilities towards the project lead.

Figure 8.4 Matrix organisation

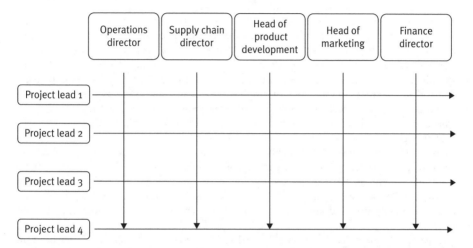

Virtual organisations: Wagner and Hollenbeck (2014) refer to this as the 'best of everything' organisation structure, and say it makes the very best of the aptly named 'efficiency vs flexibility' trade-off. Through this model, expertise is brought in as necessary through collaborations and partnerships with other organisations, rather than creating permanent functions that must be managed. This may work very well for some types of organisation – for example for small organisations or start-ups, enabling them to manage growth and costs.

This differs from outsourcing (which usually permanently moves a business function, such as payroll, outside the organisation), as the collaboration may take place to meet a temporary need relating to a specific project, or two organisations with 'compatible' services or business goals may choose to work together in a strategic partnership. The name 'virtual organisation' suggests that people/employees are dispersed rather than sitting together in one office, possibly using technology coupled with occasional face-to-face meetings.

The flexible firm model corresponds to some extent with the matrix and virtual organisation structure. We will consider this concept in a little more detail, as it may have a role to play in increasing an organisation's agility – but also throws up some interesting considerations for the HR practitioner. Perhaps the best known model is Atkinson's flexible firm (1984). Atkinson identifies three types of flexibility that can be achieved: functional (ie employees capable of carrying out more than one job role), numerical (ie the organisation's ability to change the number of employees or number of hours worked) and financial (ie the organisation's ability to adjust employment costs in response to changes in the employment market). It is interesting to consider the time in which Atkinson was writing, not long after the turbulent industrial relations of the 1970s.

His flexible firm model (Atkinson 1984) features a core group of multi-skilled, permanent employees (providing functional flexibility), who carry out the firm's core activities using skills that it is hard to 'buy in'. A 'first peripheral group' are also full-time employees, but carry out more mundane, repetitive roles that require little training, and offer less job security and fewer career prospects. Atkinson acknowledges that this type of role is likely to promote turnover, but saw this as a means to increased numerical flexibility. And finally, a second peripheral group supplement the work carried out by the core and first peripheral group at times of peak demand. This group carried out similar work to the first peripheral group, but with different work and employment patterns such as short-term contracts, subcontracting, agency temps, self-employment and outsourcing.

Readers are likely to be familiar with another flexible firm model – Handy's Shamrock model, in which a core, permanent workforce form a 'contractual core', while a 'contractual fringe' of self-employed professionals, contractors, and so on are hired in for specific projects, and a contingent workforce (performing routine jobs) help to meet demand at different times of year (Campbell and Craig 2005). Handy's model is more recent and perhaps reflects the 'buying in' of expertise to a greater extent than Atkinson's, whose original work focused more heavily on a manufacturing environment.

Although a full-blown critique of the flexible firm model is beyond the scope of this chapter, there are some clear benefits to the flexible firm model, such as the ability to bring in particular skills for a fixed period of time (such as a TUPE specialist working alongside a permanent HR team), or seasonal peaks (for example the end of the tax year, or the Christmas season in the retail sector). Both of these measures increase an organisation's agility, and ability to meet its customers' needs in the most cost efficient way.

Megatrends identified by the CIPD (2013b) also suggest that increased flexibility in working patterns may be welcomed by many employees too, for example as a result of caring responsibilities that are likely to come with an ageing population, and flexibility may also help organisations to combat future skills shortages by offering different working patterns.

However, these patterns of flexibility have also been criticised for creating a challenging work environment (for example, the fact that high turnover can hinder team cohesion), creating very different employment experiences for the various tiers, and not providing job security. If badly executed, a flexible firm model could leave also an organisation without some of the skills and capabilities it needs to function, and could create additional costs (such as an overreliance on agency workers).

Recent years have also seen a rise in the use of zero-hours contracts, which have received some bad press. These could be described as blurring the boundary between the first and second peripheral group, as the employee has a permanent contract, but the employer is not obliged to provide them with work. Zero-hours contracts are not automatically unfair – in fact CIPD research (CIPD 2015e) shows that employee satisfaction is the same and in some cases greater as a result of the extra flexibility provided.

In summary, while a flexible firm model can do much to improve an organisation's agility, for the HR practitioner, it is clear that there's a great deal to consider, firstly, when moving towards a flexible firm model, and secondly, ensuring that all legal and ethical considerations are addressed.

8.2.8 HOW OD HAPPENS: PROCESS AND OUTCOME

The CIPD advocates a simple four-stage framework for OD, the **ADIE framework**: Assess, Design, Implement and Evaluate. It broadly corresponds to other approaches to

OD, and the tools and interventions required to manage an OD process fit into it. Helpful detail on each stage can be found in the CIPD's *Organisation design and capability building toolkit* (Cannon et al 2010), and the CIPD Profession Map (2015d), and also in various other publications. Broadly speaking, the assess and design stages correspond with the OD process, and the implement and embed/evaluate stages correspond with OD outcome.

Assess: This stage focuses on gathering facts and data about the organisation in order to establish the status quo, to diagnose areas for improvement and the root cause of these. The conclusions reached at this stage will be critical to the success of the OD project, and will help to clarify priorities, obstacles and the best approach to design and implementation. Cannon et al (2010) identify six facets of organisational capability that should be assessed: strategic alignment, structural design, leadership, competence (that is, the skills, knowledge and behaviour within the organisation), culture and climate, and communications. Once an OD model has been chosen, data should also be collected to assess all areas within it, and the information collected in this stage will determine the choice of organisational structure.

Tools that can be used in this stage include:

- financial and other performance metrics
- a risk log, containing risk analysis and mitigation
- stakeholder analysis
- benchmarking with other organisations and/or a competitor analysis
- other diagnostic tools, for example for culture, strategic alignment
- employee surveys, to assess engagement levels
- appreciative enquiry and fact-finding conversations
- analysis tools such as SWOT (strengths, weaknesses, opportunities, threats) and PESTLE (political, economic, social, technological, legal and environmental) for scoping the internal and external environment.

The contingency approach to OD emphasises the significance of external, situational factors in determining the best structure for an organisation. First and foremost, structure must align with business strategy, and its objectives, goals and operating principles (Connor et al 2012), especially any element directly relating to structural change, such as downsizing, outsourcing or off-shoring functions, or opening new markets. Other situational factors to consider will vary by sector, but should be addressed in the 'assess' stage of OD. These include:

- Stakeholder demands and requirements: stakeholders will vary by organisation but can include employees, customers/service users, local or national government, regulatory bodies, shareholders, interest groups (such as environmental charities).
- Changing consumer demand and preferences: increased demand from consumers, a sizeable stakeholder group, for example for personalisation and excellent service.
- Stability of market, for example how quickly does an organisation need to be able to change and react? Wagner and Hollenbeck (2014) cite Blackberry as an example of going from being a market leader in producing mobile devices for the business sector, to almost going bust after being rapidly overtaken by quicker and more innovative firms, predominantly Apple. They highlight the trade-off that must be made between consistency/control and flexibility.
- Size and complexity of organisation, for example global manufacturing firm versus a tech start-up with 30 employees.
- Stage of maturity of the organisation. The Greiner growth model (1972) shows the phases that companies go through as they grow and develop, and a corresponding series of crises that they move through that are linked to organisational structure.

These include crises in leadership, autonomy, control, red tape and growth. The maturity of people systems will also impact the organisation's ability to change.

- Extent to which international cultures are involved (Connor et al 2012). Factors such as power distance (respect for hierarchy) in some cultures, such as Japan, may mean that flatter, more informal organisation structures are not as effective.
- For the public sector, cuts in government funding and requirement to do more with less.
- Demographic change, leading to multi-generational workforces with differing priorities, as well as changes in consumer demands.
- Technological trends within the sector.
- Extent of regulation, affecting the need for organisational control.

Design: This stage confirms the goals and objectives for the OD project. It includes both the *process* (for example how project will be run, communications plan, which OD model will be used) and the *outcome* (for example a 'to be' map of the organisation system, and specifications for the other key elements in the chosen OD model, such as people and process).

Tools that can be used in this stage include:

- 'to be' organisational structure/hierarchy charts
- 'to be' process maps
- analysis of costs and ROI
- KPIs and performance measures aligned to structure and strategy
- OD principles (organisation specific)
- project and communications plan, informed by change management best practice
- further fact-finding eg through conversations, brainstorming
- further stakeholder analysis and engagement, for example using a tool such as a RACI chart (responsible, accountable, consult, inform)
- input from external experts, such as legal professionals.

Other interventions and changes may be identified in this stage, for example:

- New processes may be underpinned by new infrastructure or technology, such as introducing an HR Information System (HRIS) which may negate the need for many HR administration processes, and may change how HR processes are followed by employees, for example writing and logging performance appraisals online.
- Changes to the *physical aspects* of the organisation, such as opening new offices or sites, changes to the working environment and space (for example moving from offices for individuals or teams to open plan).

Implement: This stage is the transition to the 'to be' organisation structure, through change management and the implementation of OD project and communication plans, with ongoing monitoring of progress. The success of this phase depends heavily on the quality and effort that has gone into the 'assess' and 'design' stages. Many risks can befall a badly planned and executed process, for example drops in staff motivation (and ultimately staff turnover), poor service to customers, failure of expensive IT systems which were not correctly designed to facilitate organisational processes; reputational damage as a result of all or any of these; and unexpected (and potentially very large) costs to put things right, to name just a few.

Regardless of the model chosen, and whether 'people' features in it, from an HR perspective there are many areas which will require careful planning, alignment, and implementation such as performance management and reward, role specifications and the standardisation of job roles, pay bands and structures, knowledge management, employee communication and employee relations (especially where redundancies occur).

The changes that OD can bring can also impact the *psychological aspects* of organisation, including levels of employee commitment and job satisfaction, and may impact the psychological contract – the unwritten set of expectations that employees have of the employment relationship. Interested readers should look into the principles of change management, which should guide the implementation phase.

Evaluate and embed: After the ongoing monitoring of the implementation stage, in this stage the OD project is assessed in its entirety, along with lessons learned, sharing these, making any further adjustments required and celebrating success and recognising the organisation. Tools that can be used here include financial and performance metrics (including employee measures such as turnover), the key deliverables in the project plan, a RACI chart (to guide stakeholder feedback), and review meetings.

8.3 PART 2: ORGANISATION DEVELOPMENT

8.3.1 WHAT IS ORGANISATION DEVELOPMENT?

We touched on a definition of ODV at the start of this chapter. Perhaps one of the first things to emerge when you start the study of ODV, is that compared to many other areas of HR practice, it involves some intangible concepts, doesn't have clearly marked parameters, and can be fairly challenging to define. ODV is not a narrow function. It does not have standard activities and practices that are clearly visible and consistent across organisations, and many organisations may not be practising ODV at all (or may be using the term ODV to describe another function, such as learning and development). A quick trawl through online job descriptions being used to recruit ODV managers or directors will show how very differently organisations interpret this area and remit.

Contrast ODV with recruitment, for example, where the need to recruit is usually very clear, and the process that follows almost always involves creating a job description, advertising the job role, using one or more established selection tools (such as interviews, psychometric tests, assessment centres), and making a decision to hire the candidate that best fits the original specifications. The most junior HR practitioner, and probably most employees from other parts of the business, could have a fair stab at describing what recruitment is, not least because almost everyone has been on the receiving end of a recruitment process, and is pretty sure when it has happened. ODV, on the other hand, isn't a function but a field of practice, covering a range of tools and techniques. It has roots in behavioural psychology, an association with change management and more recently a specific focus on improving organisational performance (CIPD 2015c).

It is widely recognised that there isn't a single definition of ODV. Broadly, it can be considered as a holistic approach to improving organisation effectiveness, often led by HR but operating across functional boundaries (CIPD 2015c). It is focused on identifying and resolving organisation problems, but on an ongoing basis rather than a finite one (CIPD 2015c). (Contrast this with OD which is a large-scale but one-off intervention.)

The CIPD (2015b) defines ODV as an organisation's 'planned and systematic approach to enabling sustained organisational performance through the involvement of its people'. However, this focus on organisational performance is a more recent development. Even as late as the 1990s, when debate around ODV was broad and well-established (for example to include culture, teams and facilitation), improving organisation performance in terms of adding value to the bottom line was not always a stated goal of ODV (Marsh et al 2009).

For example, French and Bell (1999, p26) describe ODV as 'a long-term effort, led and supported by top management, to improve an organisation's visioning, learning, and problem-solving processes, through an ongoing, collaborative management of organisation culture – with special emphasis on the culture of intact work teams and other team configurations – utilising the consultant-facilitator role and the theory and technology of applied behavioural science, including action research.'

Looking further back, Richard Beckhard in one of the original definitions from the 1960s describes ODV as 'an effort 1) planned, 2) organisation wide and 3) managed from the top, to 4) increase organisation development and health through 5) planned interventions in the organisation's "process" using behavioural science knowledge' (cited in CIPD 2015b and Marsh et al 2009).

Around the same time, Warren Bennis, one of the first major figures associated with the ODV field, described it as 'a response to change, a complex educational strategy intended to change the beliefs, attitudes, values and structure of organisations so that they can better adapt to new technologies, markets and challenges, and the dizzying rate of change itself' (cited in Marsh et al 2009). This definition had a closer link with organisational performance than many others, and was also an early example of OD being considered as an ODV intervention.

More recently, Michael Beer (cited in CIPD 2015b) described ODV fairly comprehensively as 'a system-wide process of data collection, diagnosis, action planning, intervention, and evaluation aimed at (1) enhancing congruence among organisational structure, process, strategy, people and culture; (2) developing new and creative organisational solutions; and (3) developing the organisation's self-renewing capacity. It occurs through the collaboration of organisational members working with a change agent using behavioural science theory, research and technology.'

As some of the definitions above may suggest, one of the criticisms sometimes levelled at ODV is that it has a tendency to be 'touchy feely' (CIPD 2015b), loses track of the bottom line of the business (Marsh et al 2009) or that practitioners implement interventions as means in themselves, without a tangible business benefit.

This is also reflected in the set of values which ODV was founded on. Robbins and Judge (2008) summarise these values as respect, trust, power equalisation (ie a move away from hierarchical control), confrontation (ie addressing problems in the open) and participation (ie involving those affected by change in the change process).

French and Bell (1999, p69) cite research conducted with OD practitioners, who collectively identified the most important values as: increasing effectiveness and efficiency; creating openness in communication; empowering employees to act; enhancing productivity and promoting organisational participation. However, when asked about what the important values *should* be, they collectively cited: empowering employees to act; creating openness in communication; facilitating ownership of process and outcome; promoting a culture of collaboration and promoting inquiry and continuous learning. The 'ideal' values are based on humanistic and democratic concerns, while the actual values also relate more explicitly to organisational effectiveness.

Although ODV may at this stage still appear rather intangible, this chapter will discuss ODV and its processes and interventions in more detail, and will aim to show that when ODV is well-executed, this is not necessarily the case. To conclude, some common themes can be drawn from the various definitions, which the CIPD (2015b) summarises well:

- ODV is *systemic*, and applies to change in an entire system, for example the entire company, a single site in a multi-site firm, a department. Although it may involve individual-level interventions, these must be set in this context. An individual going on a time management course to address their own training needs, for example, would not constitute ODV.
- ODV is based on the use and transfer of *behavioural science principles and practice*, such as leadership and group dynamics, in a sustainable way.
- This helps the organisation to *carry out and manage planned change* more effectively and flexibly in the future, and enables it to embed or 'institutionalise' it.
- ODV aims to *improve organisational effectiveness* by helping members develop the skills and knowledge needed to solve organisational problems, involving them in the

change process, and by promoting high performance (such as financial, quality of service and products, productivity, continuous improvement).

- It also considers the *needs and motivations of individuals* within the system, and aims to provide a high quality of working life.
- ODV is *long term, dynamic and continuous*: it is not a 'static "mapping" process' like OD (Marsh et al 2009), nor a one-off initiative, but an ongoing process, a continuous cycle of diagnosis and review (CIPD 2015c), that feeds data back into the system, guides future strategy and develops organisational change capability.

The CIPD observes (2015b) that practising ODV isn't just the tangible steps and interventions taken, but also 'the mindset that is brought to bear on the work'. This means that the reach of the OD practitioner is wide and many actions can be described as an 'intervention', as long as they are system-wide and support strategy. In the event of HR practitioners working as internal ODV consultants, this could mean working with operations and finance to ensure that performance and reward systems align individual and organisational goals and performance. HR could implement a new performance and reward system, but as a stand-alone initiative, without alignment with strategy or other parts of the organisation, participation, or consideration of the specific organisation problems it needed to address, it would not constitute ODV.

In the section on OD above, we summarised some of the things that can trigger an OD project, and looked at *why* it takes place. As the definitions and theoretical basis (below) of ODV may suggest, it's harder to identify such specific triggers. ODV is intended to be an ongoing process, in which organisational problems are diagnosed and solved through the involvement of people. ODV interventions can occur in a 'business as usual' context, or as part of a larger, more formal change process.

These are some types of organisational challenge or opportunity that ODV interventions could aim to address:

- a disconnect between head office support functions and front-line staff in a company that owns and runs
- dissatisfaction among franchisees with service levels provided to support them in a franchise organisation that provides play activities to pre-school children
- failure to reach customer satisfaction metrics or other performance measures
- a peak in employee turnover
- a requirement to increase productivity and cut costs in a government department
- a drive to improve front-line customer service in a budget airline, in line with an advertising campaign to promote this.

French and Bell (1999) also provide six detailed case studies, describing the full ODV process from start to finish in very different organisations.

We have also looked at the need for organisational agility in some detail; some of the obstacles to this cited by business leaders and the CIPD (such as difficulties with organisation culture, fear, skills gaps) can be addressed by ODV interventions. Given the broad and slightly intangible nature of ODV outlined above, it's clear that HR and ODV practitioners must use great skill, judgement and influencing skills when designing and implementing these.

8.3.2 HISTORY AND THEORY OF ORGANISATION DEVELOPMENT

ODV has a much broader and more diverse history and theoretical base than OD, with roots in behavioural science, social psychology, motivational theories, systems theory, learning theory, and more. It is therefore challenging to give a detailed account of the history of ODV and the theories that have informed it. Readers interested in studying this area further could find the exceptionally clear chronology provided by Cannon and

McGee (2008) useful. A more detailed account of ODV's history and theory can also be found in French and Bell (1999).

There are a couple of interesting points to make about the early roots of ODV back in the 1940s and 1950s. Firstly, many of the early theorists knew each other and many worked on the same research. Names which most students of HR will know – such as Likert, Argyris, McGregor and Lewin – worked together and often influenced each other.

Secondly, many of the ODV interventions that were created, tested and put into use, are *now* things which a majority of us take for granted as part of working life, especially in an office environment. For example, 'T-groups' (training groups) in the late 1940s examined how people communicate and behave in meetings and aimed to optimise this. French and Bell (1999) cite a delightful story about the first ever use of a flip chart: in a T-group meeting in 1946, Lippit and Bradford got a local newspaper to donate the blank paper at the end of press runs (they also used butchers' paper), which they cut into equal sized pieces and stuck round the room (and later onto a frame) to capture outputs, having got frustrated with the blackboard. Now, capturing thoughts on a flipchart, or on a screen via PowerPoint is second nature to us, and we would even expect to see this in a meeting or training session. But in the post-war period, when most organisations were bureaucratic and hierarchical, having group discussions where everyone could contribute and sticking these thoughts up on the wall was a very big challenge to the way organisations and society operated. Although ODV may be criticised for being 'touchy feely' or vague, its lasting contribution to the way that individuals and groups behave and interact shouldn't be underestimated.

ODV as we know it today originated from several 'stems' or research and theory back in the 1940s to 1960s, and we'll draw a summary of these stems from French and Bell (1999):

Laboratory training: Also known as T-groups, these were small, unstructured group situations in which participants learned about group dynamics, leadership processes and their own behaviour within this, for example through feedback from a third-party observer. These were based on the premise that behavioural problems were caused by individuals' perceptions, assumptions and feelings about events and people around them, so the solution was therefore to alter these elements through facilitated feedback in a group. Lewin was heavily involved in the inception of T-groups, and although he died in 1947, many others (such as Argyris, McGregor, Bradford) developed this area of team interaction further over the following years. For example, in 1957 Argyris set up and ran the first teambuilding session with a CEO and executive team.

Survey research and feedback: Feedback is a specialised form of action research (described below). The 1940s and 1950s saw many developments into how feedback about organisations and the people in them was collected and measured. For example, Likert created innovations in measuring attitudes (Likert scales are still used today). Survey research also fed into T-groups, for example, in measuring participant reactions.

Action research: This originated with John Collier (a man of practical affairs, the US Commissioner for Indian Affairs 1933–45) and Kurt Lewin (a man of science). Action research takes a scientific (and sometimes an academic) approach to investigating specific organisational problems with a view to solving them, with extensive participation from the multiple stakeholders in this process. It can take several forms, and there are many 'varieties' of action research, which have evolved over the years. Lewin distinguishes between investigating general laws and diagnosing specific situations. Chen, Cook and Harding go further, and distinguish between diagnostic, participant, empirical and experimental action research. Appreciative enquiry is also a form of action research (that is, looking for the positives in a team or organisation's current situation to create a positive vision of 'what could be'), as is survey feedback and research.

Sociotechnical and socioclinical: These interventions originate in the group therapy work carried out in the Tavistock Clinic in England as early as the 1920s, with soldiers suffering from post-war neurosis, as well as with families.

During the 1940s and 1950s, various other theories and theorists were coming to the fore in the areas of behavioural science, social psychology and motivational theory which also informed ODV. Many of these are well-known, such as Maslow's hierarchy of needs (including the concept of 'self-actualisation'), Vroom's expectancy theory, and Herzberg's Quality of Working Life movement, incorporating his work on job enrichment (Buchanan and Huczyinski 2010).

? REFLECTIVE ACTIVITY 8.2

Consider the contrast between some of these theories and those that underpin organisation design, for example Weber's bureaucracy and scientific management.

What are the principal differences that you can see?

Considering the environment of the post-war period up to the 1960s, why do you think these theories evolved? What do you think their impact would have been at that time?

Theories on change management that are still in use today also emerged during this period, notably Lewin's 'unfreeze-move-refreeze' model which is particularly relevant to ODV, and the Burke-Litwin model of organisational change, which we touched on in the OD section above.

These models were designed by ODV theorists and align with many of ODV's principles and values. The correlation between ODV and change management generally is complex but interesting, and Cummings and Worley (2015) explain this quite clearly, stating that while all ODV involves change management (as we'll see in the model below), not all change management involves ODV. They add that ODV distinguishes itself from change management in various ways. Its behavioural science foundation means that ODV has values of human potential, participation and development at its core, in addition to performance and competitive advantage. It is concerned with the transfer of knowledge and skill so that the organisation is more able to manage change in the future, and achieves this through meaningful involvement of people through ODV interventions. Conversely, they describe change management as having a narrower focus on values of cost, quality and schedule, along with mechanistic assumptions, through which people are involved in the process only as steps in a plan. This ties in with the observation made earlier (CIPD 2015b), that ODV is a mindset, as well as a tangible series of interventions.

French and Bell mark the 1980s and 1990s as a tipping point. Economic turbulence led to dramatic change in many organisations, with rapid and extensive change in technology and innovation, an increase in mergers, buy-outs, bankruptcies, as well as thousands of small companies being set up. A decade or two on, and this situation is even more extreme, with the commercial environment sometimes described as '**VUCA**' – volatile, uncertain, complex, ambiguous.

They refer to 'second generation' ODV which emerged during and after this period. The features of second generation ODV include:

- a move towards 'organisational transformation', that is radical, revolutionary, or massive, and a move away from incremental change
- an increased interest in organisational culture, and growing sophistication in defining, measuring and changing this, for example the work carried out by Schein

- developments in the 'learning organisation', and the conditions in which individuals and organisations learn and develop best, for example Argyris carried out research into the 'defensive routines' shown in meetings that block communication and productivity
- an intensified interest in teams, especially as organisational structures have evolved, for example high-performance teams, cross-functional teamwork, self-managed teams
- a growing focus on **Total Quality Management** – an organisational climate in which employees are committed to the continuous improvement of product or service quality. This requires a particular and authentic set of values that ensure individuals' roles in the organisation are clear, and they are truly involved, engaged and free to provide feedback and input
- various other areas, such as managing diversity in teams and organisations, a new interest in Quality of Working Life (QWL – which some companies try to address through well-being programs), and aligning reward systems with teamwork.

8.3 3 HOW ODV HAPPENS

In the section on OD, we looked at potential triggers of OD, or reasons why an OD project is initiated. While it does not have triggers as clear as those for OD, ODV interventions are likely to be initiated in response to an organisational problem or challenge. We've also referred to ODV as a continuous process, in which an organisation continually learns and improves – so it may seem slightly paradoxical to address the point(s) of initiation. ODV is a process of planned change that can be carried out both as 'business as usual', as part of an ongoing improvement process, or to drive a larger change initiative.

The ODV process can broadly be divided into distinct stages, and some consistencies exist across the various approaches to this. The CIPD Profession Map (2015d) divides the core activities that make up the ODV process into: defining the strategy, assessing organisation capability, building ODV interventions, and managing change (including evaluation).

Broadly aligned with the CIPD model (and others), Cummings and Worley (2015) refer to six phases:

1   entry and contracting

2   diagnosing

3   collecting, analysing and feeding back diagnostic information

4   designing interventions (human process, technostructural, HRM and strategic change)

5   managing change

6   evaluating and institutionalising change.

This is similar to Warner Burke's seven-phase consulting model, cited in French and Bell (1999), who describe it as the 'program management' component of ODV. These models are designed to ensure that the right interventions are made, at the right level of the organisation (that is, individual, group, organisation-wide) at the right time. Each of these phases has a set of tools and processes that can be used to ensure that this happens. These steps also correspond with the assess, design, implement, evaluation approach to OD that we addressed in section 8.2.8.

In practice, and more so than with OD process which is more linear, the stages of the ODV process may blur together, with activity in different stages taking place concurrently depending on the organisation and what it is trying to achieve.

8.3.4 STAGE 1: ENTERING AND CONTRACTING

When considering entering and contracting, it is interesting to consider the role of key organisational actors in the ODV process. It is widely acknowledged that ODV must be managed, or as a minimum supported by senior management and/or at board level, to ensure its reach across the whole system (CIPD 2015b). To be truly effective it needs sponsorship and active involvement of senior executives, and must be multi-disciplinary, involving different parts of the organisation as required.

Although ODV features on the CIPD Profession Map (2015d) and is well-established in the field of HR, ODV frequently relies on external consultants, and has only recently been considered as a mainstream discipline of HR (CIPD 2015b), and many works (such as French and Bell 1999) refer as a matter of course to the contracting process with an external practitioner.

Marsh et al (2009) state that HR is very well placed to lead ODV, because as a function it is already in the position of having to work and influence across all areas of the business (although they acknowledge that some HR practitioners may lack skills and confidence when it comes to OD and ODV). ODV has historically focused on people, and has grown from humanistic values, so fits fairly logically with HR. It also draws on many HR processes, and also people data to diagnose organisational problems and challenges, and to design the interventions that will create the desired change (CIPD 2015c). French and Bell (1999) acknowledge that the HR practitioners can and do act as internal consultants, and where organisations have an HRD, they are either responsible for hiring the consultant or an integral member of the 'client team'. However, the extent of HR's involvement may depend quite heavily on the credibility and engagement of this function within the organisation.

There can be advantages to working with an external practitioner, such as a fresh perspective, someone to role model new behaviours, experience from many other organisations and sectors, and development opportunities for the HR team. However, this very strategic area of HR provides a big opportunity for HRDs and their teams to add great value to the organisation through leading and facilitating effective, planned change. There is also scope for HR functions to develop the skills of collecting, analysing and acting on data and information, and providing insight across the business (CIPD 2015b).

Whether ODV is carried out by an internal or external practitioner, the entry and contracting phase covers the early dialogue and diagnostics between the main stakeholders, and the early identification of the organisational problem or challenge. It is critical for scoping the intervention's goals, and identifying key stakeholders and their expectations. It can involve several activities, including:

- group discussions with/between HR, organisation leaders, managers
- identifying and clarifying the organisational issue(s) to be addressed, for example falling sales, business growth. This may be based on early diagnostics and what is known now about the business, and as the ODV process progresses, new information is likely to come to light that highlights the root cause of this, or an alternative issue which is the real driver.

Whether the OD practitioner is internal or external, there are several ethical issues that they must be mindful of, including confidentiality, over-promising, colluding, applying an intervention that is familiar rather than appropriate, and accurately eliciting and feeding back findings (French and Bell 1999).

8.3.5 STAGE 2: DIAGNOSING

After the initial discussions about the organisational problem or challenge, this is the fact-finding stage which involves collecting then analysing organisational data. This enables the OD practitioner to build up a clear and accurate picture of the situation and its root causes. Although it may focus on different areas, this process is not dissimilar to the 'assess' stage of OD which we looked at above. Interventions available to assist diagnosis include (French and Bell 1999):

- interviews, for example to establish strengths and weaknesses within a team or function
- observations, for example of how meetings are conducted, how team members interact

- questionnaires and survey feedback
- examining organisational documents
- 'projective' methods such as asking a team to draw a team crest or logo.

8.3.6 STAGE 3: FEEDING BACK DIAGNOSTIC INFORMATION

This involves feeding back the findings from the diagnosis stage to the client, for example feedback gathered in individual interviews is categorised and presented back by the ODV practitioner. The 'client' could be one leader in the organisation, but is more likely to be a client group (such as a senior project team, the executive board), or the group(s) that is the target of the ODV intervention. The OD practitioner discusses the findings with the client group to check for understanding and accuracy, seeks clarification where necessary and they collectively draw insights and conclusions about the situation, problem or opportunity (French and Bell 1999).

This stage may require the ODV practitioner acting as a coach, a facilitator, a mediator (in the event of conflict) and a teacher (they may provide short 'lectures' on key, relevant topics to the group)

8.3.7 STAGE 4: DESIGNING INTERVENTIONS

This can also be referred to as planning change, such as French and Bell (1999), who define interventions as 'sets of structured activities in which selected organizational units (target groups or individuals) engage in a task or a sequence of tasks with the goals of organizational improvement and individual development' (p145).

This is the stage where practitioner and client decide what actions to take, and the practitioner ensures they fit together into an intervention strategy. In practice, interventions can target several levels within the organisation: individual, teams and groups, inter-group relations and the total organisation. Theoretically, the many interventions available are sometimes most suitable for one of these levels in particular; there isn't scope here to go into this level of detail, or even to provide full explanations of each intervention. More detailed accounts can be found in Cummings and Worley (2015), and also French and Bell (1999) and who cite (among many others) these potential interventions:

- teambuilding activities
- conflict resolution or mediation activities
- learning and development interventions (individual or group)
- career or life planning activities
- inter-group activities (referred to as 'organisational mirroring')
- survey feedback activities in which groups review and discuss results of surveys they have participated in
- process consultation activities, such as where the client gains insight into various organisational processes and how to diagnose and manage them
- coaching and counselling activities, for example to help individuals to learn and embed new behaviours
- HRM activities, for example redefining reward strategy to increase motivation and performance
- planning activities, for example a facilitated goal-setting workshop
- strategic management activities, for example a facilitated executive meeting where the organisation's strategic plan is evaluated and redefined
- organisational transformation activities, for example system-wide changes like the introduction of total quality management.

In these interventions, the ODV practitioner may be acting in any number of roles, such as a coach, a facilitator, a trainer or a mediator, and will require a robust understanding of ODV practice, the group or organisation they are dealing with, and organisational performance generally.

8.3.8 STAGE 5: MANAGING CHANGE

ODV is a planned change initiative, like OD, and in many respects this stage is similar to the 'implement' stage of the ADIE approach to OD. Unlike OD though, it is likely that many employees will already have participated in the change process during the previous stages, which are very likely to overlap, and some of the interventions designed or chosen in the previous stage may already have taken place. Although ODV processes should be supported by a project plan with agreed timelines, outcomes and so forth, to the average employee this change process would appear more fluid and inclusive than one surrounding an OD project.

As mentioned previously, Lewin's 'unfreeze-move-freeze' is very relevant to ODV-related change, fitting well with the fluid and dynamic nature of these 6 steps required to bring it about. The Burke-Litwin model, although more detailed, also supports the ODV process. French and Bell (1999) also reference other established change models. They cite one designed by Cummings and Worley in 1993, who identify five sets of activities required for successful change management: motivating change (or creating change readiness), creating a vision, developing political support, managing the transition and sustaining momentum. They also reference Kotter's eight-step model which overlaps with this, and also includes ODV-friendly concepts such as 'empowering' employees to act on the vision.

8.3.9 STAGE 6: EVALUATING AND INSTITUTIONALISING CHANGE

If we think back to one of the criticisms made of ODV, that its practitioners often lose track of the organisation's bottom line and are over-involved with the ODV process, this may appear to be a challenging stage of the process. Whilst OD may have more tangible metrics associated with it (for example, cost savings, increased output), some of the aims of ODV interventions are intangible and rather harder to measure. Nevertheless, to ensure that ODV remains focused and relevant in an age where organisations face growing pressures to innovate, be agile and streamline costs, it is recommended that ODV practitioners (whether internal or external) either set some KPIs (key performance indicators) or targets, ideally linked to the organisation's strategic plan, or clearly define some outcomes that they are setting out to achieve.

So whilst it is not impossible to establish organisation performance metrics to measure the outcome of ODV interventions, or to clearly define outputs, there are other, less quantifiable outcomes which may be expected from ODV interventions and which add value to the business. These include further feedback (which may be fed back into the continual process of ODV); increased interaction and communication (leading to positive change in attitudes and behaviour); more frequent and visible confrontation (helping to remove obstructions); increased participation in problem-solving, goal-setting, and so on; increased accountability and increased energy and optimism (French and Bell 1999).

The ODV practitioner may remain involved with the project for months or even years, for example returning periodically to observe and feed back on a group meeting, or to run an annual planning workshop. The high level of employee participation that ODV involves aims to create lasting behavioural change at individual through to the organisational level, and ultimately cultural change. This factor helps to embed change, as do other aspects of OD, such as the cyclical and fluid nature of OD itself, and its focus on satisfying individual motivators and increasing personal development which raises commitment to the new way of doing things.

CASE STUDY 8.2

HOLACRACY AT ZAPPOS?

Tony Hsieh (pronounced 'Shay') is the CEO of Zappos, an online shoe retailer based in the US recognised for outstanding customer service to customers buying shoes through its website. Hsieh invested in Zappos in 1999 after selling his first business, LinkExchange, to Yahoo for $265m, and became CEO of Zappos shortly after. Although gross sales were minimal back in 1999, when consumers were still getting used to the Internet and online shopping was still a new concept, Hsieh turned the business around completely, and just a decade later in 2009, sold it to Amazon for $1.2bn.

As if this wasn't enough, he achieved this by running Zappos in a unique way, putting organisational culture, training and development, and customer service at the heart of the business, sustaining these through the change in ownership, and using many innovative interventions to bring these to life. For example, in the Zappos office you might find a nap room, a petting zoo or makeshift bowling alley. All new employees receive four weeks' training, and are offered $2,000 to resign after the first week, to make sure that only truly committed employees stay with the business. There are no time limits on calls that come in to the customer service centre, so employees have time to engage with callers and fully resolve their query. Customers and employees are delighted, and the business results show that this approach has created high levels of organisational performance.

In early 2014, Zappos made a surprising announcement: it planned to eliminate job titles and traditional managers from the company. Rather than being accountable to one boss in a hierarchy, employees would report and be accountable to colleagues in their 'circle',

each of which has a specific organisational goal. This was a move toward a new philosophy of how to run a company called 'holacracy' (see www.holacracy.com for further details). Holacracy is a truly dynamic organisational model. It changes the structure of an organisation by taking power away from a management hierarchy, and distributing it across various job roles. Both roles and organisational structure are adjusted regularly, decision-making is delegated to 'circles' responsible for specific goals, and all employees are bound by the same, visible rules, including the CEO.

By the end of 2014, 80% of Zappos' 1,500 employees did not have a manager. In March 2015, Hsieh offered 3 months' severance pay to any employee who felt they could not get behind this radical new management system. 210 employees (around 14%) took him up on this offer (McGregor 2015).

Questions

1   Are you surprised that 14% of employees (already accustomed to working in an 'unusual' culture) chose to leave the organisation? Why/why not?

2   What steps do you think Zappos needed to take to implement (a) this radical new structure and (b) the working practices which went with it?

3   From an ODV perspective, when they introduced holacracy, what risks do you think Zappos' leadership team faced in upsetting the existing culture? Do you think that the existence of a very strong culture was a help or an obstacle in this change initiative?

4	Could holacracy work in your organisation? What are the pros and cons of doing away with traditional authority in the form of line management?	For further reading on Zappos see Hseih (2010) or various newspaper articles e.g. Hollander (2013). For further reading on holacracy, see www.holacracy.com

We've looked at both OD and ODV in some detail: their histories and theoretical bases, what they are, how they happen in organisations, and some of their similarities and differences. Both aim to improve and sustain organisational performance in the current and future business environment, and in line with the contingency theory that we referenced earlier, OD and ODV must consider and respond to various external factors in their process and outcomes – especially the need to create and support an agile organisation.

As we have touched on previously, this is also a fascinating time to be thinking about how organisations will sustain their performance in the future. Organisations have an ongoing and growing need to be more agile, and OD and ODV can impact this through their various interventions: engaging employees, organisation structure, job design, systems, processes to name a few.

As we reach the end of this chapter, we will look at some other trends, established and emerging, which may impact the way that OD and ODV must operate in order to achieve their end goals, some of which we have already touched on in this chapter.

? REFLECTIVE ACTIVITY 8.3

There is not scope here to provide significant detail on these trends or to expand on them, and they are included to provoke thinking about OD and ODV within your own organisation. Consider:

1 How could each of these trends affect your organisation in the decade ahead?

2 Which one would have the biggest impact?

3 What steps could your organisation take from (a) an OD, structural perspective and (b) an ODV perspective to prepare for these changes?

8.4.1 TECHNOLOGICAL CHANGE

Technological change has had a significant impact on work and organisations since the industrial revolution, and later the advent of mass production. In more recent decades, increasingly sophisticated technology has impacted work and life in almost every sector, from the way pilots fly planes, to automating accounting and payroll processes, to booking a holiday through an app, to finding love, and endless more examples.

However, developments in the world of robotics mean that in the foreseeable future, it's not only repetitive tasks or set processes that can be automated, as machines and robots are increasingly capable of using delicate judgement in the way that a human would and making decisions. At the time of writing, newspapers are publishing articles with titles such as 'Could a robot do your job' (*Daily Telegraph* 2015).

Frey and Osborne (2015, p3), experts in this field, sum this up as follows: 'Technology is now enabling not just the automation of repetitive tasks but also cognitive tasks involving subtle and non-routine judgment. Through robotics, big data, the digitisation of industries and the Internet of Things the nature of occupations and whole industries is changing and also the dynamics of economic growth.'

Although this may still seem like the stuff of science fiction films, it raises a multitude of questions. From an OD perspective, what do you think the impact could be on the process element of your organisation, or others that you are familiar with? How might it impact job design where you work?

From an ODV perspective, consider the complexity and organisational challenges that the automation of such complex tasks may bring; the impact of this on workforce structure; the impact on employee motivation and engagement; and the challenges of diagnosing this opportunity, designing interventions and managing change in a manner true to the values of ODV.

8.4.2 NEW AND EMERGING BUSINESS MODELS

In the OD section, we looked at some more dynamic organisational structures, such as virtual, matrix and flexible structures. But another emerging trend is a change in the type of organisations and the business models they operate in. In 2014, 5.2m small and medium-sized enterprises (SMEs) accounted for 60% of private sector employment in the UK, with 99.3% of these being 'small' rather than 'medium' (DBIS 2014), a figure which is steadily on the rise.

Douglas McWilliams (2015) has written a book called *The flat white economy*, referring to a relatively new and fashionable type of milky coffee and more importantly the cafes in which, stereotypically speaking, it is consumed in great quantities by young creative types working on Apple laptops. Although it may be mainly an East London-based phenomenon, McWilliams argues that the flat white economy has created four times more jobs than the City lost in the global financial crisis, and it is becoming a prototype for digital cities around the UK and the world.

Thinking from an OD perspective, why do you think this population is drawn towards freelance jobs or roles in small, informal start-ups? Is this a geographical phenomenon limited to London? As these organisations grow, what kind of organisational challenges might they face, from both an OD and an ODV perspective?

8.4.3 CHANGES IN CUSTOMER EXPECTATIONS

While customer expectations vary from sector to sector, many common themes in this area are reported in the mainstream press as well as in research. For example, Solomon (2014) refers to changed perceptions of what is 'fast' (for example delivery and response times), an increased demand for accuracy, an expectation of extended availability (often 24/7), greater awareness of consumer rights and an expectation of money back, an appetite for authentic, non-scripted service, and greater 'empowerment' and personalisation. How can OD interventions ensure that an organisation's structure and processes facilitate efficient operations to meet evolving customer expectations?

8.4.4 DEMOGRAPHIC CHANGE

An Internet search on this topic will reveal a multitude of trends impacting the UK in this area (for example CIPD 2013b), including gender representation and immigration (leading to increased multiculturalism in organisations). Another one is population ageing; this means there is not only an approaching 'workforce cliff' of labour and talent shortages, but that organisations will soon be dealing with multi-generational workforces containing baby boomers as well as members of generations Y and Z.

Whilst being mindful that this is an area fraught with stereotypes, what are some of the challenges arising from this that ODV can help to address? How might the different populations experience different organisation structures, the extent of hierarchy within them and the working patterns that they involve?

8.4.5 OPPORTUNITIES FOR THE HR PROFESSION

At different points in this chapter, we've touched on the role of HR in these very strategic business processes, and highlighted that perhaps HR is not involved in OD and ODV from the outset, or is overlooked in favour of an external practitioner. Although this presents a profession-wide opportunity, it also presents a personal one. In concluding this chapter, the reader is encouraged to review the CIPD's Profession Map (2015d), tackle some of the reflective questions and consider how to increase their own effectiveness in this area, through their continuing professional development (CPD) and in their own organisation.

REFERENCES

ATKINSON, J. (1984) Manpower strategies for flexible organisations. *Personnel Management.* pp28–31.

BUCHANAN, D. A. and HUCZYNSKI, A. A. (2010) *Organisational behavior.* 7th ed. London: Prentice Hall.

BURNS, T. (1963) Industry in a new age. *New Society,* 31 January. Vol 18. pp17–20, cited in PUGH, D.S. (ed.) (2007) *Organisation theory: selected classical readings.* Harmondsworth: Penguin.

CAMPBELL, D. and CRAIG, T. (2005) *Organisations and the business environment.* Oxford: Elsevier Butterworth Heinemann.

CANNON, J. A. and MCGEE, R. (2008) *Organisation development and change toolkit.* London: Chartered Institute of Personnel and Development.

CANNON, J. A., MCGEE, R. and STANFORD, N. (2010) *Organisation design and capability building toolkit.* London: Chartered Institute of Personnel and Development.

CIPD (2013a) *Hacking HR to build an adaptability advantage.* Research Report. London: Chartered Institute of Personnel and Development.

CIPD (2013b) *Megatrends: the trends shaping work and working lives.* London: Chartered Institute of Personnel and Development.

CIPD (2014) *HR: Getting Smart about agile working.* Research Report. London: Chartered Institute of Personnel and Development.

CIPD (2015a) *Organisation design.* Factsheet. London: Chartered Institute of Personnel and Development.

CIPD (2015b) *Organisation development.* Factsheet. London: Chartered Institute of Personnel and Development.

CIPD (2015c) *HR's role in developing OD solutions for change.* London: Chartered Institute of Personnel and Development.

CIPD (2015d) *CIPD profession map.* London: Chartered Institute of Personnel and Development.

CIPD (2015e) *Zero-hours and short-hours contracts in the UK: employer and employee perspectives.* Policy Report. London: Chartered Institute of Personnel and Development.

CONNOR, G., MCFADDEN, M. and MCLEAN, I. (2012) Organisation design. In: STEWART, J. and ROGERS, P. (eds). *Developing people and organisations.* London: Chartered Institute of Personnel and Development.

CUMMINGS, T. G. and WORLEY, C. G. (2015) *Organization development and change.* 10th ed. Stamford, CA: Cengage Learning.

DAFT, R. (2007) *Understanding the Theory and Design of Organisations.* Mason, OH: Thomson South Western.

DAILY TELEGRAPH [online] (2015) Could a robot do your job? Not if you're creative enough. Available at: www.telegraph.co.uk/finance/businessclub/11552787/Could-a-robot-do-your-job-Not-if-youre-creative-enough.html [accessed 2015].

DBIS (2014) *Business population estimates for the UK and regions.* Sheffield: Department for Business Innovation and Skills.

EIU (Economist Intelligence Unit) (2009) *Organisational agility: how business can survive and thrive in turbulent times.* London: Economist Intelligence Unit.

FRENCH, W. L. and BELL, C. H. (1999) *Organisation development: behavioural science interventions for organisational improvement.* 6th ed. Upper Saddle River, NJ: Prentice Hall.

FREY, C. B. and OSBORNE, M. A. (2015) *Technology at work: the future of innovation and employment.* Oxford Martin School, University of Oxford/Citi GPS: Global Perspectives and Solutions.

GREINER, L.E. (1972). Evolution and revolution as organizations grow. *Harvard Business Review*, 50, 4, 37–46

HOLLANDER, J. (2013) Lessons we can all learn from Zappos CEO Tony Hsieh. *Guardian Online.* 12 March.

HSIEH, T. (2010) *Delivering happiness: a path to profits, passion, and purpose.* New York: Grand Central Publishing.

MARSH, C., SPARROW, P., HIRD, M., BALAIN, S. and HESKETH, A. (2009*) Integrated organisation design: the new strategic priority for HR directors.* White Paper 09/01. Lancaster: Lancaster University Management School.

MCGREGOR, J. (2015) At Zappos, 210 employees decide to leave rather than work with no bosses. *Washington Post.* 8 May.

MCWILLIAMS, D. (2015) *The flat white economy.* London: Duckworth Overlook.

PWC TECHNOLOGY INSTITUTE (2015) *Building enterprise agility.* PWC Technology Institute, September.

RHODES, C. (2015) *Manufacturing: statistics and policy.* Briefing Paper Number 01942, 6 August. London: House of Commons Library.

ROBBINS, S. P. and JUDGE, T. A. (2008) *Organizational behaviour.* 12th ed. Upper Saddle River, NJ: Pearson Education.

SOLOMON, M. (2014) 10 Trending changes in customer service expectations. *Forbes Online.* 8 August.

WAGNER, J.A. and HOLLENBECK, J.R. (2014) *Organizational behaviour: securing competitive advantage.* New York: Routledge.

WORLD BANK (2015) *Manufacturing, value added (% of GDP).* Available at: data. worldbank.org/indicator/NV.IND.MANF.ZS [accessed 2015].

WORSTALL, T. (2012) The story of Henry Ford's $5 a day wages: it's not what you think. *Forbes Online.* 12 March.

CHAPTER 9

Improving Organisational Performance

STEPHEN TAYLOR

CHAPTER CONTENTS

- Introduction
- What is high performance working?
- Linking high performance working and organisational performance
- Explaining the link
- Criticisms of the research on high performance working practices
- Formal performance management systems
- Problems with performance appraisal
- 360-degree feedback
- HRM and formal performance management
- Refreshing and updating traditional performance management
- Building a high performance culture

KEY LEARNING OUTCOMES

By the end of this chapter, you should be able to:

- understand the concept of high performance working
- explain why many analysts believe that high performance work practices lead to superior business performance, while some others remain sceptical
- set out how typical performance appraisal systems operate, including 360-degree approaches, and the role that HR managers play in supporting them
- identify the major criticisms that are made concerning traditional appraisal systems and advise about how they can be made more effective
- participate in activities aimed at building a high performance culture at work.

9.1 INTRODUCTION

Improving and seeking to maximise employee performance in a workplace is a central objective of human resource management. Once an organisation has secured the services of people with the skills and experience that it requires through effective recruitment, selection and employee retention practices, its next aim is to find ways of getting the best out of those people. Accomplishing this is something which HR managers undertake in collaboration with line managers, assisting and advising them where possible, while also providing them with training and tools which help them to secure higher performance from individual employees. We have discussed many elements of this process elsewhere in this book, particularly in our chapters on reward management, human resource development and employee engagement. In this chapter we are therefore going to focus on the management of employee performance at the level of the team rather than the individual employee. The most successful organisations not only seek to improve the level of performance achieved by each individual that they employ, they also work towards the creation and sustenance of 'high performance working' across their operations. Achieving this is always very challenging, requiring an organisation's people to demonstrate commitment, initiative, enthusiasm and determination to meet and exceed objectives. Ultimately it requires an organisation to build a high performance work culture and to maintain and strengthen this over time. Human resource managers are generally expected to lead initiatives in this area, but the achievement of genuine high performance working is always a collective endeavour. Senior leaders play a crucial role, as do team leaders at all levels, as well as employees without any management responsibilities.

Over the past twenty years the terms 'high performance work systems' and 'high performance organisations' have achieved considerable prominence in research into HRM carried out all over the world. Much of this work strongly suggests that sustained, superior organisational performance is the outcome when such an organisation is created. Moreover, there is also evidence to suggest that employees benefit as well as their organisations when they participate in high performance working. While these claims are compelling, it is important to remember that they are not without their critics. It is thus inaccurate to suggest that this broad approach to HRM has universal support or to assert that it will invariably have a positive impact in all business scenarios.

Formal performance management systems have a much longer history, but are still widely recognised as having a potential role to play in enhancing employee performance, particularly when it comes to ensuring that key organisational objectives are met. Like high performance work practices, traditional performance appraisal systems are not without their critics. In this chapter we will therefore explore these debates and also discuss ways in which formal reviews of individual performance can be adapted to make them more fit for purpose in contemporary organisations.

Finally, we consider the types of approach and management philosophy that are required to build a sustained high performance culture in organisations. This is challenging for any management team at the best of times, but is potentially much harder still when business environments are volatile, meaning that long-term job security can in no way be guaranteed. In this final section we draw on the ideas of Holbeche (2005) to discuss ways in which high performance can be achieved and sustained even in unpredictable and highly competitive environments.

9.2 WHAT IS 'HIGH PERFORMANCE WORKING'?

For more than a century now consultants and academic researchers have expended a great deal of effort trying to establish whether or not any simple set of management principles can be identified which will enhance an organisation's performance when applied in practice. Frederick W. Taylor and his contemporaries started this process in the 1890s and the early years of the last century with the development of 'scientific management' principles. These revolutionised the way that the manufacturing industry was organised across the world with the development of time and motion studies, Gantt charts and assembly lines. Productivity increased substantially in the process. Later, as the service sector grew and manufacturing plants became more technologically sophisticated, different sets of principles came to prominence and were widely applied. Most influential was human relations thinking which argued in favour of management systems and job design principles which motivated people, making working life more interesting and enjoyable. This also led to productivity improvements as employees became more committed, less inclined to leave jobs and to take periods of unauthorised absence. In the late twentieth century, as globalisation and rapid technological advances created a business world that was less predictable, less stable, more competitive and, in many countries, post-industrial, the question of how organisations could best maximise the performance of their people was again revisited. While research in this area is still very much ongoing, the set of principles which have proved to be most enduring and influential are those that underpin **high performance work systems** (HPWS).

HPWS are best understood as comprising a bundle of distinct human resource management policies and practices which are introduced in an organisation at the same time and which are mutually reinforcing. The precise make-up of the bundle has never been agreed definitively. Different studies have included a wide variety of different elements (Paauwe et al 2013, pp7–8). However, there is a broad consensus that any list should include the practices which are most likely to promote employee commitment and involvement. The following elements are most commonly included in analyses of HPWS (see Boselie et al 2005; Datta et al 2005; Marchington and Wilkinson 2012):

- Rigorous and sophisticated recruitment and selection practices, whereby an organisation encourages applications from a broad field of candidates, going on to make an evidence-based choice based on who is most likely to perform well in the job being advertised.
- High levels of investment in training and development, so that employees are kept up to date with developments in their field, improve their capability and are able to advance their careers.
- Relatively high levels of pay, but payment systems which make the amount received contingent on performance. This approach serves to attract strong performers, retains staff in whom the organisation has invested and provides an incentive for employees to maximise their contribution.
- Internal promotion systems based on merit which encourage investment in HRD while providing people in whom that investment has been made to remain employed in the organisation for longer than they might otherwise choose to.
- Team-based approaches to work which enable groups of employees to determine for themselves how exactly they achieve their objectives and empower them to make improvements. Team-based incentive reward systems are also often included.
- Grievance procedures that can be used without fear so that employees who believe they have been treated unjustly can raise the issue with senior managers without having to resign and seek alternative employment. The result should also be a reduction in the incidence of injustice.
- A high degree of participation in decision-making enabling employees to help determine organisation policy and practice. This enhances commitment while also often improving the quality of decision-making. The more autonomy that individuals have over their own areas of work the more engaged they will be.
- Information sharing whereby managers are as transparent as possible about the issues the organisation faces and their future plans. This is a prerequisite for effective employee involvement and also signals an intention to treat people in a mature manner.
- An effective performance appraisal system to help ensure that everyone employed in an organisation has goals to work towards which align with the organisation's objectives which they are expected to meet.
- Flexible working, particularly multi-skilling so that people can be deployed efficiently and can adapt rapidly when new opportunities arise.
- A high degree of job security. This serves to attract and retain strong performers while also underpinning commitment and engagement.
- Provision of a good work–life balance so that employees enjoy a high level of personal well-being, do not become overstressed or run the risk of 'burning out'.

- A high level of harmonisation in respect of terms and conditions of employment so that status differentials are minimised and the same rules apply to everyone, however senior. Examples might include standard holiday entitlement, hours of work, pension arrangements and access to on-site facilities such as car parking and restaurants.

The contents of the bundle can be seen as comprising a range of HR and general management principles which are typically viewed as 'best practices', being both sophisticated and designed to attract, retain and engage employees. They are believed to be associated with relatively high levels of organisational performance for two main reasons. First, because people want to work in organisations that take this 'best practice' approach when managing their people, an employer that does so is better able than others to build up a positive reputation in the labour market. It can then achieve 'employer of choice' status and will be able to attract and retain the best staff. Second, once employed those staff are more likely to be actively and positively engaged in their work. This will maximise their level of commitment and should encourage them to demonstrate 'discretionary effort', going further and exerting more energy than is required under their contracts of employment. Some argue that HPWS also make it more likely that employees will embrace change rather than resist and also that it promotes innovation and creativity (see Holbeche 2005).

9.3 HIGH PERFORMANCE WORKING AND ORGANISATIONAL PERFORMANCE

A huge amount of research has been carried out all over the world in recent years which has sought to test the proposition that the adoption of 'high performance working practices' leads to superior business performance. The results have generally been encouraging, although not all are convinced by them.

The first studies of this kind were carried out among larger private sector companies based in the USA during the 1990s. Jeffery Pfeffer (1994, 1998) of Stanford University examined in what ways the HR practices used in the most successful and fastest growing companies differed from those of their less successful competitors. He concluded that a mix of policies along the lines of the 'best practice bundle' set out above were used in the majority of these companies, going on to argue that in his view they had something significant to offer all organisations operating in all sectors:

> Contrary to some academic writing and to popular belief, there is little evidence that effective management practices are 1) particularly faddish (although their implementation may well be), 2) difficult to understand or to comprehend why they work, or 3) necessarily contingent on an organisation's particular competitive strategy. (Pfeffer 1994, p27)

At around the same time Mark Huselid at Rutgers University was exploring the same issue, but on a much bigger scale and using a questionnaire-based methodology. The paper he published in 1995 reporting his results went on to become the most widely cited academic article on an HR subject in the world. Its influence cannot be understated. Huselid (1995) sent detailed questionnaires concerning all types of HR policy and practice to 968 firms from a range of industries. All employed over 100 people. He then compared the results with measures of company performance as set out in their published annual reports. He looked at staff turnover rates, but more importantly he also considered a measure known as 'Tobin's q' which is defined as the market value of the firm divided by the book value of its assets, and also at gross rates of return on capital invested. His conclusions were striking. Huselid was able to show that the more use of sophisticated HR practices there was in a firm, the lower its labour turnover, the higher its market value and the higher its profits. His precise calculations were as follows:

A 1 standard deviation increase in HR practices yields:

- a 7.05% decrease in staff turnover

- $27,044 in increased sales per employee

- $18,641 more in market value per employee

- $3,814 more in profit per employee.

For the first time a robust academic study had thus apparently demonstrated that enlightened, people-focused HRM paid off in financial terms. Here was the proof that HRM really added value, and significantly too.

In the years following the publication of Huselid's seminal article, his work was replicated and refined in many further studies carried out around the world. Not all had quite such striking results, but in the vast majority of cases the conclusions have been broadly comparable with those of Huselid's original study (see Paauwe et al 2013, pp2–4 for a summary of this body of research). Of particular importance was Combs et al's (2006) meta-analysis which took account of 92 separate studies undertaken in the wake of Huselid's. Some of these had quite small sample sizes, but when taken together in aggregate with all the other smaller studies the results have greater validity. Combs et al concluded that 'high performance work practices' are on average associated with a 4.6% increase in return on assets and a 4.4% reduction in staff turnover.

On the face of it this large body of research is highly compelling, and unsurprisingly it has been widely publicised by HR managers and organisations that are keen to advance the case for approaches to management that are progressive and sophisticated in their treatment of staff. As a result it is now widely accepted that 'best practice HRM' in the form of the bundle of practices discussed here are of considerable potential benefit for all types of organisations operating all over the world in any industry. Not only will their introduction substantially increase an organisation's performance, but it can help to sustain competitive advantage for longer, while also increasing the well-being and satisfaction of employees.

9.4 EXPLAINING THE LINK

In more recent years the research on links between HRM and business performance has moved on. Having established the existence of an apparent link between the way people are managed and business performance, researchers have been keen to try and understand the nature of that link. In other words, they have sought to explain why exactly the adoption of the bundle of best practices appears to have such a benefit for the organisations concerned. This work is still very much in progress and will undoubtedly reveal new insights in the future. But already we can point to a number of findings which have been very influential.

In the UK the most prominent research has been that carried out by John Purcell and his colleagues at Bath University with funding provided by CIPD. These are often labelled 'the black box studies' to reflect their key aim of exploring the unknown reasons for the performance–HR link. Working over a six-year period, the team of researchers started by started by identifying organisations that were either already well known for having sophisticated HR policies and practices in place or had recently embarked on a strategy of doing so. Twelve UK-based organisations from a mix of industrial sectors finally participated. The team then undertook a very extensive series of interviews with employees and managers in specific areas of these businesses. They also revisited several times so as to be able to record reaction to new initiatives as they were introduced over time. The first results were published in 2003 (see Purcell et al 2003). There were three major findings:

1 When an organisation has in place a bundle of 'progressive' or 'high performance' HR policies and practices there is a positive response from employees (expressed in terms

of job satisfaction, motivation or organisational commitment) which leads them to work harder and to strive to improve their performance. In such circumstances 'discretionary effort' results, meaning that employees tend to work beyond contract, going the extra mile without having to be coerced into doing so.

2   A characteristic shared by the most successful organisations is some form of 'big idea' that underpins what their mission is and what values that mission is based on. Moreover, this big idea and these values become embedded in the organisation's policies and practices, helping to glue the organisation together. Employees tend to buy in to the idea and respond by working with enthusiasm, some pride and effort. Another way of expressing this is the presence of a 'strong sense of shared purpose' between managers and employees.

3   Having the right HR policies and practices in place was not enough. These have to be 'brought to life' by the line managers with whom staff interact on a day-to-day basis. Effective line management is thus a crucial component of 'the black box'. Unless employees respect and are motivated positively by their immediate supervisors, the positive impact that 'progressive' HR policies have will not be realised. Indeed one finding was that poor implementation of policies and practices by line managers who have not bought into them is often worse for the organisation than not having any policies at all.

The black box studies therefore found good evidence that the right approach to HR, implemented effectively, will bring about superior organisational performance (ie the output). In other words, they found good, robust evidence across several organisations that demonstrated strong support for a causal link between HRM activity and superior business performance. Importantly, however, they concluded that there was no automatic link. Other conditions must also be satisfied if a bundle of best practices is to underpin high levels of performance.

The black box studies are also celebrated for their advocacy of the **AMO** model – one of the conditions that needs to be in place. AMO stands for:

- the **a**bility to perform well
- the **m**otivation to perform well
  and
- the **o**pportunity to perform well.

It is this, along with the other conditions, which permits organisations to benefit fully from good HR practices.

Another highly influential body of research in this field has emanated from the Gallup Organization (see Harter et al 2002). Their findings were derived from an analysis of data collected over a number of years across the world using a simple 12-question instrument. This simple employee engagement questionnaire had, by 2002, been administered to 198,514 people in 7,939 business units operating in all manner of industries over a 30-year period. The 12 questions simply comprise statements such as:

'I know what is expected of me at work'

and

'In the last seven days, I have received recognition or praise for doing good work'.

Respondents are then asked to say whether they strongly agree, agree, disagree, strongly disagree or neither agree nor disagree, and scores then being generated for a unit's employees' level of engagement. The sheer size of this dataset gives the analysis credibility. What is more, it enables statistically significant correlations to be sought between the extent of employees' emotional and cognitive engagement and other variables such as profitability, productivity, customer satisfaction and employee turnover rates. Some of the key findings are as follows:

1   There is greater variation in terms of the level of employee engagement between different business units within the same organisation than there is between organisations. This is significant because it implies that the variability in levels is not related to the type of industry or characteristics of employees – but is in most cases due to the quality of line management.

2   Impressive correlations were found to exist between relative levels of employee engagement in a business unit and the success of business units. Business units with the highest rates of employee engagement are doubly successful than those with the lowest when measured against indicators such as productivity, customer responses and profitability.

3   A particularly strong relationship was found between levels of employee involvement and rates of staff turnover. The size of the dataset allows separate analysis of high turnover industries and low turnover industries. In high turnover business units (above 60% turnover rate), staff turnover was, on average, 29% lower in units which scored in the upper quartile for employee engagement, than in the lower one. The variation, however, ranged between 14 and 51 percentage points. In low turnover units the average difference was 10% (ranging from 4 to 19 percentage points) between upper and lower quartiles.

The message from the Gallup Studies is thus strikingly similar in many respects from that of the black box studies. HR policies and practices help to generate superior business performance because they help to motivate employees positively to perform well in their individual roles. The black box studies use the term 'discretionary effort' to describe this, while the Gallup Studies use the term 'employee engagement'. But both contend that Huselid's link can largely be explained by the fact that most employees respond positively to the presence in their organisations of the 'best practice bundle' of high performance work practices, and that this tends to lead (provided other important conditions are also in place) to improved individual work performance. When this is true of the preponderance of employees, the net result is substantially improved organisation performance.

The most recent studies have tended to analyse different aspects of human performance to see if any particular ingredient can be found to explain more of the link than others. There has, for example, been a lot of work carried out on the concept of 'employee well-being', the suggestion being that the best practice bundle promotes well-being and this is then the major source of improved performance. Others have focused on the development of human capital and the employee relations climate (Peccei et al 2013). As yet, however, no definitive conclusions have been reached about how far these more narrowly defined concepts might be especially significant in explaining Huselid's link.

9.5 CRITICISMS OF THE RESEARCH ON HIGH PERFORMANCE WORKING PRACTICES

The research into high performance work practices and its link to superior business performance has been very widely disseminated and has proved highly influential in underpinning changes in organisational practice. However, it is also important to point out that some remain unconvinced by it. While no-one has yet authoritatively argued that the bundle of HRM 'best practices' has no positive impact whatever on business performance, some have argued that attempts to quantify the impact in financial terms are deeply flawed, while others have questioned the true extent to which this body of research *proves* anything.

The major criticisms have come from those who have concerns about the way that the existence of a clear correlation between HRM activity and business performance is taken to indicate that the first is the cause of the second. Correlation does not prove causation, even if that may appear to be the obvious explanation. Their work suggests that in reality it may be the case that superior performance leads to the introduction of high performance working and not the other way around. In other words it could be the case that once a firm is successful, it uses some of its surplus profit to invest in a first-class HR function with state-of-the-art policies and procedures. This is plausible when we look at the approach to HRM that is favoured by the most successful technology companies such as Google, Microsoft and Apple (at least in their US operations). They have used the financial fruits of their success, in part, to create a superb employee value proposition, making them highly rewarding places to work in all respects.

Another entirely plausible explanation for the correlation could be the existence of a third interdependent variable which the researchers have failed to control for and which can explain both the presence of HPWS and the superior business performance. Achieving a good reputation among financial analysts and opinion-formers is one possibility here. It may be that an organisation that is professionally and efficiently managed is able to generate income for investment. This then in turn both explains its good performance relative to others and, potentially, its relatively generous approach to employment practices. Yet there may be no actual direct link between the two.

Another group question the existence of HPWS practices at all, arguing that there is a big distinction to be made between management rhetoric in respect of HRM and the reality of work as experienced by employees (for example Legge 1995). The argument here runs as follows. The presence of sophisticated 'high commitment' and 'high involvement' HR practices is mere window dressing which masks what is actually going on in these organisations; namely increased work intensification and greater exploitation of workers. The companies concerned are using the language of HRM to cover up the reality which is longer hours, tight wage settlements, additional stress for staff, more management control and lower job quality. It is these, so the argument runs, that are really responsible for the stronger business performance and not the nice HR rhetoric that covers up the ugly reality. We can also perhaps point to organisations in the public sector in the UK where pay is high and terms and conditions of employment generous, but where there appears to be no evidence of sustained high performance or even much by way of high productivity.

The most sophisticated critique to date has been that published by Steve Fleetwood and Anthony Hesketh (2010). In their book entitled *Explaining the performance of human resource management* they warn against uncritical acceptance of the findings of studies that link HR practices to business outcomes. Ultimately, they point out, it is the people who work in organisations who are generally responsible for the achievement of sustained superior business performance. The book is long and closely argued, but it is possible to summarise their key points in a few sentences:

1 It is not possible to predict in financial terms what impact new HR interventions will have on business performance.

2 The studies focus too much on the 'HR architecture' and not enough on 'the role of individuals in shaping the performance of organisations'. It is people who deliver superior organisational performance, not HR systems, policies or practices. The research tends to focus on this architecture and not sufficiently on the people.

3 Too much trust is placed in the conclusions of studies that seek to demonstrate how HR *causes* improvements in performance. This is too great a claim. Instead we should think in terms of HR playing an *enabling* role.

Paauwe et al (2013, pp6–7) call for much more longitudinal research now to be carried out in order to address the concerns of critics. This would mean measuring business performance before the introduction of HPWS and then again afterwards while controlling for all manner of other possible factors, and doing so repeatedly in many different organisations and industries. Only then, assuming the results were positive, will we be able to claim with a high level of confidence that HPWS causes an increased level of business performance.

9.6 FORMAL PERFORMANCE MANAGEMENT SYSTEMS

In most organisations performance management is seen as being a process that carries on continually as individual line managers seek to engage and motivate their staff on a day-to-day basis using whatever approaches work best for them. Aside from some involvement in training and more extensive involvement when performance slips so far that disciplinary action is necessary, HR managers have only a limited role to play in this ongoing, informal side of the management of performance. However, in most organisations there is also a formal performance management system of some kind which operates alongside these more informal day-to-day activities. It is here that the HR function generally plays a more central role.

Formal performance management systems have a variety of titles, reflecting the particular emphasis that organisations choose to give them: 'performance appraisal', 'performance evaluation' and 'personal development review' are some of the most widely used. While these systems also vary in the way that they operate, they have some common features. Firstly, they involve individual employees meeting with their line managers or first line supervisors on a regular basis (most often annually or bi-annually), to discuss their performance. Secondly, the outcomes of such review meetings are recorded and placed on file. Thirdly, action points of some kind typically result which employees then work towards achieving ahead of their next review. As a result of this formality, employees tend to take the process seriously and perhaps approach its preparation with some caution.

Bloom et al (2012) reported the results of a ten-year-long international study involving teams of researchers across the world carrying out interviews with thousands of managers in a variety of organisations, some highly successful, others less so. They found strong evidence across both the public and the private sectors that organisations were on average 23% more productive when they had in place formal performance management practices which met *each* of the following three basic criteria:

- *Targets.* Individual employees are set 'tough but achievable' objectives to achieve by benchmark dates.
- *Incentives.* Employees were given sufficient incentives in the form of praise, recognition, payments or career development opportunities to make it worth their while achieving their targets.
- *Monitoring.* The organisation collects and analyses performance data so as to enable it to identify where improvements can be made.

There is nothing new about formal performance appraisal involving these kinds of principles. There is evidence that such systems were widely used in the time of the Wei Dynasty in Third Century China, the approach has long been used in military organisations and in the Civil Service in many other countries. In the UK its routine use in business organisations dates from the 1980s and rather more recently in the public sector. Many reasons have been suggested for this growth. Some believe it to be linked to the adoption of individualised performance-based pay systems filling the gap left by the collapse of industry-level collective bargaining. Bach (2005, p297) cites the stimulus given by the requirements of the Investors in People Award, and the development of organisation-wide competency frameworks. Other factors that may be significant are the need for organisations to respond to intensified competitive conditions and the need to find ways of managing accelerating change. Theoretically performance appraisal helps in both scenarios because it encourages employees to focus their attention on management objectives.

Performance appraisal procedures are primarily intended to have a positive impact on individual and collective performance. There are, however, other objectives too such as raising morale, clarifying expectations and duties, improving upward and downward communication, reinforcing management control, identifying developmental opportunities and improving a workforce's understanding of wider organisational goals. They can also provide information on which to base the selection of individuals for promotion and redundancy, not to mention a major potential role as the foundation of incentive-based payment systems.

Unfortunately, the practice rarely lives up to these high theoretical expectations. Research into the outcomes of performance appraisal systems shows that, far from improving motivation and performance, they can in fact very easily have the opposite effect – particularly when they form the basis for decisions about an individual's remuneration. Indeed, reading the results of some studies, it can easily be concluded that performance appraisal is in practice more of an organisational curse than a panacea. At the very least it can be shown that there is no actual relationship between organisation success (as measured financially) and the presence of performance appraisal (Redman 2001, p62). Opinion differs as to why this is the case, with some writers on the subject questioning the system itself and its underlying philosophy, and others blaming the manner in which it is actually carried out in organisations. Undoubtedly, part of the problem is quite simply that appraising people is fiendishly difficult to do well. Its formality, in so far as it reminds the participants that their working relationships are hierarchical, can serve to set back or even destroy the development of genuine and fruitful relationships between supervisors and subordinates. Furthermore, the frankness and openness that the parties have to show during performance appraisals are a feature of the process with which many are understandably uneasy. Rice (1985) quotes an acquaintance as saying that appraising a work colleague is 'the equivalent of walking up to a person and saying "Here's what I think of you, baby"' – an uncomfortable activity that most would avoid if they could.

One of the problems with traditional forms of performance appraisal arises from the fact that most systems try to achieve two rather different things simultaneously. On the one hand they are used as a means of formally evaluating each employee's personal performance over a period of time, while on the other they aim to identify future developmental opportunities. A potential incompatibility arises from the different ways in which employees perceive each of these objectives. When the purpose appears to be evaluative, there is naturally a tendency for appraisees to talk up the good aspects of their performance and perhaps to be less forthcoming about the poorer ones. As a result, they tend not to open up about their developmental needs. This is no great problem if the objective of the exercise is indeed evaluative. Managers know that employees are unlikely to tell the whole truth, and can make allowances for this in reaching judgements about each individual's performance. However, it is clearly a problem when there is a wish also to focus on future performance and on any need employees may have for additional training or experience in order to achieve future goals. In order to persuade subordinates to give a wholly frank picture of their own performance, it is necessary not only to stress the developmental aspects of appraisal but also to make quite sure that information gained is not used for evaluative purposes. As soon as employees suspect that their appraisal results are informing decisions about pay, promotion or redundancy the likelihood of an open and honest exchange of information diminishes considerably. For this reason a number of writers have suggested that organisations should make a choice about whether their appraisal system is to be principally used for evaluation or developmental purposes, on the grounds that it is not possible to achieve both effectively (see Murphy and Cleveland 1995, pp107–09).

There is also a divergence of view between those who advocate the measurement of performance on the basis of results or outputs and those who believe it is more effective to focus on behaviours or the way that results are achieved. As a result we can identify two principal varieties of performance management system, one based on behavioural assessments and the other on output-based assessments.

9.6.1 BEHAVIOURAL ASSESSMENTS

Here the manager reaches a judgement about an individual's performance on the basis of his or her evaluation of the employee's general conduct during the assessment period. Although specific outputs may come into the calculation, they are subordinate to a consideration of behaviour, and are used principally to provide evidence of its effective and ineffective aspects. Hence, the appraiser may decide that an appraisee has performed particularly well in the field of customer care, and will justify this judgement with reference to evidence from a number of sources. Some of these will relate to observation of the employee at work, while others will be derived from formal output measures such as the number of customers who stated that they were very satisfied with the service they received from the employee concerned.

The behavioural approach is often associated with a requirement on managers to consider performance against certain criteria already defined and determined elsewhere in the organisation. Typically, this will require a standard form to be completed which obliges the appraiser to comment on, or score, different aspects of performance. Although the use of such forms can be helpful in guiding managers to those aspects of individual performance that they should consider, they can also be very inflexible, because they do not focus on the specific requirements of individual jobs.

A more sophisticated approach, which is also a good deal more time-consuming, involves using competency frameworks. The starting point is the identification of the particular behaviours or competencies which are most important for employees in particular jobs or departments to display. In selection processes these frameworks are used as the basis for reaching judgements about likely future performance; by contrast, their use in this context involves assessing past performance. Employees are thus appraised according to how far, in the judgement of their immediate supervisor, they are actually meeting or exceeding the basic requirements of the job in question. Hence, if the competencies identified include conversational French, good interpersonal skills, the ability to work under pressure and an interest in law, then it is against these criteria that the appraisee's actual performance is judged.

9.6.2 OUTPUT-BASED ASSESSMENTS

In the case of some kinds of job it is possible to appraise people on the basis of quantifiable data. The most common examples are those in which employees repeat the same procedure or activity continually, allowing clear measures of their efficiency or effectiveness to be obtained. Such an approach is thus possible in the case of groups such as fruit-pickers, some manufacturing employees, clerical workers who process paperwork, and a wide variety of salespeople. Often such employees will be set some form of target to work towards and against which they are later formally appraised.

The other form of output-based appraisal seeks to apply the target-setting principle to a far wider range of jobs. Under such schemes, specific performance objectives or goals that the employee agrees to complete are set at the start of the appraisal cycle. At the end, the employee's performance is then appraised according to how many or how fully these objectives have in fact been achieved. At each annual or six-monthly meeting, the manager reviews past achievements with the employee and then moves on to determine the objectives for the next appraisal period. The level of employee involvement in the determination of objectives varies from organisation to organisation. In some, they are basically set by supervisors, and clearly reflect organisational needs, whereas in others the responsibility is placed on employees to devise their own objectives and to state what action they intend to take to ensure that these are fulfilled. In most cases, a mixture of these two approaches is used, supervisors and subordinates agreeing a set of appraisal objectives which satisfies both the operational needs of the employer and the personal goals of each individual employee concerned.

SMART OBJECTIVES

The acronym SMART is frequently used in the context of performance appraisal to indicate the type of objectives that managers should set. These are as follows:

- S – specific
- M – measurable
- A – achievable
- R – realistic
- T – time bound

As a general guide this comprises useful advice, helping to create clarity so that everyone knows exactly where they stand and what is realistically expected of them.

However, in recent years, as the competitive environment for many organisations has become more turbulent, managers have begun to question whether objective-based appraisal is any longer appropriate. In a fast-changing context it is not possible to set objectives for a year, or even six months, ahead which have any kind of utility. Organisational priorities are continually shifting, so what was important a year ago may well now be unimportant. Staff who aim to meet these objectives rather than those reflecting the new realities, are thus as likely to be damaging the organisation's performance as much as helping to maximise it. In such environments, according to Rose (2000) objective-setting is better characterised by an alternative acronym: DUMB:

- D – defective
- U – unrealistic
- M – misdirected
- B – bureaucratic

Here, greater flexibility is required and different types of objectives which relate to those priorities which do not change such as the need to provide a good service to customers and the need to innovate.

9.7 PROBLEMS WITH PERFORMANCE APPRAISAL

A number of research studies have drawn attention to the way in which appraisal is carried out in organisations and, in particular, to unfair bias in managerial assessments of performance. Rowe (1986) identified the following problems with rating systems:

- the tendency to give a good overall assessment on the basis that one particular aspect has been accomplished well
- a tendency to avoid giving low ratings, even when deserved, for fear of angering or upsetting a weak performer

- the tendency to give a poor overall assessment on the basis of particularly poor performance in one area
- the tendency to rate employee performance as 'average' or 'good' rather than to use the end-points of rating scales
- the tendency to give particular weight to recent occurrences in reaching judgements about individual performance
- the tendency to give high ratings to people who have performed well historically, whatever their performance over the previous year
- a tendency to refrain, on principle, from giving particularly high ratings
- a tendency to rate subordinates at a lower level than the appraiser achieved when in their position.

Beer (1985) draws attention to problems that can occur in the interview itself. In particular, he criticises the tendency for managers to do all or most of the talking, leaving insufficient opportunity for appraisees to respond or to participate in addressing future objectives. According to Philp (1990), other common problems that can reduce the effectiveness of appraisal interviews result from poor management preparation, leaving insufficient time for a proper discussion to take place, and allowing interruptions to occur during the interview. With flatter hierarchies and fewer managers per subordinate a more general problem of ignorance can arise. The manager doing the appraisal may simply be insufficiently familiar with what the employee concerned does or how they perform to carry out a reasonable appraisal exercise (Williams 2002, p8).

The specific problems described above can in many instances be reduced, or even eliminated, with effective appraisal training and regular evaluation of how appraisal interviewing is working in practice. By contrast, the more general practical problems are rather harder to put right. The first of these is a reluctance of managers to carry out appraisals. A number of reasons have been put forward to explain this phenomenon, ranging from a general dislike of passing judgement on others to an inability to handle the emotional responses that often arise when appraisal ratings are less impressive than employees expected. The appraisal interview, as an activity, does not often fit in very well with individual management styles, and this too may explain some managerial reluctance. Where a supervisor has a close and open relationship with his or her subordinates, the formality implicit in appraisal interviewing may well serve to create greater distance between appraiser and appraisee. In such situations, especially ones in which an individual's performance is substandard, supervisors may well feel that a formal appraisal interview is an inappropriate forum in which to discuss performance issues. Instead, subtler approaches are preferred. By contrast, where a supervisor prefers to manage employees from a distance, eschewing close personal contacts, appraisal interviews can reduce distance by providing employees with the opportunity to force a frank and open exchange of views.

Another practical criticism relates to the inevitably political nature of some appraisal decisions. In their research into US executives' perceptions, Longenecker et al (1987) found that such political considerations very often led to the 'generation of appraisal ratings that were less than accurate'. What is so interesting about their findings is that this did not arise because of ignorance or carelessness on the part of appraisers, but was carried out quite deliberately after careful consideration. In other words, it appears to be a problem inherent to the appraisal process and thus not easily solved by the provision of better training or standardised paperwork. The general message is neatly summed up by one of their interviewers:

> There is really no getting around the fact that whenever I evaluate one of my people, I stop and think about the impact – the ramifications of my decisions on my relationship with the guy and his future here. I'd be stupid not to. Call it being politically minded, or using managerial discretion, or fine tuning the guy's ratings,

but in the end I've got to live with him, and I'm not going to rate a guy without thinking about the fallout. There are a lot of games played in the rating process and whether we admit it or not we are all guilty of playing them at our discretion.

This research brings strongly into question the extent to which appraisal can ever be carried out in anything approaching an objective manner. The implication is that it is therefore bound, as sure as night follows day, to result in a degree of demotivation and dissatisfaction on the part of some employees.

9.8 360-DEGREE FEEDBACK

A method of appraising managerial employees that has received a great deal of attention in recent years is **360-degree** appraisal (also known as multi-rater feedback), whereby ratings are given not just by the next manager up in the organisational hierarchy, but also by peers and subordinates. Appropriate customer ratings are also included, along with an element of self-appraisal. Once gathered in, the assessments from the various quarters are compared with one another and the results communicated to the manager concerned. The idea itself is nothing new. Management writers, particularly in the USA, have long advocated the use of upward and peer appraisal as a means of evaluating management performance, but such views have taken a good deal of time to become generally acceptable. The past few years have seen the publication of the first major studies of practice in this area, allowing us to reach judgements about the processes involved on the basis of solid evidence.

In theory, 360-degree appraisal is, like many innovations, very attractive. Who better to provide constructive feedback on a manager's performance than his or her own staff? What better source could there be for suggestions about personal developmental needs? What better criteria for promotion to a senior management role than proof of the respect and admiration of peers and subordinates? In practice it is, of course, far harder to achieve well. First and foremost, there is the problem of objectivity. How is it possible to ensure that peers and subordinates are not rating someone in such a way as to promote their own interests? It would be very tempting to take the opportunity to exercise personal vindictiveness against a manager whom one personally disliked rather than to give a balanced account of their work performance. Similarly, where two peers are competing for one promotional opportunity, it is inevitable that they will be tempted into rating each other poorly, however little justification there is for doing so. Secondly, there is the potential for managerial reprisals against subordinates perceived to have rated them (the managers) poorly and thus set back their careers, or indeed the potential for the reward of subordinates who give 'false' favourable ratings. Thirdly, there is a range of problems that can arise when managers, in a bid to gain high ratings, are tempted to take action that is popular but not necessarily right for the organisation. Finally there are practical problems associated with the delivery of feedback to individuals and the setting-up of formal follow-up meetings to evaluate future progress. The giving of feedback has to be done with a high degree of sensitivity as it is not just one person's view of the individual's performance that is being communicated. Considerable skill is needed to carry out this job and subsequently to use the information as the basis for the development of some form of meaningful personal improvement plan.

It is impossible to remove all these practical problems from the process but, with careful thought and planning, progress can be made. Two conditions in particular stand out as necessary if any such initiative is to be successful:

- It must be stressed that the appraisal process is entirely to be used for developmental purposes. In other words, a situation must be engineered in which no one perceives that promotion or pay are directly linked to the outcome of the process. Although it is true that the result of the developmental process might be better performance, and thus promotion, the link should be no more direct than this.

- It is necessary to ensure complete confidentiality, so that employees are left in no fear whatsoever that their manager will be able to victimise them on account of the ratings they give or remarks they make. For this reason, the only realistic approach is to produce standard appraisal forms to be used across the whole organisation and returned, once completed, to a central office.

Evidence of participant reactions collected by Mabey (2001) suggests that where safeguards such as these are in place managers being appraised using the 360-degree approach responded favourably and believed the experience to be useful for them and their organisations.

9.9 HRM AND FORMAL PERFORMANCE MANAGEMENT

The day-to-day practice of performance appraisal is not an area of management work that HRM specialists spend a great deal of time undertaking. By its nature, this is primarily a job for line managers. With the obvious exception of the appraisal of their own staff, the HR manager's role is largely restricted to policy-making and the giving of advice. However, there are two areas in which the HR function often takes a more hands-on role: in the design of standardised appraisal documentation and in training other managers to carry out effective appraisals.

9.9.1 DOCUMENTATION

The extent to which there is a need for standard documentation clearly varies, depending on the type of performance-appraisal system operated. The more individual the appraisal criteria, the less role there is for any standard form for appraisers to complete. Where appraisal is based on specific objectives or goals set for each employee, the need for documentation is limited to some mechanism whereby managers confirm that they have carried out each appraisal interview. A good deal more is usually required where behavioural approaches are being used, particularly when employees across the organisation are appraised against similar generic criteria.

Those who have sought to identify best practice in the field of appraisal, such as Beaumont (1993, pp81–2) and Fletcher (2004, pp47–8), argue that a strong element of self-appraisal should be a feature of any well-designed system. Standard documentation has an important role to play here, as it gives employees a clear framework within which to assess their own performance. Typically, the self-appraisal form will be sent to employees at the same time as their supervisors are sent theirs. Both parties then complete these before comparing the content of each other's forms at the appraisal interview itself. Some organisations issue identical forms to appraiser and appraisee, but because the purpose of the self-appraisal is different from that of the employer appraisal, it is probably better if rather different forms are designed. Self-appraisal forms have two main purposes. The first is to provide a means for employees to communicate their own perception of the job and what they believe their strengths and weaknesses to be. The second is to provide an opportunity for appraisees to look forward and state how they would like their career to progress, were they to be given the right training and experience over the coming months. The kind of questions that are included are as follows:

- What parts of your job give you most satisfaction?
- What parts of your job give you least satisfaction?
- How would you assess your technical skills?
- How would you assess your ability to communicate with your colleagues?
- How would you describe your working relationships?
- What do you feel are your main achievements over the past year?

- What did you fail to achieve? Why?
- In what areas do you believe you have the ability to improve?
- What training courses would you like to attend in the coming year?
- What are your career objectives for the coming year?
- What suggestions do you have for ways in which the organisation of work in your department could be improved?
- How might communication in the organisation be improved?

The list is not exhaustive and can clearly be added to and made specifically relevant to particular employee groups, but these questions illustrate the type of approach that is generally taken to self-appraisal forms. The questions are open-ended and thus cannot simply be answered with a simple yes or no. Once completed, therefore, the form provides the basis for constructive discussion in the appraisal interview itself.

Standard forms for appraisers to complete cover similar areas, but also usually include some sections that require formal scoring or rating of performance to be recorded. Hence, while appraisees are asked simply to comment at some length on their communication skills, supervisors will both comment and score them. In addition, other sections require objectives or targets agreed with the appraisees to be recorded, along with developmental initiatives that are to be taken to assist in their achievement. Typically, appraiser forms also require specific mention to be made of areas that need attention (that is, those in which performance is weaker than it should be) and room for the supervisor to write a general summary at the end. The advantage of this last part is the chance it gives to finish on a high note. In other words, where faults or poor performance have been noted early in the form, there is an opportunity for a more general positive statement to be made in order that morale is not too badly damaged.

9.9.2 APPRAISER TRAINING

If there is one issue that all writers on appraisal agree about, it is the vital importance of effective training for the people who are going to be carrying out appraisal interviews. The general message is that a badly done appraisal is worse than no appraisal at all in terms of the adverse effect that it has on motivation, job satisfaction, commitment and trust between managers and subordinates. Furthermore, as has been made clear, getting it right is no easy matter. It is not, as some managers like to believe, something that cannot be taught. Just as it is necessary to learn how to interview candidates for new positions effectively, managers also have to learn basic appraisal skills. Aside from the particular features of the scheme in operation, including the use of standard documentation, the following points need to be included in training courses designed to help supervisors develop appraisal interviewing skills:

- the importance of objectivity and consistency
- the need to avoid passing judgement on any aspect of an employee's personality or attitudes that does not relate 100 per cent to his or her performance at work
- the need to prepare thoroughly for all appraisal interviews
- the need to be able to justify with factual evidence any negative comments that are made
- the importance of putting employees at ease and encouraging them to do most of the talking
- the need to stress good aspects of performance as much, or more than, poorer aspects
- the need to take a constructive approach to weaknesses in the employee's performance and to make positive suggestions as to how matters may be improved
- the need to end appraisal interviews on a forward-looking, positive and constructive note.

Appraisal training sessions themselves tend to be highly participatory, exercises of one kind or another being undertaken as a means of developing the key skills of active listening, the giving of constructive feedback and effective counselling. These take a number of forms. Firstly, there is the kind that involves showing a video to course members in which a particular set of tasks is performed (some well and some badly) by an actor. The group then works out how it would be best to handle an appraisal interview with that individual. Secondly, there are exercises in which course members or leaders undertake some task in front of a group of others, such as making a short presentation, and are then formally appraised on their performance. Thirdly, there are role-playing exercises in which course members appraise each other according to the contents of briefs provided by the course leader. In this case, participants can also be asked to give feedback to the appraisers on their performance. In each of these exercises there is scope for introducing unusual or particularly difficult scenarios that appraisers have to tackle. Wherever possible, this should include the appraisal of an employee with a particularly poor performance record, caused in part by emotional or personal difficulties. The importance of developing effective counselling skills is thus emphasised.

9.10 REFRESHING AND UPDATING TRADITIONAL PERFORMANCE MANAGEMENT

In the previous section we considered some of the common specific criticisms that are made about traditional performance appraisal systems. Another more general criticism that is often made is that these approaches do not in practice serve any useful purpose in organisations. First, it is argued that their actual impact on individual performance is limited. A strong performer will do well and a weak performer poorly however often and however formally they are appraised. Other aspects of the way an organisation is managed determine these things in practice. Second, it is often said that performance appraisal is a largely bureaucratic exercise that is treated by managers and staff as 'an end in itself'. We go through the motions because we think it is necessary to do so, but in practice the records made are rarely revisited and do not generally inform wider decision-making. Moreover, of course, in a faster moving competitive environment, there are good grounds for questioning how fit for purpose any formal management systems are which operate on an annual basis.

Some HR thinkers and writers have taken up the challenge of suggesting ways in which performance management systems can made more relevant, effective and well-suited to a faster-moving and more competitive world. Baker (2013), for example, argues that traditional performance appraisal is now outdated. It served us well in the twentieth century, but has now run its course and needs to be replaced with a new framework which is better able to meet organisational objectives. In particular, he contends, because organisations now tend to be less hierarchical and are managed more democratically than was the case in the past, new approaches need to be introduced of managing performance in workplaces which are much more flexible, informal, innovative and unpredictable. Baker's solution is his **Five Conversations Framework**. The idea is that instead of having one big annual appraisal meeting with your line manager, you should have five separate conversations each six months (that is, ten over the course of a year), each being focused on a different aspect of performance at work. The five topics he suggests form the basis of each 'conversation' are job satisfaction and commitment, training and development, improving efficiency and effectiveness, improving individual performance and longer-term career aspirations. None of these topics would be out of place in a formal performance appraisal, but Baker is not seeking to re-invent the wheel. Rather, he is suggesting that a more flexible, focused, frequent and informal approach is required. It is possible to retain the best aspects of traditional performance appraisal, while losing the poorer aspects.

Another notable contribution has recently been made by Buckingham and Goodall (2015). They argue for a system in which team leaders formally review each team member's performance quarterly at least, and more frequently when a major project is completed. Their proposed system involves a single rating being given using the following four criteria and a basic Likert scale (strongly agree, agree, neither agree nor disagree, disagree, strongly disagree):

1 Given what I know of this person's performance, and if it were my money, I would award this person the highest possible compensation increase and bonus.

2 Given what I know of this person's performance, I would always want him or her on my team.

3 This person is at risk of low performance.

4 This person is ready for promotion today.

9.11 BUILDING A HIGH PERFORMANCE CULTURE

We can conclude that organisations are most likely to maximise their performance, achieve their objectives and even over-achieve, when they operate effective and appropriate formal performance management systems alongside the recognised 'bundle' of high performance work practices and, employee-centred styles of line management that seek to bring out the best in each individual employee. However, in order to sustain high levels of performance over time there is also a need to embed a culture of high performance into an organisation's culture. Ultimately this means creating a situation in which the vast majority of staff are genuinely committed to helping the organisation to excel and are prepared as individuals to go the extra mile in this ambition. It is not at all easy to create such a culture, particularly in a fast-changing, highly competitive and unpredictable business environment in which long-term job security cannot by any means be guaranteed. If people feel that the organisations' commitment to them is qualified, they are unlikely to feel able to give it their total commitment in return. In such situations, therefore, senior managers have no choice but to invest a great amount in building high-trust relationships with their staff and in communicating honestly with them.

Holbeche (2005) draws on decades of research in performance management to argue that it is possible, even for organisations operating in very volatile business environments, to foster the development of a sustainable high performance workplace culture. She places particular emphasis on the need to build positive psychological contracts with employees, by which she means establishing positive and deliverable sets of expectations. However tempting, it is important for managers to avoid pretending that they are in a position to promise more than they can. If long-term job security cannot be provided, that needs to be made clear so that false expectations are not built up. Similarly if it is likely that employees are going to be asked to retrain regularly and operate flexibly so that the organisation can achieve greater agility, that too needs to be communicated openly and repeatedly. However, this does not mean that such employers cannot also ensure that they provide their employees with all kinds of other positive experiences which are both career-enhancing and intrinsically motivating. Holbeche's positive psychological contract includes treating people with respect, listening to their views, allowing them as much autonomy as possible to determine how, when and where they work, a decent work–life balance, alongside plenty of opportunities to develop both personally and professionally. She also advocates the benefits of being perceived to be 'a values-based organisation' which commits to principles of fairness, diversity, environmental sustainability and more generally 'making peoples' experience of work become more meaningful'.

Holbeche (2005) also argues in favour of an approach to the management of change which involves all employees. Instead of imposing change from above, she argues, which tends to lead to resistance from staff, as far as possible managers need to hand over the job of leading change to employees. They are then much more likely to react favourably to it, to see it as a positive challenge and to demonstrate flexibility when confronted with the need to change. She also advocates encouraging innovation and creativity across the organisation, inviting employees to come up with new ideas and facilitating this by breaking down organisational barriers and silos so that people from across a business are enabled to mix and share their knowledge. The nub ultimately is both to empower people and to encourage them to make full use of their talents by seeking 'to unleash rather than to constrain employee potential.'

 GOOGLE

CASE STUDY 9.1

Since it was founded in 1998 Google has been one of the world's most successful enterprises. In less than twenty years it has grown from being a small start-up technology company into one of the most widely consumed and well-recognised global brands employing over 50,000 people and turning over more than $60 billion each year, mostly earned from advertising. Google is the most visited website in the world. People use its search engine two million times every minute, meaning that it carries out around a two-thirds of all Internet searches. These vast revenues are mainly being used to invest in cutting-edge research and development activities which have the capacity to help Google grow into one of the world's biggest multinational corporations. The company has for some years now been acquiring or starting up two or three companies each month ranging from major technology firms such as Motorola to small enterprises such as Calico which researches ways of slowing down the ageing process. It is also a major player in the development of self-programming computer devices and driverless car technologies.

From the start Google's founders, Larry Page and Sergey Brin, had a clear vision as to the way they wanted to manage the people that they employed. Above all they wanted to establish a company that was highly attractive as a place for 'geeks' to work, while also providing them with every opportunity possible to make full use of their creativity and capacity to come up with innovative ideas. They have been very successful in this endeavour. Google receives 1,300 job applications every day, has a staff turnover rate of less than 5% and has been named as America's 'best company to work for' by *Fortune Magazine* for five years in succession.

Google does not, however, pay its employees particularly high salaries. Some have made a lot of money by exercising their right to buy shares in the company, but base pay is not high in comparison with other leading technology companies. Instead the appeal of working at Google is explained partly by the pleasant, lavish working environment that employees enjoy. Built to resemble a university campus with plenty of green spaces, its California HQ provides staff with a range of free restaurants to dine in, access to top-quality medical and dental facilities, gymnasia, banks and car maintenance/valeting services. Staff are also encouraged to undertake a minimum of 120 hours training each year to keep them up to date with technological developments, while also improving their personal effectiveness, leadership skills and foreign language proficiency. Google's employees are entitled to 27 days holiday each year (which is very high by US standards) and also enjoy very generous sickness, maternity and paternity payment arrangements.

Google famously allows its employees to spend 20% of their time (that is a day each week) working on projects of their own choosing that may or may not be directly related to their usual work. The company organises quarterly conferences for all staff at which corporate strategy is discussed by senior leaders, the last quarter's activities reviewed and objectives set for the coming quarter. Opportunities are provided here for employees to ask questions and make suggestions. In addition, shorter and less formal weekly 'Thank God it's Friday' gatherings are held at the end of the working week at which managers review the past week and preview the coming week while taking questions. In addition regular anonymous surveys of employees are carried out to measure levels of satisfaction and gather suggestions.

Questions

1   How far would you say that Google operates a 'high performance' working environment?

2   Would Google's approach to HRM be appropriate in all industries? Why/Why not?

3   What features of HRM at Google serve to sustain its high performance culture?

REFERENCES

BACH, S. (2005) New directions in performance management. In: BACH, S. (ed.). *Managing human resources: personnel management in transition.* 4th ed. Oxford: Blackwell.

BAKER, T. (2013) *The end of the performance review.* Basingstoke: Palgrave Macmillan.

BEAUMONT, P. B. (1993) *Human resource management: key concepts and skills.* London: Sage.

BEER, M. (1985) Note on performance appraisal. In: BEER, S. and SPECTOR, B. (eds). *Readings in human resource management.* New York: Free Press.

BLOOM, N., SADUN, R. and REENEN, J. V. (2012) How three essential practices can address even the most complex global problems. *Harvard Business Review,* November.

BOSELIE, P., DIETZ, G. and BOON, C. (2005) Commonalities and contradictions in HRM and performance research. *Human Resource Management Journal.* Vol 15, No 3. pp67–94.

BUCKINGHAM, M. and GOODALL, A. (2015) Reinventing performance management. *Harvard Business Review,* April.

COMBS, J., LIU, Y., HALL, A. and KETCHEN, D. (2006) How much do high performance work practices matter? A meta-analysis of their effects on organizational performance. *Personnel Psychology.* Vol 59, No 3. pp501–28.

DATTA, D., GUTHRIE, J. and WRIGHT, P. (2005) Human resource management and labor productivity: does industry matter? *Academy of Management Journal.* Vol 48, No 1. pp135–45.

FLEETWOOD, S. and HESKETH, A. (2010) *Explaining the performance of human resource management.* Cambridge: Cambridge University Press.

FLETCHER, C. (2004) *Appraisal and feedback: making performance review work.* 3rd ed. London: CIPD.

HARTER, J., SCHMIDT, F. L. and HAYES, T. L. (2002) Business–unit–level relationship between employee satisfaction, employee engagement and business outcomes: a meta-analysis. *Journal of Applied Psychology.* Vol 87, No 2. pp268–79.

HOLBECHE, L. (2005) *High performance organization: creating dynamic stability and sustainable success.* London: Routledge.

HUSELID, M. (1995) The impact of human resource management practices on turnover, productivity and corporate financial performance. *Academy of Management Journal.* Vol 38, No 3. pp635–72.

LEGGE, K. (1995) *Human resource management: rhetoric and realities.* London: Routledge.

LONGENECKER, C. O., SIMS, H. P. and GIOIA, D. A. (1987) Behind the mask: the politics of employee appraisal. American Academy of Management Executive. Reprinted in FERRIS, G. R. and BUCKLEY, M. R. (eds) (1996) *Human resources management: perspectives, context, functions and outcomes.* 3rd ed. Englewood Cliffs, NJ: Prentice Hall.

MABEY, C. (2001) Closing the circle: participant views of a 360 degree feedback programme. *Human Resource Management Journal.* Vol 11, No 1. pp41–53.

MARCHINGTON, M. and WILKINSON, A. (2012) *Human resource management at work: people management and development.* 5th ed. London: CIPD.

MURPHY, K. R. and CLEVELAND, J. N. (1995) *Understanding performance appraisal: social, organisational and goal-based perspectives.* Thousand Oaks, CA: Sage.

PAAUWE, J., WRIGHT, P. and GUEST, D. (2013) HRM and performance: what do we know and where should we go? In: PAAUWE, J., GUEST, D. and WRIGHT, P. (eds). *HRM & performance: achievements and challenges.* Chichester: Wiley.

PECCEI, R., VAN DE VOORDE, K. and VAN VELDHOVEN, M. (2013) HRM, well-being and performance: a theoretical and empirical review. In: PAAUWE, J., GUEST, D. and WRIGHT, P. (eds). *HRM & performance: achievements and challenges.* Chichester: Wiley.

PFEFFER, J. (1994) *Competitive advantage through people.* Boston, MA: Harvard Business School Press.

PFEFFER, J. (1998) *The human equation.* Boston, MA: Harvard Business School Press.

PHILP, T. (1990) *Appraising performance for results.* 2nd ed. London: McGraw-Hill.

PURCELL, J., KINNIE, N., HUTCHINSON, S., RAYTON, B. and SWART, J. (2003) *Understanding the people and performance link: unlocking the black box.* London: CIPD.

REDMAN, T. (2001) Performance appraisal. In REDMAN, T. and WILKINSON, A. (eds). *Contemporary human resource management: text and cases.* London: FT/Prentice Hall.

RICE, B. (1985) Performance review: the job nobody likes. *Psychology Today.* Reprinted in FERRIS, G. R. and BUCKLEY, M. R. (eds) (1996) *Human resources management: perspectives, context, functions and outcomes.* 3rd ed. Englewood Cliffs, NJ: Prentice Hall.

ROSE, M. (2000) Target practice. *People Management.* 23 November.

ROWE, T. (1986) Eight ways to ruin a performance review. *Personnel Journal* (January).

WILLIAMS, H. (2002) Strategic planning for human resources. In: LEOPOLD, J. (ed.). *Human resources in organisations.* London: FT/Prentice Hall.

Glossary

360-degree feedback A performance management technique which involves people receiving constructive feedback on their own performance from everyone working closely with them. This will typically include managers and subordinate staff as well as peers and other work colleagues.

ADIE framework A four-stage framework for organisation design advocated by the CIPD: assess, design, implement, evaluate.

AMO A simple, commonly used model popularised by the black box studies. It suggests that individual performance will only be maximised in an organisation if employees have the ability, the motivation and the opportunity to excel.

Behavioural science The study of individuals and their interactions, which has informed much of the theory that underpins organisational development.

Benchmarking The comparison between one organisation and another of an internal process, system or method in terms of its efficiency, effectiveness and/or cost.

Call centre Dedicated centres which use voice-to-voice contact with employees to support a range of employee relations issues, usually through computer-based systems. They can be in-house, outsourced and off-shored.

Claimant A person who, using a claim form, brings a case against an organisation before an employment tribunal.

Cognitive engagement Mental interest in and focus on work.

Common law Law created as a precedent by a judge in a court rather than by Act of Parliament. The common law evolves as cases are brought before the courts (and if necessary through progressively higher courts). Court decisions and rulings then become binding precedents that lower courts must always follow.

Competency framework A written set of attributes or competencies that an organisation is looking for in staff who work in particular jobs. In many cases, but not all, such frameworks are derived from a systematic study of the characteristics of top performers in those jobs within the organisation.

Constructive dismissal A situation in which an employee resigns as a direct result of an actual or anticipated breach of contract on the part of his or her employer. If the breach is proven, the courts may award remedial compensation to the 'dismissed' employee.

Contingent reward Pay based not on any established scale or measure but on what an organisation most values at the time and is prepared (and able) to pay for.

Continuing professional development The means by which employees continually improve the knowledge and skills related to their occupational area.

Contract of employment A legally binding agreement made between an employer and employee detailing specific facts about a specific job, the written and implied terms of which are enforceable in the courts.

Corporate universities An educational entity that organisations use as a strategic tool to assist in the cultivation of learning and the achievement of corporate learning goals.

Discretionary effort Additional effort voluntarily put into work by employees that goes beyond what is expected by their managers or set out in their contracts. Employees exercise discretionary effort when they are highly engaged in their work and committed to their organisations.

E-learning Learning conducted through electronic media.

Emotional engagement Emotional involvement and attachment to work.

Employee engagement The positive emotional input with which employees are committed to an organisation and to their work, and willing to work hard to achieve objectives. Prime indicators are good communication systems and evidence of partnership working.

Employee involvement A form of employee voice intended to elicit ideas and input from employees. Examples include upward and downward communication, and problem-solving groups.

Employee participation A form of employee voice intended to share power between management and employees. Examples include joint consultation committees and works councils.

Employee self-service A secure web-based computer system accessed via a company's intranet or the Internet, which enables employees to manage their own personal records and payroll details.

Employer branding A 'set of attributes and qualities, often intangible, that makes an organisation distinctive, promises a particular kind of employment experience, and appeals to those people who will thrive and perform best in its culture'.

The Employment Appeal Tribunal (EAT) The first court of appeal to which appeals from employment tribunals are taken by parties who wish to contest a ruling on a point of law.

Employment tribunals Courts which have statutory jurisdiction in handling employment-related matters and which are presided over by employment judges.

Engagement gap The gap between the desired levels of engagement for high performance and the typical levels of engagement amongst employees.

European Court of Justice The European Union's high court based in Luxembourg: the final court of appeal for cases that relate to European law.

Extrinsic reward Reward expected following the completion of work. Examples of extrinsic rewards include pay and status.

Five conversations framework An alternative approach to traditional performance appraisal that is associated with Tim Baker. It involves managers meeting employees individually five times every six months to discuss distinct aspects of their performance, their career aspirations and personal development needs.

Flexible firm A type of flexible organisation structure that aims to help an organisation meet its goals by having a 'core' workforce of permanent employees, and a 'periphery' of temporary employees (for example, outsourced functions, contractors), which can be more easily changed to meet organisational requirements (for example, more workers at peak times, or with project-specific expertise).

Grade/pay structure A collection of pay grades, levels or bands linking related jobs within a hierarchy or series, that provides a framework for the implementation of reward strategies and policies within an organisation.

Grievance procedure A formal process developed by an organisation which can be used by employees as a means of raising a complaint when they consider that they have been badly treated in some way, for example being bullied or harassed unacceptably.

Gross misconduct A breach of an employer's rules that is so serious as to justify summary dismissal (being sacked on the spot) without notice.

Hierarchy The number of management layers in an organisation – a tall organisation has many layers, a short organisation is flatter.

High performance work systems (HPWS) A bundle of human resource management practices which are implemented together at the same time re-enforcing one another in such a way as to encourage superior performance on the part of the organisation's employees.

Human capital Knowledge, skills and experience possessed by an individual, or group of individuals, expressed in terms of value to an organisation.

Industrial action Sustained measure (in the form of activity or inactivity) taken by a group of workers – usually organised by a trade union – aimed at securing concessions from an employer. Strikes are the most common form.

Insight-driven Guided by the power (generally on the part of management) to discern and understand, involving imagination, practical knowledge and enlightenment.

Intrinsic reward Reward that comes from and is inherent in the work itself. Examples of intrinsic rewards include a sense of accomplishment and opportunities for advancement.

Involuntary turnover The proportion of the total number of employments that come to an end, which were terminated at the behest of the employer.

Job evaluation A systematic process for defining the relative worth or size of jobs within an organisation.

Labour market The pool of potential workers available to an organisation – they might be local, national or global.

Labour turnover The rate at which employees leave an organisation, usually expressed as a proportional percentage. A labour turnover rate of 10% means that one in every 10 employees leaves per year (either voluntarily or involuntarily).

Learning needs The gaps that exist between the current state of an employee's knowledge, skills or attitudes and the desired state of knowledge, skills or attitudes.

Loose labour market A labour market in which there are a large number of individuals looking for employment, and job vacancies are in relatively short supply.

Management style The ways in which managers use their power and authority in the workplace. Examples are listed in Purcell and Sisson's (1983) typology of management style.

Mediation A process for resolving conflict in the workplace involving a third party, which aims to find a resolution that is acceptable to both parties involved in a dispute.

Menus of intervention Schedules of useful positive actions intended to be taken.

Multinational organisation An organisation that has facilities and assets in at least one country other than its home country.

Off-shoring The moving of the operations of a company to another country for reasons such as lower labour costs or more favourable economic conditions in that other country.

Organisation design The process and the outcome of shaping an organisational structure, to align it with the purpose of the business and the context in which the organisation exists.

Organisation development A planned and systematic approach to enabling an organisation's sustained performance through the involvement of its people.

Organisation structure The framework, pattern and position of job roles, teams and functions within an organisation, and the relationship(s) between these.

Organisational change Ways and processes in which an organisation moves from where it is now towards where it wants to be. This may involve changes to its structures, systems and culture, which may in turn alter the nature, shape and skill sets of its workforce.

Pay determination The complex process of calculating and deciding on how much employees should be paid for their work.

Performance appraisal A process requiring line managers to make a formal record of each of their employees' performance over a defined period – typically a year. The process usually involves a formal meeting at which individuals' personal performance is discussed and the setting of performance objectives for the coming period agreed.

Physical engagement Willingness to go above and beyond what is expected or required.

Pluralist Describing the view that conflict is an inevitable feature of employment relationships owing to the different (plural) interests of managers and of employees/trade unions. Following the theory derived from the work of Fox (1966) relating to the ways in which managers view employment relationships, pluralists emphasise the need for the management of conflict at work.

Psychological contract The employment relationship regarded primarily as an exchange of obligations and understood commitments between employer and employee.

Recruitment Methods by which potentially suitable employees are sought – including advertising and head-hunting – located, and eventually introduced to an organisation.

Redundancy Termination of employment because there has been, or is going to be, a collapse of the business, a closure of the workplace, or a diminution in the need for employees.

Retirement Termination of his or her employment by an individual who has decided to leave the labour market because of advancing age. There is no longer a default retirement age, so that the timing of retirement is now largely a matter of employee choice.

Reward management The operation of strategies, policies and processes required to ensure that the contribution of people to an organisation is appropriately recognised by both financial and non-financial means.

Selection Methods by which the most suitable individual for a job vacancy is chosen from the pool of individuals who have applied.

Self-service technologies The means by which managers are able to directly access technology-driven HR assistance, enabling them to carry out a range of HR activities independently.

Shared services A way of handling routine HR administrative services, mainly utilised by large organisations, across multiple business units, organisations and/or multinationally.

SMART A well-known management acronym setting out the criteria that should underpin a performance objective if it is to be effectively met. The letters stand for specific, measurable, achievable, realistic and time bound.

Span of control The number of direct reports assigned to a manager; a narrow span means fewer direct reports and greater specialisation, while a broad span means more direct reports with wider/more general responsibility.

Stability Measure of the length of time employees in general remain with an organisation (more properly known as the stability index). It is commonly used in conjunction with staff turnover.

Staff turnover The proportion of employees who leave the organisation over any specified period of time, expressed as a percentage of the total number of staff employed. It is commonly used in conjunction with stability.

Stakeholder A person or group with an interest or a concern in something.

Statutes Laws that are passed by Parliament and that are enforced in the courts. Statutes take the form either of Acts of Parliament or of Regulations issued by Ministers under the terms of individual Acts.

Structural transformation The process in which the structure of an organisation is reorganised to reflect the changing demands placed upon it.

Supreme Court Formerly the House of Lords, the highest court to which appeals can be made in the UK's judicial system. Only if a matter concerns European Law is a further appeal possible.

Tight labour market A labour market in which there are a large number of employers looking for workers with certain skills, and these workers are in relatively short supply.

Total quality management A management approach that aims to secure an organisation's long-term success through the commitment of each employee to the maintenance of high standards of operation and the continuous search for improvements.

Total reward A strategy that incorporates additional components such as learning and development, together with progressive aspects of the working environment, within the overall reward/benefits package.

Trade union An organisation independent from employing organisations that represents the individual and collective interests of its members in relation to the terms and conditions of employment.

Transactional Describing the day-to-day business conducted within existing arrangements and processes. In HR terms this would include payroll and pensions, legal services, recruitment and selection, employee assistance and training.

Transactional engagement Involvement and attachment to work on a superficial rather than deep-rooted level.

Transformational Describing activity centred on changes to the structure, processes, systems and ways of working to better reflect changing demands and pressures.

Unitarist Describing the view that the relationship between employers and employees is basically harmonious (unitary) and co-operative, united behind the authority of the manager in pursuit of the organisation's goals. It is an alternative perspective to the pluralist view.

Voluntary turnover The proportion of the total number of employments that come to an end, which were terminated by the choice of individual employees.

VUCA Volatile, uncertain, complex and ambiguous – an acronym sometimes used to describe the external or strategic environment that an organisation operates in.

Work specialisation The degree to which tasks in organisations are divided into separate job roles, and consequently whether roles are specialised with a narrow remit, or are general with a broader remit.

Index